WOMEN IN IRAQ

WOMEN IN IRAQ

The Gender Impact of International Sanctions

Yasmin Husein Al-Jawaheri

LYNNE
RIENNER
PUBLISHERS

BOULDER
LONDON

Published in the United States of America in 2008 by
Lynne Rienner Publishers, Inc.
1800 30th Street, Boulder, Colorado 80301
www.rienner.com

First published in 2008 by I.B. Tauris & Co. Ltd.

Library of Congress Cataloging-in-Publication Data
Al-Jawaheri, Yasmin Husein.
  Women in Iraq : the gender impact of international sanctions / Yasmin
Husein Al-Jawaheri.
  Includes bibliographical references and index.
ISBN 978-1-58826-598-2 (hardcover : alk. paper)
ISBN 978-1-58826-574-6 (pbk. : alk. paper)
  1. Women—Iraq. 2. Women—Iraq—Social conditions. 3. Economic
sanctions—Iraq. I. Title.
  HQ1735.A795 2008
  305.48'89275670090511—dc22

                                                          2008006786

Printed and bound in the United States of America.
This book was produced from camera-ready copy supplied by the author.

 The paper used in this publication meets the requirements
of the American National Standard for Permanence of
Paper for Printed Library Materials Z39.48-1992.

5 4 3 2 1

CONTENTS

TABLES

ACRONYMS AND ABBREVIATIONS

ABSP – Arab Ba'th Socialist Party

AFESD – Arab Fund for Economic and Social Development

AHD – Arab Human Development

AHDR – Arab Human Development Report

AIP – Annual Investment Programme

AMF – Arab Monetary Fund

BISA – British International Studies Association

CARDRI – Committee Against Repression and for Democratic Iraq

CEDAW – Committee for the Elimination of all Discrimination Against Women

CESR – Center for Economic and Social Rights

CIA – Central Intelligence Agency (US)

CPA – Coalition Provisional Authority (Iraq)

DHS – Demographic and Health Survey

ECLAC – Economic Commission for Latin America and the Caribbean (Chile)

EDSWG – Educational Sectoral Working Group

EIU – Economist Intelligence Unit (London)

EPC – Economic Planning Commission (Iraq)

ERF – Economic Research Forum for the Arab Countries, Iran and Turkey (Cairo)

FAO – Food and Agriculture Organization (UN)

GDP – Gross Domestic Product

GER – Gross Enrolment Ratio

GFIW – General Federation of Iraqi Women

GNP – Gross National Product

HDR – Human Development Reports

HRW – Human Rights Watch (Non-Governmental Organization)

IEA – Iraqi Economists' Association (Iraq)

IKBDC – Iraq-Kuwait Boundary Demarcation Commission (UN-Iraq)

ILO – International Labour Organization (UN- Geneva)

IMF – International Monetary Fund (Washington, DC)

IST – International Study Team (Non-Governmental Organization- New York)

MEED – *Middle East Economic Digest* (London)

MEES – *Middle East Economic Survey* (London)

MENA – Middle Eastern and North Africa (region)

MoU – Memorandum of Understanding (UN- Iraq)

NDP – National Development Plan

ODI – Overseas Development Institute

OFF – Oil-for-Food Programme

PRB – Population Reference Bureau

RCC – Revolutionary Command Council (Iraqi Government [1968–2003])

SC – Security Council of the United Nations

SCR – Security Council Resolution

UNCC – UN Compensation Commission (UN, Geneva)

UNCHR –UN Commission on Human Rights (UN, Geneva)

UNDHA – UN Department of Humanitarian Affairs (UN, Geneva)

UNDP – United Nations Development Programme

UNEA – UN-controlled Escrow Account (UN, Geneva)

UNEDBAS – UN's Regional Office for Education Based in the Arab States

UNESCO – UN Educational, Scientific and Cultural Organization (UN, Paris)

UNFPA – United Nations Population Fund

UNHP – UN Humanitarian Panel

UNICEF – UN's Children Fund (UN, New York)

UNIFEM – United Nations Development Fund for Women

UNILC – United Nations International Law Commission

UNMOVIC – UN Monitoring and Verification Commission (UN, Iraq)

UNOCHR – UN Office of the Humanitarian Coordinator for Iraq

UNOIP – UN Office for Iraq Programme (UN, Iraq)

UNSCOM – UN Special Commission (UN, Iraq)

WB – World Bank (New York)

WFP – World Food Programme (UN)

WHO – World Health Organization (UN)

WIDER – World Development Study Series (UNU- UN University, Helsinki)

WMD – weapons of mass destruction

ACKNOWLEDGEMENTS

The study of the impact of international sanctions on Iraqi women is the product of almost five years of fieldwork and quantitative data analysis. Much of the information contained in this book was based on empirical research with a large number of Iraqi women. I am profoundly grateful to all Iraqi women participants for their patience and trust, and I feel great sympathy and respect for their continuous struggle for survival in the distressing circumstances of the political and humanitarian situation in Iraq, both under sanctions and latterly under the effects of occupation and terrorism. Given the extremely sensitive political circumstances in Iraq and also because of my promise to protect their anonymity, I am unable to thank them by name, but without their exceptional support and openness towards me, this research would not have been possible.

I wish to express my sincere appreciation and gratitude to a number of individuals associated with the making of this book. I am sincerely grateful to Dr Nadje Al-Ali, Cultural Anthropology, for her excellent knowledge and support and to Professor Tim Niblock, Political Science and International Relations, for help and advice. My special thanks to my friend Cynthia Cockburn, Professor of Social Science, for being an immeasurable source of knowledge and support. Particular thanks too, to Dr Kamil Mahdi, Political Economy, for his support throughout my study at Exeter University. I am grateful to Professor Gudmundur Alfredsson, Professor of International Law, and Professor Katarina Tomasevski, Professor of Political Science and International Law, Lund University in Sweden, for their kind assistance.

Especial thanks to my friend Lindy Ayubi for her proofreading and excellent assistance and for her enduring support. I am also grateful to my friends Dr Julia Drober and David Morgan for their assistance. The help and support provided by Dr Mudhafar Amin, the post Head of the Iraqi Interests Section in London, in facilitating my trips and my fieldwork in Iraq is also gratefully acknowledged.

My appreciation goes to the Institute of Arab and Islamic Studies at the University of Exeter for financial support through the Sir Anthony Parsons scholarship (1999–2002), and to the Danish Research Agency for their scholarship funding (2000–2003). Professor Kirsten Hastrup, Social Anthropology and Social Science, Institute of Anthropology, Copenhagen University, supported my application for this scholarship, and her constant encouragement helped me to establish the initial proposal and direction of this research.

I would also like to express my sincere gratitude and appreciation to the readers for their helpful and inspiring comments. Special appreciation in this regard is dedicated to Denis Halliday, the former UN Humanitarian Coordinator for Oil-For-Food programme, who resigned in 1999, in protest about the injustice of the programme. I would also like to thank the two anonymous readers from I.B.Tauris Publications for their thorough and supportive comments. I should also like to thank my typesetter and project manager, Carolann Martin and Matthew Brown, for their extremely skilful work. My thanks go also to my commissioning editor, Abigail Fielding-Smith, for her wonderful coordination and support.

Finally, my deepest thanks to my family in Iraq for their generosity and for their indispensable contribution to my research.

1

THE UNITED NATIONS SANCTIONS ON IRAQ

Introduction

The immediate response to the Iraqi invasion of Kuwait in August 1990 was the imposition of a direct and comprehensive set of sanctions by the United Nations (UN). However, even after Iraq's withdrawal from Kuwait, the sanctions were prolonged for almost 13 years (1990–2003), based on the claim that Iraq was not cooperating with the inspection teams looking for the weapons of mass destruction (WMD) that the country was accused of possessing. Iraq's compliance, particularly with regards to its alleged WMD, was never considered satisfactory.

The UN sanctions on Iraq were not removed until Saddam Hussein's regime had been overthrown by the use of military force and Iraq had been occupied by the allied powers of the United States and the United Kingdom in March 2003. In May 2003, the lifting of sanctions was ordered by the UN Security Council's Resolution (SCR) 1483, according to which Iraq was allowed the free flow of oil exports. The resolution also gave the USA and Britain control over Iraq until such time as a democratic government had been formed in Iraq.

The removal of Saddam's regime and the occupation of Iraq in 2003 put an end to doubts about the real objective of sanctions in Iraq. The WMD that Iraq was alleged to be concealing were never found, and eventually the work of the inspectors who were looking for evidence of these weapons was officially terminated by the UN in January 2005.

This Introduction provides a brief chronology of the UN sanctions on Iraq and their general impact on the economy of Iraq and livelihood of its population. It includes also an overview of samples of research and location, as well as the structure of the book.

Sanctions and War Scenarios

Initially, it should be mentioned that, from its formation as a modern state in the 1920s, Iraq was dependent mainly on the export of oil for its exchange earnings, with oil production as the country's biggest industry (see Appendix Table 1.1). By the end of the 1970s, Iraq had become the second largest oil-exporting country after Saudi

Arabia in the Organization of Petroleum-Exporting Countries (OPEC).[1] The United Nations' immediate response to Iraq's invasion of Kuwait in August 1990 was a complete ban on trade to and from Iraq, exempting only 'supplies intended strictly for medical purposes, and in humanitarian circumstances, foodstuffs' (Security Council Resolution 661, 6 August 1990, para. 3c). The importing of foodstuffs was thus forbidden except on humanitarian grounds. However, this resolution was amended by SCR 666 of 13 September 1990, which permitted the supply of food-stuffs to the civilian population 'if circumstances should arise that made it necessary to do so'.

In this way, the impact of the economic sanctions on Iraq's economy was initially demonstrated in the shocking fall in the state's oil revenues and in all sorts of other income sources. The immediate stoppage of oil exports and the later restrictions on such export caused severe shortages of foreign exchange earnings that have had a tremendous impact on all aspects of life in Iraq.

However, the impact of sanctions on Iraq's economy and people can only be viewed in the context of the scale of destruction carried out by the allied war against Iraq in January 1991.[2] It is believed that a prominent aim of the Gulf War in 1991 was to inflict severe damage on Iraq's civilian infrastructure in order to aggravate the impact of the economic sanctions.[3]

The six-week bombing campaign that began on 16 January 1991 did not distin-guish between military and civilian targets.[4] In addition to its military objectives, the coalition bombing comprehensively targeted the civilian infrastructure, including oil facilities, oil pipelines and refineries, electric power stations, transport and tele-communications networks, water treatment facilities and water distribution systems, fertilizer plants, food processing plants, food warehouses, iron and steel plants, bridges, hospitals, storage facilities, industrial plants, irrigation sites, and civilian buildings.[5] These facilities were either rendered completely useless or were exten-sively damaged. Several United Nations officials, as well as independent observers, explicitly denounced the impact of the intensity and scale of the bombing:

> It should … be said … that nothing that we had seen or read had quite prepared us for the particular form of the devastation which has now befallen the country. The recent conflict had wrought near-apocalyptic results upon what had been, until January 1991, a rather highly urbanized and mechanized society. Now, most means of modern life support have been destroyed or rendered tenuous. Iraq has, for some time to come, been relegated to a pre-industrial age, but with all the disabilities of post-industrial dependency on an intensive use of energy and technology.[6]

A moderate estimate put the value of the assets destroyed during the 1991 bombing at $US232 billion.[7] However, it did not take into consideration the value of loss of export earnings including oil revenues, the value of lost output, the replacement of military equipment and related supplies, inflation-related losses, depreciation of the Iraqi currency, and lost imports.[8] A single example serves to reveal the scale of the damage inflicted upon Iraq's infrastructure; it was estimated that the replacement of the country's power-generating systems would cost Iraq $US20 billion.[9]

Among the whole body of Security Council resolutions on the crisis, the Cease-Fire Resolution (SCR on 3 April 1991) was one of fundamental importance because it imposed and maintained the sanctions regime on Iraq, and was considered as 'one of the most comprehensive sets of decisions ever taken by the SC'.[10] While the resolution demanded Iraq's unconditional compliance in many areas,[11] it did not put any time-ceiling for lifting the sanctions, leaving the sanctions regime in Iraq without a specific timetable for completion of the UN's tasks (disarmaments commissions) in the country.

However, the immediate blockage of Iraq's oil exports and all financial transactions caused a cash crisis that also affected tasks undertaken by the UN in Iraq, i.e., humanitarian assistance and inspection costs, not to mention the deteriorating living conditions for the wide majority of the Iraqi population.[12]

In June 1991, in an attempt to provide some cash, the Security Council adopted Resolution 699 which called on the international community to assist 'in cash and in kind' in order to support the UN's work in Iraq. However, after this had yielded a very limited response, the SC took another initiative which modified the sanctions regime by allowing Iraq the export of a limited amount of its oil.[13] This was the so-called 'Oil-For-Food' Programme (OFF).

However, the government of Iraq was reluctant to implement these resolutions or to take up these half-way solutions. It claimed that Iraq had fulfilled all the requirements imposed on it by the Cease Fire SCR 687, and therefore demanded the total lifting of all oil export restrictions.[14]

Following Iraq's refusal to act on these resolutions, the problem of financing the UN's operations in Iraq was temporarily solved by using Iraqi funds abroad.[15] However, these measures did not solve the problem of financing the UN's many committees and their staffs in Iraq while the UN was also trying to remedy the unfolding humanitarian situation arising from sanctions.

The Oil-for-Food Scenario

In this context, the OFF initiative actually perpetuated the sanctions regime while at the same time allowing for generous funding of the UN's intentions and tasks in Iraq.

In another attempt to circumvent the Iraqi government's objections to the previous OFF resolutions (sovereignty issue),[16] the UN adopted SCR 986 on 14 April 1995. This allowed the export of US$2 billions-worth of oil every six months on condition that all transactions would be channelled through the UN Escrow Account (UNEA).

In spite of the unfavourable reaction of the Iraqi government to this resolution, it did, however, open the gate for further negotiations within the same framework. The negotiations ended on 20 May 1996 with the adoption of the Memorandum of Understanding (MoU) on the implementation of SCR 986, allowing Iraq to sell US$1 billion-worth of oil during successive 90-day periods. The proceeds had to be placed in the UNEA, to which Iraq had no access. The MoU specified that of the US$4 billion of revenues that would be generated over one year, 30 percent was allocated for Gulf War reparations for countries, companies and individuals, 5–10 percent for financing UN operations in Iraq, another 5–10 percent for the maintenance of Iraq's oil pipelines, and 15 percent for humanitarian supplies for the three million Iraqi Kurds in Northern Iraq.[17]

In early 1998, the Secretary-General reported to the SC that the $US2 billion-worth of oil exports was not sufficient to cover 'reasonable' humanitarian goods, and suggested that Iraq needed to be allowed to export a larger quantity of oil.[18] The SC responded by allowing Iraq to increase oil exports to $US5.2 billion-worth every six months (SCR 1153, 20 February 1998). However, it was impossible for Iraq to have exported oil worth US$5.2 billion every six months because of the serious damage that had been inflicted on its oil industry by the Gulf War in 1991. Furthermore, the UN-established Sanctions Committee was refusing to enable any adequate restoration of production by systematically denying Iraq full access to funds and to imports of essential spare parts and equipment needed to repair and maintain its oil industry.[19] Because of these obstacles, Iraq's oil-export revenues did not even come close to the amount of $US5.2 billion approved by the Security Council. The first time that Iraq's oil revenue achieved that level was in mid-1999 when international oil prices rose from as low as $US7 per barrel to $US17 per barrel, and especially because Phase VI had been extended from 19 November to 6 December 1999.[20] Even though the OFF programme was set according to six-monthly 'phases' of oil exports, these phases were often interrupted or delayed, and sometimes they even stopped completely. There were different reasons for this, including the holding back and delaying of contracts by the Sanctions Committee, allied air strikes, and disputes about the OFF programme and sanctions (see Appendix Tables 1.2 and 1.3).

By the end of 1998, and after four days of intensive US and British air strikes (16–19 December 1998), international criticism and disquiet over the operation of sanctions and their adverse impacts on the Iraqi population was intensifying. The lack of accountability in the sanctions policy towards the Iraqi people's human rights had put the UN's credibility in a precarious situation. Affected by international censure but determined to keep sanctions intact, the UN took an initiative at the end of 1999 to lift the ceiling on Iraq's oil exports completely, and SCR1284 was adopted on 17 December 1999. However, while paragraph 36 of the Resolution suggested lifting the ceiling on Iraq's oil exports, it retained the procedures regarding control over Iraqi finances through the Sanctions Committee and the Escrow Account.

This new resolution (SCR 1284) did not bring about any substantial change in the humanitarian situation in Iraq because Iraq's oil exports continued to be hostage to the Sanctions Committee's holdbacks, delays, and rejections of requests for the spare parts and equipment needed to restore the oil industry.[21]

The continuous calls of Iraq and the Secretary-General for an increased allocation of funds for the importation of spare parts remained unanswered until March 2000, when the Security Council raised the amount from US$300 million to US$600 million (SCR 1293, March 2000). The result was that Iraq's oil production and export levels continued to suffer, with consequent effects on the status of humanitarian contracts. The tightening up of already detailed verification procedures that accompanied each delivery of contracted aid required a commensurate increase in the number of observers, in order to satisfy the Sanctions Committee that items were being used for their stated purpose.[22]

In summary, in a period of seven years (May 1996–May 2003) Iraq had over US$100 billion-worth of oil transactions through UN-controlled sales. However, only US$37 billion-worth of contracts for food and services was approved by the UN Secretariat.[23] The value of holds and good arrived under number of the OFF phases is shown in Tables 1.4 and 1.5 (see Appendix).[24] Iraq's revenues from the sale of oil through the UN Escrow Account was exposed to abuse and frauds, not only through the payment of numerous unjustified war compensations and lucrative salaries, but also through the huge costs of the UN operations in Iraq. The extent of Iraq's OFF revenues lost or held back by the UN remains unclear up till the time of writing (summer 2006).

The OFF Programme also involved a scandal that became publicly known only in 2004. The UN Secretary-General, Kofi Annan, appointed a commission of enquiry (the Volcker Commission) to investigate allegations of theft and bribery, and of the association of UN high-ranking officials with payoffs (vouchers) for the purchase of millions of barrels of Iraqi oil on extremely favourable terms, as well as oil smuggling by the Iraqi regime.[25] The Volcker Report showed that in fact the amount used for the reconstruction of public services and civilian infrastructures was rather less than half of the real proceeds received from the sale of Iraq's oil. In addition to the excessive deductions – made to cover UN operations in Iraq and compensation claims – the actual use of Iraq's available funds for rebuilding the civilian infrastructure and services was seriously hampered by the UN Sanctions Committee's systematic holds, delay, and rejection of imports and delivery contracts.

The Independent Inquiry Committee issued its definitive Report (Volcker) on the overall management and oversight of the OFF Programme on 7 September 2005. It detailed the results of its investigations into specific aspects of the OFF Programme, stressing that things had gone wrong, and that the reputation and credibility of the UN had been damaged. It called for the United Nations to establish a stronger executive leadership, institute a comprehensive administrative reform, and introduce more reliable controls and auditing. However, the Committee avoided placing responsibility for the difficulties with the OFF Programme exclusively at the door of the UN Secretariat. It stated that Members of the Security Council and its 661 Committee had to take their share of the blame for providing uneven and wavering direction in implementing the OFF Programme. The OFF Programme scandal and its implications for the actors involved is still an issue needing further investigation.

The Report also emphasized that the lack of clarity in the OFF Programme had been exacerbated by permitting the Iraqi regime to exercise too much involvement in the design and subsequent implementation of the Programme; 'as a result, neither the Security Council nor the Secretariat leadership had been in overall control'.

The cruel irony however was that Saddam Hussain and his henchmen, over more than thirteen years of sanctions, grew obscenely rich as a direct result of sanctions that were meant to punish them.[26] While these illicit crimes were taking place, Iraq's economy and its helpless civilian were made to suffer hunger, disease, and death as a result of those very sanctions that were said to be helping them.

Destruction of Iraq's Economy and Welfare Scenarios
Inflation
One of the devastating impacts of sanctions on the Iraqi economy was the sharp depreciation of the exchange rate of the Iraqi dinar (ID) and the escalation of the inflation rates. It should be noted that during the 1970s, the Iraqi dinar was one of the strongest currencies in the region, underpinned by oil revenues and rising levels of reserves stemming from the comfortable surplus on merchandise and trade. By the mid-1980s, however, the exchange value of the ID had been markedly weakened for many reasons, including the Iraq-Iran war, the collapse of oil prices, and the effect of international inflation.[27]

Prior to the invasion of Kuwait, in July 1990, although inflation was running at 45 percent, with an exchange rate of US$1 to ID 4 (unofficial), the official exchange rate remained at US$1 to ID 0.3.11.[28]

Following the imposition of sanctions, the foreign exchange market did not immediately reflect the full magnitude of the shock. The reason for this relative 'stability' was that the embargo was initially almost impermeable and affected imports as well as exports, thereby curtailing the demand for foreign currency. Compared with later years under sanctions, depreciation of the ID's value during the first few months of sanctions was 'mild', with 'black market' exchange rate of US$1 to ID 8, while the official exchange rate remained the same.[29] In other words, during the first year of sanctions, the ID lost only 50 percent of its market value against the US dollar, compared with later years under sanctions, when much more rapid depreciation of the Iraqi currency indeed fuelled inflation.

By December 1993, at the height of the economic crisis that preceded the enactment of the OFF agreement, the Iraqi government, in an attempt to narrow the budget deficit had resorted to printing money, a strategy that led to an inflationary spiral. Following this move, inflation rate reached 1000 percent, and by December 1995, the exchange value of the ID had hit a low of US$1 to ID 3,000.[30]

Political circumstances, especially those that reflected the relationship between the Iraq government and the UN, were immediately reflected onto rates of inflation and values of exchange rates. As an immediate reaction to the OFF agreement, especially as previously scarce goods began to become more widely available in the market, the inflation rate fell to an average of 60 percent in 1997 from an estimated 200 percent in 1996.[31] Similarly, the unofficial exchange rate of the ID reached US$1 to ID 1,900 in 1997.[32] However, despite the wider availability of goods in the Iraqi markets as a result of the OFF programme, prices of foodstuffs and other basic necessities rose by 23 percent as compared with levels of foodstuffs prices by the end of 1996.[33]

The same scenario was repeated prior to the 2003 war and the invasion of Iraq by the US and UK armies and its aftermath. In January 2003, the unofficial exchange rate of the ID depreciated from its black market rate of US$1 to ID 2000 to about

US$1 to ID 3000 in March 2003. This trend continued throughout 2003, when the exchange rates of the ID witnessed a period of significant fluctuation, trading at rates between US$1 to ID 2000–3000.[34]

Food and Medicine Crisis

The UN sanctions set off an escalating humanitarian crisis in Iraq, revealed through the drastic increases in prices of foodstuffs that were further worsened when the government terminated price subsidies because of the budget deficit.

During the 1970s and 1980s, prior to sanctions, Iraq's oil revenues had enabled the Iraqi government to implement polices that sought to continue high civilian levels of spending that gave particular priority to the health and education systems, as well as to food and other commodities that were directly subsidized and controlled by the state distribution system. Iraq also depended heavily on imports, and 75–80 percent of all consumed foodstuffs were imported.[35]

Iraq's welfare state was described as having been 'until recently among the most comprehensive and generous in the Arab World ... which ensured that Iraq had the highest caloric consumption per head in the Middle East by the end of the 1980s'.[36]

However, after the imposition of sanctions, the Iraqi government instituted a food rationing system in September 1990 that was considered internationally to be 'crucial' in sustaining the survival of the Iraqi population over years of sanctions, and in preventing an imminent famine. Even Max Van der Stoel, Special Rapporteur on the Human Rights Situation in Iraq, who was pro-sanctions and also one of the UN officials most critical of the Iraqi regime, was impressed by the sufficiency of the rationing system:

> The food warehouses and stocks of medicine in all cities are intended for all citizens, without any discrimination ... The state has been applying a comprehensive and exemplary system to ensure that its citizens receive a minimum allocation of basic foodstuffs ... the monthly allocation of foodstuffs is distributed on the basis of ration cards, which have been supplied to all Iraqi families in all parts of the country and also to Arab and foreign residents of Iraq.[37]

With the drastic increase of foodstuff market prices and the shrinking purchase value of the ID due to high inflation, basic subsistence for the majority of the Iraqi people was only attained through access to the government's rations, which were provided at nominal prices. The high rate of inflation was most directly reflected in food prices – especially of basic foods such as flour, meat, eggs, etc – that rose and fell following the value of the Iraqi dinar. For example, by the end of August 1990 the average food prices in shops were 850 times higher than the level in July 1990, and between 1991 and 1995 were 4,000 times higher.[38]

By September 1998, the UN's Department of Humanitarian Panel estimated that four million Iraqis (about 20 percent) were living in extreme poverty.[39] In condemning the OFF programme the UN Secretary-General pointed out that, in the period from July 1995 to October 1998, Iraq was left with only US$5.2 billion for humanitarian purchases, and noted that this amounted to about US$75 per capita annually for Iraq's 20 million people.[40] It appeared that Iraq's per capita income was far below the World Bank's threshold of absolute poverty at US$1 per day.[41] In March 2001 Anan reported to the Security Council that:

> The humanitarian programme was never intended to meet all the humanitarian needs of the Iraqi population or to be a substitute for normal economic activity. Also the programme is not geared to address the longer-term deterioration of living standards or remedy declining health standards and infrastructure.[42]

In a 1999 report, the UN Humanitarian Panel observed that the OFF had not prevented the humanitarian crisis in Iraq.[43] It found that even if the programme worked perfectly, the humanitarian situation in Iraq would continue to be disastrous in the absence of a sustained revival of the Iraqi economy, which in turn could not be achieved solely through remedial humanitarian efforts.

In protest about the OFF programme, Denis Halliday, the UN Humanitarian Coordinator, resigned in 1999. Halliday was followed in 2001 by Hans von Sponeck, who rejected the OFF programme as a solution for the dire humanitarian situation in Iraq under sanctions. Von Sponeck remarked that:

> The OFF provides me with US$177 per person per year – 50 cents a day – for all of the needs of each Iraqi citizen. Now I ask you, US$177 per year? That's not a per capita income figure. This is a figure out of which everything has to be financed, from electrical service to water and sewage, to food, to health – the lot ... that is obviously a totally, totally inadequate figure.[44]

As he was preparing to leave Baghdad, Von Sponek said: 'I can no longer be associated with a programme that prolongs suffering of the people and which has no chance of meeting even the basic needs of the civilian population'.[45] Later he declared: 'Lawlessness of one kind does not justify lawlessness of another kind', and asked 'how long must the civilian population be exposed to such punishment for something that they have never done?'[46]

Wages and Income Levels

The Iraqi state during the 1970s and 1980s directed its energies towards extensive state/nation-building programmes that included generous resource allocation to the public sector, including industry, agriculture and commercial services, in addition to education, health and social services (see Appendix Table 1.6 and 1.7).

The welfare state in Iraq thus became the centre of all aspects of life in Iraq, including the economic, political social and cultural domains. As such, the state was directed towards benefiting a large proportion of the population, especially the labour force, through governmental bureaucracies, and the educational and health systems. This led to the emergence of a large middle class that owed its very existence to the state. The *Middle East Economic Digest* (MEED) described the government's role in providing various services as 'remarkable', noting that:

> Prices of basic necessities were stabilized by state subsidy; the minimum wages greatly increased over the rate of inflation; new labour laws provided complete job security; the state became an employer of last resort for all graduates; free education and health care was provided; per-capita national income increased from ID 195 [equal to US$587, based on the exchange rate at the time] in 1970, to ID 7,564 [equal to US$22,692 in 1979].[47]

Immediately after the imposition of sanctions and the cut in revenues from oil exports and sales, the Iraqi government responded by limiting or putting a total stop on nominal expenditures to all economic sectors. Moreover, due to the shortage of revenues and because of channelling the available revenues into consolidating the power of its elites, the state was unable to preserve its central role in the economy, i.e., through direct control of production and distribution, fixed wages, direct subsidies of goods, and price fixing.

In the early years of sanctions, the state began to lay off large number of public sector employees since it had to shut down many of its public sector enterprises, down-size others, and sell off the rest to the private sector and to individuals. However, the most drastic measure taken by the Iraqi government was the removing of price subsidies of all goods and foodstuff above the food ration. These measures led to escalating prices of basic necessities, including fuel, as well as the imposition of high fees and taxes for many services, such as education, health, and for other services that had previously been provided free or for subsidized prices.

Under these circumstances, wages could not cover the most basic essential needs. The economic conditions of the vast majority of Iraqis of middle and lower-middle class began to decline, reflected by deteriorating living standards, a surge in unemployment, and diminishing incomes.

The extreme economic recession thus created a number of particular vulnerable groups, and people dependent on the government for their main source of income, such as civil servants and pensioners, no longer received an adequate income to survive. The gap between monthly salary and levels of food prices is described as followed:

> During 1993, average monthly salaries for civil servants ranged from ID 200–500, two or three times more than their level in August 1990. Meanwhile, Iraq's food price index increased nearly 75-fold over the same period of time. In 1995, food prices were 4,000–5,000 times more than their August 1990 levels, while average monthly salaries were only ID 3,000–5,000 [US$2–2,5]. Consequently, families' real earnings have fallen to less than 5 percent of their pre-sanctions level, as measured by food purchasing power.[48]

Throughout the 1990s, regular surveys by the Food and Agriculture Organization (FAO), the World Food Programme (WFP), the UN Children's Fund (UNICEF), and the World Health Organization (WHO), in addition to numerous reports by independent institutions and non-Governmental organizations (NGOs), continued to document the tremendous collapse in living standards, including health, education, employment, food insecurity, and many others.[49]

The UN sanctions imposed on Iraq created widespread unemployment and severe shortages of specialists and skilled people, due to the migration of many individuals either outside Iraq or into non-related professions, often as taxi drivers or petty traders. As Boone et al. reported for the Center for Economic and Social Rights (CESR):

> It is apparent that there has been a very dramatic rise in the number of people who engage in 'bottom line' economic activities such as casual labour and petty trading. There is free entry into these activities, so long as a person is reasonably healthy, but rates of remunerations are extremely low.[50]

UN officials and other independent observers confirmed the scale of the suffering endured by the Iraqi people due to the economic crisis.[51] Deteriorating wages and rising unemployment drained away many of the brightest and best among Iraq's educated elite, as mass emigration became the only way to a better life. The Security Council became increasingly aware of the steadily unravelling social cohesion in Iraq over the years of UN sanctions. Theft, bribery, juvenile delinquency, begging and prostitution, despite the horrific punishments attached to such crimes, increased to an alarming level.[52]

Gendered Analysis of Sanctions

In spite of the widely documented impact of sanctions on the economy and the people of Iraq, there has been notable absence of material addressing the gender-specific impact of sanctions on Iraqi women. This absence, however, is in line with assumptions that politics and international politics are gender-neutral, i.e., affecting women and men on the same level.[53] Although these assumptions are increasingly being challenged, empirical investigation about how politics, in different ways and circumstances, is ingrained in the lives of women is still limited.[54] Nevertheless, investigation of the relationships between women and politics has raised questions about how women are differently affected from men by international politics, and how women relate to economic and social forces, both within and outside society.

It is known that while images of men or women may vary across culture and history, in most cultures, gender differences do signify relationships of inequality of power and resources distribution, and relationships of domination between women and men.[55] Therefore, inequalities between the sexes are embodied in a whole system of social relations. As such, even in normal circumstances, women are at an economic disadvantage relative to men; i.e., women's work in formal and informal sectors is undervalued and unrecognized (especially household responsibilities and child rearing), and women often play several roles together (at work as well as in the home).

Experiences from other cases reveal that dislocation, disruption in the supply of food and water, and health services are particularly felt by women who often have to replace the destroyed infrastructure. The effect of war and political strife, and the implications of these processes, including 'insecurity', 'violence', 'poverty', etc., are thus also gendered processes and have different implications for men and women.[56]

In light of this state of affairs, this book aims not simply to analyse Iraqi women's subordination and inequality within the society, but more importantly, to examine how sanctions made themselves felt within the Iraqi society, and their effects on Iraqi women in their daily lives in society and inside the family. As such, it explores the implications of sanctions for Iraqi women in terms of sociological and ideological change in women's roles, and in their status in the society and the family. It is based on the living experiences of Iraqi women under the circumstances of sanction, not only for the provision of basic needs, but also the effects on women in their subordinate and disadvantaged situation.

The enquiry of this book thus implies an understanding about Iraqi women that goes beyond referring to the political economy of sanctions to include their implications for the socio-economic role of the state, of which Iraqi women were the prime beneficiaries. In this context, this book also includes a historical account (1970s and 1980s) of Iraqi women's relationship with the state and to the process of state-building.

Samples and Methods of Research

The investigation of the gender-specific impact of the UN sanctions on Iraqi women was based on a study of the living experiences of 227 Iraqi women aged between 15–55 years, through surveys (residential and student-specific), open-ended interviews, and case studies.[57] In response to demands by respondents for their anonymity to be protected, all the surveyed women are introduced under pseudonyms.

The respondents differed in terms of their family status (married, single, and widows), their employment status (working, non-working, and students), and their educational background.

The survey of residential areas was conducted according to a random selection of samples from three residential areas (Madinat Al-Thawra, Al-Adhamiya, and Al-Mansur) in Baghdad City. Each residence (house number) was counted as one unit, i.e., one woman. However, in cases where one residence consisted of more than one household unit, one woman (aged between 15–55 years) was selected from each household.[58] In total, 180 residents' units were visited, i.e., approximately 60 residence units in each of the three locations. All the residences surveyed were family-based, including households that were headed by women.[59] The survey of students was conducted with 50 female students from two major universities in Baghdad (Al-Mustanseriya University and Baghdad University) from different disciplines and educational levels.

The degree of response was highly successful. The number of respondents who completed the questionnaires was 227, with only 10 questionnaires rejected. However, during the initial contacts with respondents, some difficulties were encountered. Some women were initially hesitant about answering the survey. This, however, was expected. Due to the long period of political oppression in Iraq, people were reluctant to reveal personal views or expose details of their intimate family lives for fear that their lives might be endangered. Therefore, depending on the individual case, it was important to make the right introduction, in order to give respondents sufficient information and time to get to know about the research before I proceeded with questions or writing notes.

In addition to the surveys, the empirical work also involved three case studies and 90 open-ended interviews; most of these were carried out on the basis of more than one meeting (extended interviews). Open-ended interviews and case studies were of the utmost values as sources of information through which it was possible to understand the changing conditions of Iraqi women under sanctions by linking their present experiences to that of the past. In this way, it was possible to illuminate previously unexamined or misunderstood experiences, particularly Iraqi women's experiences in the pre-sanctions period.

Location of the Fieldwork

The fieldwork took place solely in Baghdad City, and the survey was carried out in three residential areas, based on Iraqi statistics from the 1970s that classified Baghdad in terms of the class and income of the inhabitants. These are described below:

Area I – Madinat Al-Thawra (Revolution City)

Al-Thawra city was created by the Revolutionary government of 14 July 1958 to shelter the influx of migrants from different parts of Iraq. These were mainly farmers from villages around Baghdad who sought employment in state institutions and in the growing industrial public sector. In the 1970s, the Ba'th government renamed the district Saddam City. However, after the Anglo-American invasion and occupation of Iraq in 2003, the area received a 'brand new' name – it was to be called Al-Sader City, in remembrance of Imam Mohammad Baqer Al-Sader, the prominent Shi'i opposition member who, with his two sons, was killed by Saddam Hussain in the 1980s.

Al-Thawra is the largest and the poorest residential area of Baghdad City. It is located on the east bank of the Tigris River, which divides Baghdad into two major parts (West/Karkh and East/Resafa). The inhabitants of Al-Thawra are mainly poor factory workers, farmers, and small, lower middle-class, retail shopkeepers with a low- to middle-level educational background. The majority of the roads in this district are unpaved and muddy, and difficult to walk through because of the sewage that over-flows into the ruined houses and the nearby roads. The empirical work in this area was carried out smoothly and without specific difficulties with the people there; rather, most problems were encountered when taxi drivers often refused to drive along these roads. In spite of the miserable condition of this area, local people were friendly and very willing to speak about their experiences of life under sanctions. In the course of this book, Al-Thawra residential area is referred to as Area I. There were 90 women participants from this area.

Area II – Madinat Al-'Adhamiya (Al-'Adhamiya City)

The second largest residential area in Baghdad City, Al-'Adhamiya district is also located in the eastern part of Baghdad City. One of the oldest residential areas of

Baghdad, it was named after the shrine of the Grand Imam (theologian and lawyer – *al-imam al-'adham*), Abu-Hanifa Al-Nu'man (699AD/80AH-767AD/150AH); the shrine is located in its centre. During the 1970s, the area was known as one of Baghdad's finest residential areas and was inhabited largely by people with middle-class and upper middle-class incomes and with upper-middle and high educational backgrounds, who were mostly professional and government sector employees. Since the 1990s conditions here had noticeably worsened. A large part of the area had become very impoverished, with crumbling houses and streets. With regard to the degree of responding to the research, more hesitancy was encountered in this area as compared with Area I. *Al- 'Adhamiya City* is referred to throughout the book as Area II. There were 75 women participants from this area.

Area III – Madinat Al-Mansur (Al-Mansur City)

Al-Mansur City is one of the oldest and finest areas of Baghdad, named after the Abbasid Caliph Abu Ja'far al Mansur, who established Baghdad city (145AH/762CE). It is located on the west bank of the river Tigris (al-Karkh side). In the 1970s, Al-Mansur City was largely inhabited by high-income professional people, most of whom were government sector employees, civil servants, and business managers, as well as a tiny segment of government officials. However, there was a major change in the area during the 1990s, when a large proportion of its original inhabitants either sold their houses to move to cheaper districts or left the country entirely, to live in other countries with greater advantages in terms of income and personal security. On the other hand, the economic crisis caused by sanctions has provided plenty of opportunities for a small section of the society to profit from the situation, and such individuals have been able to move into the area to live. At the time of the survey, the majority of Al-Mansur inhabitants consisted of families whose primary source(s) of income were either from private businesses or from their positions as high-ranking government officials. It was clear from the sample that none of the residents of this area had to depend entirely on public sector wages. Some problems were encountered in this area, particularly because many women were unwilling to cooperate and doubted the intension of the survey, while some other were more interested in knowing about life in the United Kingdom than in talking about their lives in Iraq. Al-Mansur city will be referred to in the study as Area III. The survey included a total of 62 female respondents (60 house units) from this area.

Structure of the Book

Following the present chapter, which illustrates the macro-economic impact of the sanctions on Iraq and details about the research, the second chapter illustrates dynamics of gender as constructed and sustained in Iraqi society over the two decades (1970s and 1980s) prior to the imposition of sanctions. It examines the position of Iraqi women within the state-building project during the different historical periods. The chapter offers an overview of the way in which micro-economic conditions influenced Iraqi women's legal status and their participation in the labour force during the 1970s and 1980s, as a contrast to the subsequent situation under sanctions. The aim of Chapter Two is to demonstrate how the status of women in Iraq was shaped by economic and political conditions, and how their legal and social status was related to the regulatory power of the state in its different historical configurations.

Chapter Three illustrates the impact of sanctions on Iraqi women's participation in the labour force, and their impact on the gender division of the labour force. The chapter provides insights into the kinds of power relationships in the economy and the labour market under sanctions, and examines how, and to what extent, relations of gender inequality in the labour market were moved and affected by sanctions. It sheds light on trends in the employment of females and levels of income and earnings under sanctions, particularly through study of women's participation in different economic activities (public sectors; private sector; family enterprises; and informal and self-employment).

The impact of sanctions on female education in Iraq is examined in Chapter Four, which is based on the findings of the student survey (50 female students), and the follow-up with some of the students after they had graduated. As a contrast to the status of education under sanctions, the chapter provides also a historical account (statistics) of female education, and discusses state legislation during the 1970s and 1980s that concerned female education and the related progress of female enrolment at different educational levels. The intention is to assess the implications of sanctions for female education, first through exploring constraints on various aspects of education in Iraq, and secondly through interpreting the impact of these constraints on female education, particularly with regard to its effect on social values and attitudes towards women.

Chapter Five examines the way in which aspects of the economic and political crisis under sanctions were transformed into influential factors in the reconstruction of gender relations and in the changes in women's positions inside the family. Through exploring the insights gained from three case studies of Iraqi women from different social and economic backgrounds, the chapter emphasizes that the implications of political processes, such as sanctions for women, do not enter into the difficulties of everyday life. Rather, it aims, to explore the more damaging conse-quences of these circumstances as they extend from being shortages of food, diminishing incomes, and deteriorated socio-economic services, etc to the more perpetuated consequences for women's roles and positions in the society, kinship and family kinship.

Chapter Six explores the psychological impact of sanctions on Iraqi women. It explains the psychological conditions of women in times of crisis, and the pressures they endured when the entire community suffered economic and political upheavals. The chapter illustrates aspects of Iraqi women's experiences during the crisis, such as violence, domestic responsibilities, and health conditions.

The Conclusion gives an assessment of sanctions, their political and humanitarian objectives and their effectiveness, as well as considering the development of the Iraqi case after 2003.

2

IRAQI WOMEN AND THE STATE:
A HISTORICAL REVIEW

Introduction

In exploring the changing conditions of Iraqi women under the weight of sanctions, it is essential to examine their position and the kind of gender relationships they experienced in what might be considered the more 'normal' circumstances of the pre-sanctions period.

It should be noted that although the roles assigned to women in Iraq by the Iraqi regime in the pre-sanctions period have received some attention, this particular issue has not been dealt with comprehensively. The available literature on the subject focuses largely on the issue of the state's ambivalent attitude towards women, but solely within the context of the patriarchal structures of the Iraqi society. On the whole, it is agreed that the state either attempted to weaken patriarchal and tribal structure by assigning new roles to women, or else weakened women's status and roles by trying to maintain and reassert patriarchal structures.[1]

While these arguments rest largely on socio-cultural factors as the underlying motivation for the changing roles and status of Iraqi women, the intention of this chapter is to draw upon a combination of other factors behind the excessive social change that occurred during the 1970s and 1980s. It therefore provides an analysis of economic and political dynamics during various historical periods, and the ways in which they influenced the legal status of Iraqi women and their position in the labour force. Special emphasis is given to explaining the position of Iraqi women in the national state-building project and to attempts by the nation-state to bring about changes in women's position in the economy and the family.

Recasting the Nation-State in Iraq

It is well known that by the middle of the 20th century, the Arab world had witnessed many historical momentums that culminated in the emergence of the nation-state and affected the development of Arab societies, not only at that time, but also for many years subsequently.

In the discourse of increasing challenges from colonial cultures, the nation-state became a central arena of experimentation among competing socio-political forces; this, in return, enabled the state to play an important role in society and raised expectations for positive and rapid social change.[2]

The evolution of the nation-state in Iraq began towards the end of the colonial and semi-colonial era in 1958, when a group of 'Free Officers' (*harakat al-dhobat al-ahrar*) moved swiftly in a revolution that put an end to the monarchy in Iraq.[3] However, the new government did not survive long. In February 1963, a group of officers turned against the revolution through a coup d'état, and in alliance with the Ba'thists managed to take control. Following the coup and a five-year period of political instability, the Ba'th Party came to power in 1968.[4]

The Ba'thist elites, a close-knit kinship group derived from rural and clannish lower-middle class origins and belonging to the minority Sunni sect, rose to power on the back of a nationalist, pan-Arabist, and relatively secular political ideology – the Ba'th.[5] Like other Arab nationalist political elites in Egypt (1952–70), Tunisia (1956–87), Algeria (1972–9), Syria (1963), and in Libya (1969), the Ba'thist elite in Iraq (1968–2003) saw themselves as apostles for political and social victories, not simply within Iraq but rather as a mass pan-Arab progressive movement that sought to revitalize the Arab nation and restore the historic role of the Arabs among the others nations of the world.[6]

However, the emergence of nationalist Arab ideologies was not the only factor behind the evolution of the nation-state in Iraq. The structural alteration in Iraq's oil industry in the 1970s, especially the nationalization of the Iraqi Oil Company, was the other most important factor behind the change. The ideology of the Ba'th in Iraq was tremendously empowered by the huge oil reserves, which, together with an extremely oppressive security apparatus, had enabled the broadening of the regime's narrow political base, thus turning the Ba'th into a party of the masses.

The nationalization of the Iraqi Oil Company in 1972 was followed by the sharp rise in oil prices and the consequent 'oil boom', and the government duly embarked on an extensive programme of economic growth, aimed especially at directing the economy away from agriculture into state-owned industry (the oil industry) and services. This objective was behind the mass urbanization of Iraq's cities and the consequent migration from rural areas to the big cities, where job opportunities and new life-styles were opened up to the masses.[7] Throughout the 1970s, the state directed its energies towards extensive state-building projects that included public programmes in industry, agriculture and commercial services, along with education, health, and social services (see Appendix Table 1.7).

Iraq's welfare state in the 1970s was directed towards benefiting the wider majority of the poor and lower-middle classes and turning them into a middle-class labour force of governmental bureaucracies, civil servants, intellectuals, military, police, security apparatuses, and other state agencies. In this context, the nation-state in Iraq came to acknowledge the essential position of Iraqi women in the state-building project, and their roles in the realization of a 'modern' society.

Dynamics of Gender in the 1970s

Under the slogan of equal rights for all citizens, regardless of their sex, Ba'th elites, in the 1970s, stressed that liberating women was an integral part of liberating the nation from the 'backwardness' and 'the power of darkness' of colonialism and its clique of feudalists and capitalist.[8] Establishing the status of Iraqi women was emphasized in connection with the transformation of the impoverished classes into a large, educated middle class society, thus directly linked to the state-building process and to national development. Accordingly, the ABSP Doctrine of 1974 stated:

Institutions are obliged to adopt specific economic, social, and cultural legislations and programmes aiming at promoting and encouraging women's participation in the country's economic development [work, education, cultural, political, and social domains].[9]

This political ideology was cultivated through an extremely centralized role on the part of the state in the economy. During the 1970s Iraq witnessed overall economic growth and a rapid spread of consumerism, as well as a rise in income and living standards for the vast sectors of the Iraqi population. Collectively, these factors constituted the new challenge that required Iraqi women as well as men to unite, in order to contribute to, and cope with the process of change.

However, in addition to the national challenge, other factors on both the regional and international levels, motivated the new socio-cultural outlook of the Iraqi society in the 1970s. At the regional level, social class transformation and improvement of women's rights in the society and the family became a phenomenon, especially among the broad and evolving middle-class strata in many parts of the Middle East. Liberating ideologies and notions of human rights and women's rights were widely favoured by the oppressed poor, most of whom were eager to move out of under-development and poverty towards the new opportunities that were becoming available for both women and men.

This mainstream was also supported and encouraged at the international level. During the 1970s, the balance of power throughout the world and specifically within the United Nations placed a considerable responsibility on the newly emerged nation-states. This came within the context of an emerging new spirit in the world encouraged by the UN's support for the struggles of developing countries for independence from colonial rule, and through the UN's backing for state-building projects that were taking place in these countries.

Legislation Concerning Participation of Female Labour

As an outcome of these factors, Iraq's political elites were encouraged to reflect a progressive image of women's role in their society, and this was particularly portrayed in the adoption of number of international human rights conventions.[10] The realization of Iraqi women's full potential came to be regarded as part of the 'package', and as one of the state's main tasks. Concepts of 'women's liberation' and 'equality of men and women' that often stressed in the statements of the political elites in the

1970s, were exemplified through reforms and laws that assigned rights and preferential treatment to women.[11] The most important provisions concerning women's rights in the 1970s included the following:

- Principle of Equality between the Sexes

Iraq's interim Constitution of 1970 acknowledged the right for equal enjoyment of economic, social and cultural rights without discrimination on the basis of sex, religion or race.[12] Moreover, the constitution ensured women's particular rights in areas where they were less advantaged, such as employment. The state granted every able citizen the right to work, specifying that: 'the state must guarantee good working conditions, raise the living standards of workers, and improve their professional skills, without discrimination on the basis of their sex'. In this area, the constitution placed a positive responsibility on the state (Articles 1, 12 & 19), obliging it to invest financially in the process of realizing these rights (Article 19, Paragraph C). Stipulating the principle of equality between sexes in the constitution paved the way for a series of progressive provisions (laws and reforms) that were adopted during the 1970s.[13]

- Special Provisions (Preferential Treatment)

Chapter Six and amendments of the 1970 Labour Law focused exclusively on addressing women's rights at work; e.g., ensuring good working conditions, special health security, the provision of childcare at the worksite, and baby-feeding breaks during working hours.[14] All workers were entitled to state housing: however, single breadwinners were 'especially' entitled to this right, in addition to receiving other welfare benefits, such as child allowances.[15]

- Maternity Leave Laws

The Labour Law of 1970 for the first time granted Iraqi women the right to fully paid maternity leave (one month's ante-natal and six weeks' postnatal, subject to extension in certain cases).[16] However, this right was subject to several amendments during the 1970s and 1980s, and these adjustments to maternity leave law reflect the state's direct intervention in Iraqi women's lives, namely through the regulation of women's productive and reproductive roles. Through its legal policy, the state either supported women's productive and reproductive roles or restricted one role at the expense of another.

Amendments to women's right to fully/partly paid maternity leave during the 1970s and 1980s, to an extent indicated the way specific economic conditions affected the state's attitude towards women's participation in the labour force. The economic prosperity (oil revenues) witnessed in Iraq during the 1970s[17] was reflected in the advantages given to Iraqi women through preferential treatment and other social benefits, particularly their right to fully paid maternity leave. By 1977, maternity leave had increased from one month to six weeks of ante-natal and six weeks of post-natal leave,[18] and by 1979, in addition to six weeks of fully paid leave, women had the right to six months of maternity leave on half salary for every child under four years of age.[19] Moreover, women also had the right to enjoy four periods of maternity leave during their employment services, with maternity leave to be counted towards women's pension and retirement benefits.

It should be noted however, that these rights and preferential treatment were assigned exclusively to women employees in the state (public) sector, whereas the rights of women workers in the private sector were not only minimal but were also among the responsibilities of the employers.

Family Laws and Legislation

In the process of realizing the new role of Iraqi women in the 1970s, the state ventured 'intimately' into the extremely sensitive area of family affairs. Iraqi women were focused on in terms of the family, and the family was considered as the primary element of the nation, whose specific duty was to protect and nurture it. The most important legislation in this area related to the Personal Status Code (PSC) or *qanun al-ahwal al-shakhsiya*, which had been first promulgated in Law No. 188 of 1959. However, the enactment of the PSC as a coherent legal document applying to all Iraqi citizens (of Muslim faith) occurred in 1978.[20] The code introduced important changes in some of the most sensitive areas of women's lives, including marriage, polygamy, divorce, children custody, and inheritance, as follows:

- Laws Regulating Marriage[21]

In principle, marriage was considered a 'national duty', which the state had to encourage, facilitate and supervise, while procreation was the duty of the family.[22] The PSC prohibited forced marriages, and the conditional marriage of minors (minimum 15 years) had to receive the consent of the guardians of both parties and the consent of a state-authorized judge (who was entitled to overrule the wishes of the guardian(s) if there were no adequate grounds for those wishes). Marriage without the presence of a state-authorized judge is considered illegal.

- Laws Regulating Polygamy[23]

According to the PSC, marriage to a second wife requires the first wife's consent and the permission of an Iraqi state-authorized judge. The legislation requires the official registration of all marriages in an official Iraqi court and failure to act upon these conditions entails penalties.[24]

- Laws Regulating Divorce[25]

Concerning divorce, the PSC introduced a radical change to the legal position of women. It enabled them to have equal rights with men to initiate divorce, especially in cases of persistent dispute, adultery, incurable disease or long absence of one of the spouses. In cases of adultery or marital infidelity, the state-authorized judge would be obliged to grant the ultimate divorce according to the wish of one or both spouses (see Chapter Five for other conditions where the woman has the ultimate right of divorce).[26] The 1978 Code also confirmed the 1959 Code's stipulation outlawing the practice of killing women for honour crimes (i.e., extra-marital sexual relations) a practice that, with varying degrees of severity, had been widespread among tribes in Iraq.[27]

• Custody of Children

The Personal Status Code (the same laws regulating divorce) granted custody of children less than 10 years of age to the mother, unless the court was convinced that the mother's guardianship was harmful to the child. Judges were given the right to prolong the period of a mother's custody when this was deemed desirable, until the child was between 15 and 18 years old. Until then, the child could choose which parent it wished to stay with.

• Laws Regulating Inheritance

The PSC of 1978 preserved the special stipulation of the 1959 Code that concerned a female's right to inheritance. Accordingly, women were granted equality in inheritance rights in certain special cases. A single female child was made fully eligible to inherit from her parents, and the right of her parents' male relatives to claim that inheritance was nullified (Law No. 188, Personal Status Code, 1959). The 1978 Code also preserved the 1959 provision that granted a single daughter equal rights with her brother(s) to an inheritance.[28]

Dynamics of Gender in the 1980s

By the end of the 1970s Iraq was beginning to witness a complex web of economic and political factors that took the country into a prolonged period of decline and that affected the lives and wellbeing of Iraq and its people. It started in mid 1979 when Saddam Hussain, having managed to overcome all his opponents the Revolutionary Command Council (RCC), became the President of Iraq.[29] Secondly, after less than two years in office, Saddam ignited a prolonged war with its neighbour Iran (September 1980– July 1988).

After Saddam reached the pinnacle of power in Iraq, one constant force in the leadership was embodied in his person, with nepotism becoming closely intertwined with the process of state-building.[30] Laws and legislation, including the ABSP's Doctrine that had functioned as a guideline for the party, became visibly less important than the President's speeches, which were regarded as both law and the nation's ideological guide.

With regard to Iraq's economy, the average annual growth rates of the 1970s, which had shown promising prospects for further sustainable economic development, were forced backwards in the 1980s, due to the outbreak of the Iraq-Iran war.[31] The serious damage inflicted on Iraq's oil facilities by the Iranian air campaign at the first years of the war coupled with the dramatic fall in oil prices and high levels of inflation, managed to shrink Iraq's national income from ID 15,323 billion in 1980 to ID 8,925 billion in 1981 (at exchange rate US$1 to ID 0,311).[32] The development programmes that had previously been projected had to be curtailed, while Iraq's spending on the war and on non-military imports relied heavily on loans and financial support from the Gulf States.[33]

While the Iraq-Iran war meant death, disability, and destruction for hundreds of thousands of young Iraqi men, for the majority of Iraqi women it meant heavy responsibilities both as mothers and workers.[34] During the 1980s, Iraqi women had to organize their lives according to the state's ambivalent attitude towards their roles in society and the family. The state's attitude towards women during the 1980s was portrayed through its contradictory demands on Iraqi women. In the period from 1980 to 1985 they were invited to participate more actively in productive life, with an opening-up to women of all opportunities in the wage labour force. However, the period from 1986 to 1990 saw Iraqi women being asked to concentrate on their 'natural' role as the 'producer' of the nation. In this period they were encouraged to leave their formal jobs as workers and civil servants in order to give birth to more children (to a minimum of five children).[35]

In the realizing of the state's gender policy in the 1980s, the General Federation of Iraqi Women (GFIW) took on a special role as the state's female 'arm' in both the society and the polity. As well as organizing the female constituency for the Ba'th regime, the GFIW also played an important part in supporting the state's 'contrary' demands on Iraqi women. At one point (1980–85) the GFIW was placed at the head of a national campaign aimed at increasing women's participation in the labour force while at another stage (1985–90), it obtained the leading role in another national campaign, in which, however, its role was aimed at encouraging Iraqi women to increase the birth rate.

Legislation Concerning Participation of Female Labour (1980–5)

Most importantly, the new challenges that Iraqi women had to meet in the 1980s were embodied in new legislation as well as through amendments to existing laws, especially those concerning women's right to maternity leave and women's labour movement within and outside the country. This was reflected in the following:

• Laws Regulating Civil Services[36]
The law of Civil Service (CSL) of 1975 was amended to encourage women's participation in a-typical jobs, such as introducing female workers (doctors, nurses and other servants) into military hospitals, and granting them special allowances in addition to their salaries.[37] In the same context, all female graduates were required to work for one year (civil service) in hospitals and health centres before they could be assigned to any other job in the state sector.[38]

• Law Regulating Movement of Labour Force
Aimed at encouraging women to stay at jobs, a state decree issued in December 1980, gave men employed in the state/public sector the right to accompany their wives if the wife's job required her to change work location.[39] This amendment cancelled a previous provision that gave this entitlement to working women only.

In the same context, male and female employees in the public sector were excluded from the right to paid accompanying (family) leave outside the country.[40] This decree cancelled a previous provision that had entitled qualified men and women to receive special allowances on an equal footing in such cases. However, by July 1981 a further decree had forbidden husbands or/and wives to take family (accompanying) leave outside Iraq unless they had had at least two years of (actual) service within the country.[41] Later, a new decree was adopted in 1983 that terminated the system of accompanying leave outside Iraq, regardless of the reasons.[42]

In a similar manner, applications for resignation were also subject to restrictions. In 1983 a decree was issued stipulating that civil servants (both men and women) were not permitted to hand in their resignation unless they had completed ten years of service in the public sector. The decree also obliged those applying to resign to refund the state for the cost of their education.[43]

• Laws Regulating Maternity Leave
In 1980, women's rights to fully and partly paid maternity leave were reduced from six weeks of fully paid and six months of half-paid leave to a total of 72 days (21 days of ante-natal and 51 days of post-natal leave), and they were obliged to complete at least one year's service before being entitled to another maternity leave.[44] This decree was speedily amended in 1981, with the assertion that women's maternity leave should not be 'less than six months' in total, and that they could enjoy this entitlement four times during their services for every child under four years old.[45]

However, the most radical amendment to maternity leave since the adoption of the 1970 Labour Law was a 1982 decree that abolished the right to paid maternity leave (fully and partly paid).[46] Moreover, this decree also regulated maternity leave for a period of maximum of six months, and specified that maternity leave was only granted to mothers with a child under one year old.

Dynamics of Gender in the Period 1986–90
By the end of 1986 the state, through its various institutions, had launched its second 'national' campaign of the 1980s. This time however, the aim was to encourage women to produce more children for the 'Revolution'. Many Iraqi women commented sarcastically on this campaign by taking the title of a daily television programme about Ba'thist ideology called 'The Revolution Asks and We Answer' and twisting it to 'Saddam Asks and Iraqi Woman Answers (tjeeb)'.[47] On this new mission, Saddam, during one of his visits to the GFIW, asserted that: 'the revolution demands that every Iraqi family should have at least five children (boys or girls). A family with less than four children is considered less loyal to the revolution'.[48] The Federation immediately responded with another campaign, this time aimed at encouraging women to give birth to more children and again carried out through the media and through seminars and conferences. A three-year working plan involving co-operation with the Health and Education ministries, legislative bodies, and the media, was set up by the GFIW to implement Saddam's ideas regarding the role of Iraqi women in procreation.[49]

However, it is believed that the issue had only partly to do with these assumptions and that there was another reason involved as well. The worsening economic and financial crisis of the war pushed the state into hastily-formulated pragmatic policies, one of which was the step towards privatization that led to the discharging and redistributing of a large part of the labour force, particularly women. By the end of the Iraq-Iran War, the demobilization into civilian life of large numbers of servicemen encouraged the removal of women from productive tasks. The official justification for dismissing female labour was then given a moral and patriotic image, namely that women would instead devote their time to give birth to more children, to answer 'the demand of the leader and the revolution'. Within this framework, convincing women to leave their employment became 'logical', since it encouraged the idea that developing women's reproductive role became their contribution to production.

Legislation Concerning Participation of Female Labour (1986–90)

In addition to slimming down the public sector, the state began to encourage the emergence of the private sector by lifting restrictions on labour force movement between economic sectors and facilitating early retirement and labour resignation.[50] In order to maintain and develop these trends, the state adopted new laws and amended other, as indicted below:

- Laws Regulating Civil Service

In 1987, the state allowed working women to resign from their jobs in the state sector on family grounds, especially where children were involved.[51] In addition, the state issued a decree granting full retirement rights to women who resigned, although this privilege was restricted to women with at least fifteen years of service, or to mothers with at least three children under the age of fifteen. Widows and divorced women were entitled to the same right.[52] By 1987, the state had also exempted women who had resigned from the obligation concerning the repayment of the costs of their education to the state, without this affecting their full retirement rights.[53]

These decrees were not only aimed at young women but were directed particularly towards women over thirty years of age: because they had had quite a long period of work experience (at least 15 years) and/or were already mothers of 'at least' three children, they became the target group. Obviously, the 'national duty' envisaged in women's reproductive role did not exempt older women, mothers of three or more children, and those with relatively long work experience, from carrying out their obligations. The formulation of this law was the clearest statement issued by the government about the political objectives of women's reproductive role at that particular moment.

- Laws Regulating Maternity Leave

Aimed at encouraging Iraqi women to increase birth rates, the state in 1987 granted one year of fully-paid maternity leave to mothers who gave birth to twins.[54] This was followed by another decree that entitled 'all' females in the public sector to similar privileges – six months fully-paid and six months half-salaried maternity leave – as long as they were in service.[55]

For the first time, and in the same year, the government adopted a decree that concerned women employed in the private sector. This decree amended Articles 80–89 of the 1971 Labour Law, according to which women in the private sector were entitled the same benefits granted to women in the public sector, particularly with regard to provisions concerning rights to maternity leave.[56] However, the new provisions stated that full responsibility for the payment of the 72 days of maternity leave had to be taken by private employers and not by the Social Security and Welfare organization as in the case of public sector employees.[57] However, placing full financial responsibility on private employers for payment of the special rights insurance designated by the state for working women, including training, special facilities for mothers and expectant women, and paid maternity leave, made females even less favoured by private sector employers, and thus failed to change the vulnerability of female workers in the private sector.

Female Labour Participation in Relation to Gender Dynamics

Having introduced ways in which macro-economic conditions influenced changes in the prevailing ideological images of Iraqi women's roles and status, and shown how these images were reflected through laws and legislation concerning women during the 1970s and 1980s, it is important to look at the implications of these dynamics for Iraqi women's participation in the labour force these historical moments.

Characteristics of Female Labour Participation in the 1970s

The unprecedented level of economic activity during the 1970s increased demands on the labour force to fill the new opportunities for employment. This demand coincided with the adoption of progressive labour laws and reforms that encouraged women into employment, and resulted in an unprecedented increase in female participation in the labour force. Statistics from the 1970s show that Iraq's labour force doubled, and that there was an unprecedented increase in numbers of jobs (see Appendix Table 2.1).[58] These statistics also indicate that a large number of Iraq women with varying skill levels took their first steps towards economic independence by accepting employment offered in the state sector. Female labour participation increased from 4 percent in 1967 to 17.5 percent in 1977 (see Appendix Table 2.1).

This made the public sector the main source of employment for both men and women in Iraq (see Appendix Table 2.2).[59] Official Iraqi statistics for 1977 show that 75.3 percent of the female labour force was concentrated in the production sectors, including agriculture, mining and quarrying, manufacturing industry, and the infra-structural sectors (water and electricity, construction and building) (see Appendix Table 2.1).

Iraqi women managed to enter into waged labour by occupying different professions, including so-called 'typically' men-only jobs such as technicians (32.4 percent of the total labour in the profession) (see Appendix Table 2.3). However, the rate of women in full-time jobs in 1977 was only 39.2 percent of the total labour force in the country, while the rate of females in part-time jobs was 58.6 percent.[60]

Unemployment among economically active females (excluding students) was 11 percent (i.e., 11,575 thousand) of total unemployment in the whole country.[61]

Characteristics of Female Labour Participation, 1980–5

The Iraq-Iran War meant that huge numbers of economically active Iraqi men were drafted into the armed forces. The level of economically active males in the armed forces increased from 2.9 percent (82,000) in 1975 to reach 13.4 percent (430,000) in 1980.[62] By the end of the Iraq-Iran War, the percentage of labour force draftees had reached 21 percent of the total of the economically active male population in Iraq, or one million young men.[63] These figures show that the war created critical shortages of labour, since a large proportion of manpower was directed to the front lines. Initially the draftees were replaced by foreign workers, but by 1983 the number of foreign workers had already fallen,[64] since Iraq's critical shortage of, and urgent need for hard currency had pushed the government to slow down the demand for foreign labour.[65]

The huge cost of the war with Iran and the desperate need for a cheaper workforce to replace foreign labour motivated the government to encourage and facilitate the entrance of Iraqi women into waged labour. However, the drafting of large numbers of young, economically active Iraqi men from civilian life into the armed forces remains the most important reason behind the call for Iraqi women to participate more actively in the labour force. This, in return, also affected the average income of the Iraqi family, and indeed meant that a large number of women found themselves economically responsible for the family, and had therefore joined the waged labour force.

This time, women's economic participation had been encouraged not only by laws and legislation, but most importantly also by the speeches of Saddam Hussain that often reflected the women's potential as qualified labour force. On one of his visits to the offices of the GFIW in March 1983, Saddam stated that:

> Iraqi women should participate in the production process. The roles of Iraqi women in other areas are already well recognized and the only area in which they have not realized their potential, and actually are far from doing so, is production. Women should work towards this goal in order to create a better balance between their duties and their rights.[66]

The GFIW responded by supporting the national campaign ("Campaign to Increase Women's Participation in the Economic Development Process") that was launched following a conference held by the Federation in September 1983. The Campaign involved establishing four offices for women in Baghdad and one in each of the Iraqi governorates. All ministries were required to cooperate with the campaign through special committees set up to direct the recruitment of women, and industrial plants were obliged to provide women with training courses that would facilitate their integration into the production process.

Official statistics shows that the patterns of female labour participation growth witnessed in the 1970s had continued during the first five years of the Iraq-Iran war.

Numbers of females had increased in all types of profession, including low-skilled jobs (See Appendix Table 2.5)[67], and their labour participation increased from 19 percent in 1980 to roughly 25 percent in 1985 (see Appendix Tables 2.4 and 2.5).[68]

Characteristics of Female Labour Participation, 1986–8
By 1986, at the height of the financial crisis of the state that resulted from the Iraq-Iran War and low oil prices, the government had launched another national campaign, aimed this time at increasing the birth rate. This campaign got under way as the state was embarking on new social and economic policies, including down-sizing public sector enterprises, shifting control over some public sector production and services to the private sector, removing restrictions on the movement of labour from the public to private sector, and reducing subsidies to public sector enterprises.[69]

Iraq's official statistics reveal that by the end of 1987 the number of women in the labour force had fallen markedly, despite the increased size of the economically active female population. The female component of the workforce declined from 17.5 percent in 1977 to 11.7 percent in 1987, while unemployment among economically active females (including those who never entered the labour market) increased from 2.2 percent in 1977 to 7.6 percent in 1987 (see Appendix Table 2.6).[70]

However, patterns of female participation in the labour force appeared to change during the decade, since statistics indicate that a large number of women were occupying high-ranking professional jobs, reflecting both the position of women in the labour force and also their economic status. By 1987, female employment in public administration, education, health and social services had grown markedly (see Appendix Tables 2.6, 2.7, and 2.8). This pattern also reflected a positive change in social attitudes towards women working outside the home. Indeed, the increased number of women in high professional jobs reveals that not only were Iraqi women participating in the labour force to earn an income, but they were also competing with men for better positions in the labour market.

Statistics also show an increase in the number of female workers in full-time jobs. In 1987, 82 percent of the total number of female workers was in full-time jobs, as against only 39.2 percent in 1977.[71] The percentage of women in part-time jobs declined correspondingly, from 58.6 percent in 1977 to 10.6 percent in 1987.[72]

Characteristics of Female Labour Participation, 1988–90
In July 1988, both Iraq and Iran announced the official ending of the eight years of war. A huge number of Iraqi men were released from the army and had to find jobs in the civilian domain. Even so, available statistics reveal that the rate of female parti-cipation in the labour force increased from 12 percent of total labour in 1987 to reach 24 percent by July 1990 (see Appendix Table 2.9). Nevertheless, numbers of female workers in different economic activities appear to have been heavily influenced by the state shifting its priorities in the allocation of public investments.

Following the state's attempt to privatize some of the state-owned enterprises, public investment in industrial and manufacturing sectors declined, to the advantage of the agricultural sector which also witnessed increased public and private invest-ments.[73] It appears that, in line with this adjustment, large numbers of Iraqi women found job opportunities in the agricultural sector (see Appendix Tables 2.9 & 2.10). Statistics show that female labour in the agricultural sector tripled from 15.4 percent of total female labour in 1987 to 43.4 percent by mid-1990. This increase indicates a regressive trend in women's participation in the labour force with a larger number of women finding their incomes in less skilled and low paid professions within the agricultural sector.

The shifting of the public investment allocation from the industrial and manu-facturing sectors to the agricultural sector must not be understood solely in economic terms, since this move by the Iraqi government was also politically motivated. The economic crisis induced by the Iraq-Iran War and the deterioration of Iraq's economy affected the lives and welfare of the wider section of the population, and resulted in the narrowing of support for the regime among the urban middle classes. In attempt to consolidate its power, Saddam's regime responded by appealing to tribalism and kinship support networks. Thus, a larger proportion of the available financial and human resources was redirected towards these rural and semi-rural networks, particularly in the Northwest governorates where Sunni tribes were in the majority.

Conclusion

The post-revolutionary government of Iraq, with its radical nationalist Ba'th ideology had used Iraq's huge oil wealth to create a 'strong' centralized state with institutions that were capable of penetrating most aspects of society. The institutional framework, elaborated by the Iraqi political elites in the 1970s and 1980s through the party and the state, offered citizens a range of alternatives for meeting their social, economic, and political needs. The Iraqi elites legitimized their positions by claiming to repre-sent the population as a whole.

Ba'thist elites in the 1970s acknowledged that winning the political allegiance of the masses implied, among other things, the freeing of the individual from the familial and tribal matrix and his/her reintegration into the nation-state. The state institutions came to assume more and more of the authority, prerogatives and duties traditionally assigned to the patriarch and the tribal kinsmen. This was portrayed through state policies and legislation that were clearly intended to undermine the power of the extended kin group and its hold over the life of the individual member, to separate the nuclear family from the larger extended one (which included uncles, cousins, etc.), and to reject the traditional authority of the kinsmen with regard to the women of the group.

The detailed strategies employed by the elites for state-building had important consequences for the policies and programmes directed towards women and families. The enactment of changes in family law and in legislation concerning female education and employment, and the formulation of policies affecting women's productive and reproductive choice, proved that changes in societal values and ideologies affecting gender relations and *vice versa* were, and are, closely bound to the power of the state.

In Iraq, as in any other conventional patriarchal culture, women are 'traditionally' projected as reproducers of the sacred *'umma* (nation/community),[74] and of its symbolic boundaries.[75] The Code of Personal Status (CPS) as amended in 1978 should not be understood in western terms of 'liberalizing' women. While it was intended to undermine the authority of fathers, brothers and husbands over women, the CPS strengthened the 'patriarchal' state control of the family and women. This could be clearly seen through the authority and power of the state courts and the state-authorized judge, and particularly through the right to overrule the wishes of the father(s) or the guardian(s), or to act on behalf of them, if the judge saw no adequate grounds for those wishes. By acting as a 'mediator' advocating women as active participants in public life, the state was able to re-conceptualize the position of women and their gender roles. Through its direct role in the economy and its active interference in the social field (laws and socio-economic policy), the state could manipulate the persistence of the patriarchal pattern of gender relations and sex roles.

Laws and legislation in general are not only important instruments of social change; when their implementation involves considerable public resources, they also become a key for social transformation. The state in Iraq in the 1970s and 1980s was not merely an agent of legal reform, but was also an agent for the implementing of reforms and directions through which the state managed to secure the sustainability of its central position in the society and polity. Through a combination of 'positive' legal reforms, generous public resource allocations, and effective control over the implementation of directives, it was possible to bring about important shifts in the prevailing choices and behaviour of social actors, and to encourage a rapid increase in the roles of state institutions. State-sponsored economic development, labour laws, and state-sponsored education created a significant degree of upward social mobility and increased the number of women who were willing and able to fill administrative and welfare positions.

Even though statistics are not sufficient for analyzing the status of Iraqi women during the 1970s and 1980s, they nevertheless reveal the implications of the economy and the polity for the lives of Iraqi women, and particularly for women's participation in public life. A more realistic evaluation of women's status is only possible through an interpretation of the progress achieved on the economic level, in terms of women's social position, and on the levels of family and society in terms of women's decision-making. Nor can statistics adequately measure women's work in the informal sector, such as agriculture, and in non-domestic work. Indeed, the economic value of women's participation in these activities is not counted in GNP anywhere in the world.[76] Doubts remain as to whether the participation of Iraq women in the formal labour force has been transformed into a serious challenge to the prevailing patriarchal and social attitudes towards women. Even so, patterns of female participation in public life during the 1970s and 1980s reveal that there was a close connection between the existing economic conditions, the state's gender policy, and the position of Iraqi women.

Thus, an evaluation of the implications of the prevailing economic conditions for the lives and status of Iraqi women must take account of the role of the state in the economy, especially through the public sector and the state institutions. This relationship was clearly reflected in Iraqi women's lives during the 1970s, when the country's 'relatively' stable and prosperous conditions resulted in an important shift in the legal and economic status of Iraqi females, as increasing numbers of women benefited from employment and education opportunities, and preferential treatment.

In contrast to the conditions of the 1970s, Iraq's process of economic development during the 1980s was disrupted by political conflicts, wars, and economic crisis. Indeed, while the stability of economic development in the 1970s was clearly reflected through state legislation and recruitment of women into the labour force, the economic and political instabilities of the 1980s were similarly reflected through state policies, legislation, and female employment. The weighty economic and political effects of the Iraq-Iran War were felt by both the regime and the people of Iraq. For Iraqi men, the war meant death, disability, and the destruction of their professional careers, but for Iraqi women, the impact of Iraq-Iran also reached other areas of their lives. During the first five years of the war Iraqi women were challenged by the burden of double or triple roles, as mothers, wives, workers, and also as soldiers on the home front, but in the later years of the war, they had to confine themselves to their 'traditional' roles in the household and reproduction.

The mounting political and economic frustration fuelled by eight years of war with Iran and the burden of foreign debt not only impaired Iraq's ability to resume its economic development, but also narrowed support for the Ba'th regime among the urban middle classes. These dangerous developments were behind the regime's shifting emphasis on the support of tribalist networks, the narrow clique of Saddam's kin, and specific religious groups (the most radical *Wahhabi* sects).

Most importantly, the consequence of these developments carried Saddam's regime into a further devastating action, when the Iraqi military forces were ordered to invade the neighbouring country of Kuwait in August 1990. Saddam's invasion of Kuwait marked the beginning of a new and devastating era for Iraq and for its people, who were put under fire and then subjected to more than a decade of economic sanctions.

3

IRAQI WOMEN'S EMPLOYMENT
AND INCOME UNDER
UNITED NATIONS SANCTIONS

Introduction

The analysis provided in Chapter Two indicated that the relationship between Iraqi women's participation in the labour force and the economic conditions of the country has not been one-sided. Rather, it is an interactive relationship: that is, each structure influences the other. Conceptions of the roles, rights (including legal) of women – and of men's and women's values – may influence labour market and economic processes, but they may also change as a result of economic development. It is therefore expected that a positive change in the economy and polity could lead to the growth of a labour-intensive economy that, in turn, might accelerate women's economic participation. Consequently, along with the new patterns of women's employment, the patriarchal system may change toward a more egalitarian set of gender relations where women's position as women and as workers might improve. Similarly, a negative change in the economy will lead to a change in gender relations in the society; e.g., a deterioration of the economy could decrease women's economic participation. In consequence, new patterns of women's employment and survival strategies could lead to a reformulation of the patriarchal gender system toward a more repressive set of gender relations, both in society and family.

Moreover, due to the systems of patriarchal control in Iraq as any other parts of the Middle East and North Africa region (MENA),[1] Iraqi women have in general had less economic power and have been more dependent on the nation-state than men. They are, therefore, much more vulnerable to any economic change, particularly if the change is as shocking as sanctions.

Through an empirical analysis of women's experience, this chapter illustrates the implications of sanctions for Iraqi women's labour participation, and trends in the employment of females and levels of income and earnings. This is provided in four sub-sections according to types of economic activities (public sector; private sector; family enterprises; and informal and self-employment). The final section of the chapter looks at respondents' previous employment status as compared to their employment status under sanctions.

Iraqi Women's Employment Status: Statistical Review
Official Statistics

As discussed in the previous chapter, the enhancement of Iraqi women's economic and social options has always been strongly associated with the growth of the state/public sector and the welfare state, through which women's opportunities were either increased or repressed.

Under sanctions, statistics about Iraq, including official and UN statistics about Iraqi women's labour force participation, are often inconsistent and reveal strong contradictions. UNICEF reported that the labour force composition in place at the start of the Iran-Iraq war had continued during sanctions, and that women's employment in the public sector had increased.[2] The UNDP also maintained in 2002 that the level of Iraqi women's employment in the labour force had declined from 24 percent in 1990 to 17 percent in the year 2000.[3]

However, after the imposition of UN sanctions on Iraq, an unprecedented turning point was reached for women's employment in the public sector; according to the last available Iraqi official statistics (1999), it showed a dramatic decrease. For example, by 1996 women's employment had witnessed its sharpest decline, reaching its lowest level since the 1970s (see Appendix Table 3.1). From December 1997 to December 1998, women's labour force participation in Baghdad City, with the largest concentration of female labour, declined by more than one thousand working place (see Appendix Table 3.2). Since it is difficult to test the reliability of these figures, statistical data from any source (including Iraqi official statistics) is not considered explicitly in the analyses in this chapter.

Employment Status of the Surveyed Women

The term 'employment status' is used throughout this chapter mainly to describe the involvement of the respondents (the surveyed women) in income-earning activities, including all kinds of formal and informal labour-based activities as well as family-based activities. The term 'economically active' describes the status of individual respondents, and includes those who were unemployed, provided they were actively seeking work. The term 'economically inactive', on the other hand, refers to respondents who were not employed and who were not actively seeking employment, and included students, pension recipients, retired persons, housewives, and those in undefined economic activity.

The sample of this study consisted of 148 working women; 31 unemployed women (economically active); and 98 unemployed women (economically inactive, including 50 female students).

It must be noted that women's response to the definition of their employment status did not always correspond to their actual position in the labour market, and many respondents identified themselves as not employed. However, the open-ended interview was an effective method through which a substantial number of these women revealed their desire to find jobs. One group was actively seeking employment while another was hindered by family reasons or discouraged by low salaries, or both. For instance, Aida (a 35 year old from Area II) was a graduate teacher, and had identified herself as unemployed. In an interview, she revealed that she was eager to speak about her desire to resume teaching, which she remembered passionately:

> I remember the time when I felt more worthwhile, especially when I was able to buy things for myself and for my family from my salary [ID 75 was equal to US$227 per month in 1988]. I cannot deny that it was also difficult to keep up with the two major responsibilities of home and work, but I loved my job.

Initially, Aida was hesitant about revealing her reasons for giving up her job but later on was willing to tell me that her husband had been complaining about her absence from home for a job that was 'not worthy'. Therefore she had to leave work. About her monthly salary, she said:

> I received ID 3,000 a month [US$1.50 at 1996 exchange rate]. However, in 1997, in order to encourage teachers stay in their jobs, the government increased teachers' incomes, and decided to give an additional allowance on a three-monthly basis. Anyway, the allowance I received was not sufficient to buy a pair of shoes.[4]

This suggests that number of women left their jobs for reasons such as these, but they were still keen to have a job because they needed extra income. In such cases, these women were counted as unemployed, but economically active 'discouraged workers'.

Employment Status through Economic Sectors & Geographic Location

Despite the modest level of female participation in the labour force in the sample (148 women), the survey showed that women from poor or limited-income households (Areas I and II) made up the majority of working women in the sample, while respondents from rich or unlimited income households (Area III) were less interested in waged jobs (Table 3.1- below).

Table 3.1 Respondents' formal employment status by residential areas

Location	Working	Not-working economically active	Economically inactive
	No.	No.	No.
Area I	84	2	4
Area II	49	17	9
Area III	15	12	35
Total	148	31	48

The survey showed also that 74 women, a substantial proportion, were concentrated in the public sector, 60 women were engaged in informal or self-employment, while only 14 women were in private and family enterprises. As for the distribution of these women based on the residential areas surveyed, most of the working respondents (44 women) in the poorest area (Area I) were employed in the public sector while only 5 were employed in the private sector. A smaller number of the working respondents (25 women) from the 'middle-class' area (Area II) were employed in the public sector and none in the private sector. However, the lowest female participation in the labour force (15 women) was registered in the 'rich area' (Area III), with 5 women in the public sector and 5 women in the private sector, and with similar number engaged in family enterprises (privately-owned business) as shown in Table 3.2 - below.

Table 3.2 Respondents' employment status according to economic sectors

Sector	Number of women generating income	Residential area		
		Area I Total Surveyed 90	Area II Total Surveyed 75	Area III Total Surveyed 62
1. Public sector employee	74	44	25	5
2. Private sector employee	9	4	–	5
– Family enterprises	5	–	–	5
3. Informal & Self employed	60	36	24	–
Total	148	84	49	15

Note: Working women in the informal sector are counted as nonworking (economically active).

The survey revealed that 60 of the economically active women in the sample were either employed in the informal sector or were generating income by self-employment. Many of these women identified themselves as unemployed, but in fact were actively involved in different informal economic activities as a primary source of income. It should also be noted that many respondents were involved in economic activities through self-employment for a secondary source of income in addition to their formal income as employees in the public sector. This will be explained in detail later in this chapter.

Respondents' Occupational and Income Status in the Public Sector

According to the survey, women in the public sector were employed in a wide range of occupations and salary status (Table 3.3 - below). However, it was difficult to estimate the average incomes of respondents in the different economic sectors due to the lack of comprehensive and comparable data and the reluctance of respondents to reveal such information. Therefore, an estimation of female earning levels was based on general observation and assistance from other people in Iraq.

Table 3.3 Respondents' occupation and income status as public sector employees
(October 2000 – February 2002) (at exchange rate of US$ 1: ID 2000)

Occupation	No.	Area I	Area II	Area III	Av monthly income /ID
Government institutions	5		4	1	5,000
Teacher (primary, secondary, high school)	14	4	10		3,000
University lecturer	2	–	–	2	20,000
Engineer (technicians)	8	4	4		9,000
Medical doctor	2	–	–	2	19,000
Qualified nurse	7	5	2	–	4,000
Other health related occupations	9	9	–	–	3,000
Bank employee	6	2	4	–	4,000
Librarian (university administration)	5	4	1	–	4,000
Hotel administration (other public services)	4	4	–	–	4,000
Janitors/Cleaner	5	5	–	–	3,000
Other (sales and service)	7	7	–	–	4,000
Total / Average	74	44	25	5	ID 3,500–12,500

The table shows that average monthly incomes of respondents in the public sector ranged from ID 3,000 to ID 20,000. However, respondents from the poorest and middle class areas were occupying the lowest paid jobs (ID 3,000–ID 9,000). This shows therefore that the highest average monthly income (ID 5,000–ID 20,000) was that of respondents from the rich area (Area III) even though they accounted for the lowest number of working women in the survey.

The first attempt of many attempts to regulate public salaries according to market prices was made by the state in September 1991. However, the effects of these attempts were quickly neutralized as prices rose in response. By 2002, standard monthly salaries for civil servants ranged from ID 3,000 to ID 20,000, i.e., 42 to 200 times more than their minimum nominal levels (ID 70 per month) had been in August 1990, prior to the invasion of Kuwait.[5] Compared to the exchange rate in 1990, the average salary of ID 70 was equal to US$217 per month. In 2002, in spite of the state's attempts to raise public salaries, common salaries were equivalent to US$1.50, $3.50 monthly. Looking at food prices, the price of a kilo of meat was ID 0.75 in 1990, whereas in 2002 the price had risen to ID 2,800, i.e., 3,850 times higher than the 1990 level. The same trend could be observed in the prices of all kinds of basic foods and services.

On the level of the survey, it is obvious that while all the surveyed women employees in the public sector were receiving low salaries, poor and middle-class women were those most severely hit by the crisis. According to the exchange rate in the time of the survey, their income did not exceed per month US$1.50, 4.50 per month.

Public Sector Employment: Loss of Opportunities and Incentives

As previously noted (Chapter Two), Iraqi women's entry in the formal labour force was directly related to the emergence of the state/public sector in Iraq. Sponsored by state laws that specifically ensured preferential treatment and equal payment of women, the public sector had always represented a tremendous opportunity for many Iraqi women to develop their potential. Indeed, prior to sanctions, advantageous opportunities for women in public sector jobs exceeded those available to men. In addition to good pay and job stability, women enjoyed special health insurance, distinctive benefits with regard to children's allowances, and pensions. The attraction for a woman of a job within the public sector was that it provided a level of security not found in the private sector, as well as sustainable rewards for long service in the form of pensions.

These advantages vanished after the imposition of sanctions. A large number of women left their jobs, not only because of the low wages, but also because the absence of services previously provided by the state (such as transport services and kinder-gartens) significantly discouraged women from going to work. Another underlying reason why women were discouraged from the labour force in the public sector was the mismatch between the professional skills of employees and their earning oppor-tunities. Under sanctions, professional skills ceased to be an income-determining factor. As shown above, respondents' monthly salaries within the public sector indicate that almost all occupations, including professions such as medical doctors or university lecturers, were likely to be low paid, regardless of the skills required.

The compound effects of high unemployment rates and diminishing work incen-tives did not end with deteriorating living standards for the broad majority of Iraqi middle class society. There were also other devastating consequences for employees in the public sector. Particularly notable was the level of migration of Iraqi people outside the country, especially the educated, the economically active, and those with high professional expertise. It is estimated that during the sanctions era over three million Iraqis left the country, mostly among high- and middle-level educated individuals who sought better lives and jobs abroad. However, the desperate needs of the poorest and least-educated forced them to take on any sort of job in order to generate income, and under these conditions, the constraints were even greater for the educated middle-class, both men and women.

Amira (aged 26, from Area II) a university graduate (Agriculture Engineer) was adamant that she had to find a job, no matter where. She did not want to believe that life was not going to change for the better. However, she could only get a job at the Electricity and Water Department. She described her situation:

I have no choice other than working in spite of the low wage. It does, however, make me feel that I am doing whatever I can to feel better within myself and to contribute to our household. However, with a small salary [ID 3,500 per month] I am only able to buy some vegetables and fruits every month. It is better than nothing.

In addition to the many incentives for female employees, the public sector has always been regarded by the majority of the Iraqi people as the most respectable working environment. Other economic sectors, including private enterprises (shops, factories, and firms), are perceived as areas of potential risk for women's reputations. Inhibitions among Iraqis about female employment in the private sector are often based on what are claimed to be unacceptable working conditions, e.g., working hours are too long, or the place of work is too far away. However, the real reason is that any employer other than the state is always perceived with doubt and suspicion, because such an employer is an 'unknown entity'. The problem of the exposure of Iraqi women to unknown men that is unavoidable in many private jobs is often minimized or does not exist when the employer is as 'respectable' and 'trusted' as the state.

The statements of some respondents may explain social attitudes towards women's attempts to find incomes elsewhere outside the public sector. Zahra (aged 30, from Area II) a university graduate, was living with her mother and a younger sister. They were living on her salary (ID 4000 per month) as a bank assistant, and payments sent by her brother who was living in Sweden. Despite the low remuneration, Zahra's family was proud that she was working in Iraq's largest financial institution. To my question about other job opportunities, she responded:

> Yes, once I received a good job offer and an opportunity for a better salary. One businessman who is a client of the bank was extremely grateful for my efficient services and offered me a job as finance manager in his own company. He promised me a better salary and the possibility of travelling abroad. However, I could not take up this offer because my mother caused a big problem and threatened to stop me from going to work. My mother believes it is shameful to let me work for strangers. My brother was also very angry with me because I liked the job offer. He was phoning every day from Sweden to make sure that I had refused the new job offer. Of course, I ended up obeying my family and being the way they like me to be.

It was possible to visit Zahra at her workplace, where it became apparent that the majority of the clients in the bank were men. Nevertheless, her family had never complained about the amount of contact she had with men at the bank. In general, this situation suggests that Iraqi women's access to employment revolves around notions of female protection, which is secured in the public sector. Indeed, it also explains the existence of women workers in banks, hospitals, universities and schools, etc.

Social Attitudes towards Women's Work
Obstacles to women's mobility in public have always existed in Iraq, but the protection provided by the state to women against discriminatory practices in

employment and elsewhere, encouraged women to pursue the challenges of public life. It was culturally distinctive that Iraqi middle-class men and women were directed towards obtaining a university degree and after that, a suitable profession in the state sector. A man or a woman with such 'prestigious' qualifications was considered economically successful as well as socially acceptable.

However, the situation under sanctions changed this cultural outlook. Highly educated Iraqi men, who often work in the daytime as teachers, lawyers, engineers, etc., take jobs as taxi drivers or shopkeepers in the evening in order to supplement to their incomes. While economic pressure has caused a change in social attitudes towards a man's 'prestigious' position from respect for his profession to respect for the 'size of his pocket', it has affected women by increasing their insecurity.

As women became more dependent on male providers, it was possible to recognise the changes in the language used to describe a respectable man or woman. Instead of the images that were previously utilized to describe a 'good' man, such as a 'clever' lawyer or engineer, etc., the images of a successful man were becoming rather concerned with the amount of money he could make, regardless of how he did so. A 'successful' man turned out to be the one who brought in money, a lot of money, regardless of his social and educational background. The same applied for women. Satisfactory criteria for a woman as a 'bright woman', referring to her profession and to her approach to competing beside men, turned out to be rather more concerned with her position as a 'respectable housewife' or more precisely, a girl knowing nothing about the world outside the door of her home.

With the shrinking of job opportunities, it was noticeable that a large number of men were turning to the sales and retail sector. However, it is socially unacceptable for educated women, especially from the middle class, to work by selling goods in the streets, and it was simply impossible for a young woman or even a mature woman to be seen working as a taxi driver, anywhere in Iraq. Such kinds of occupations are believed to be disreputable because they expose women to the 'risk' of interaction with strangers. It is notable that the retail sector is predominately male. Thus, apart from the peddling of a few small foodstuffs and except for a few shops managed by old women who were predominately poor migrants from villages and from the suburbs of Baghdad, it would have been difficult for women to work in retail services.

It must be noted, however, that social resistance to female occupation in retail services does not include sales jobs in outlets such as pharmacies and dispensing opticians, where middle-class men and women occupy such professions. These 'professionalist' types of sales jobs have evolved as culturally acceptable for both women and men because they usually require a college degree. However, it was evident that there were fewer women than previously in these occupations. During the 1970s and 1980s, most pharmacies and opticians' shops in Baghdad were run by women, whereas under sanctions a large number of these retail outlets became family businesses and were typically run by the head of the household, usually the man. It appears that, due to the scarcity of jobs, men were also competing with women over the few opportunities for so-called 'acceptable female jobs'.

The situation was especially hard on widows, divorced, and deserted women. These women, in general, relied primarily on pensions and other allowances given by the state, but this kind of income was rendered worthless under sanctions. Zuhur (aged 38, from Area II) was a widow with four children. She graduated as a nurse, and in addition to her work in a hospital, had built her own small shop, attached to her house. She explained:

> I have no other means to cope with this kind of life. I need to feed my children and send them to school. My salary is not sufficient to keep us going [ID 3,000 per month plus ID 1,500 pension of her late husband]. So I decided to build this shop by myself and with help of my son who is 14 years old. Since the death of my husband during the Gulf War (1991), I have become everything to my children. But life is very hard. My brother protests about my work in this shop, and has pressured me to close it three times. He claims it is disgraceful for a single woman of my age to work in a shop. Now my son helps me in the shop after school. It is very hard for a woman like me. They claim it is a man's job. I am not thinking like that. The most important thing for me is to make sure that my children will not have to go to bed without having any supper.

Obviously the increasing economic and social pressure resulted in restricting women either to their homes or to so-called 'socially acceptable', and often low-paid jobs typically in the public sector that high inflation rates were strongly reflected.

Respondents' Occupational and Income Status in the Private Sector

Initially, it must be noted that the Ba'th regime did not really favour privatization of the economy, even though the government, by the end of the 1980s, saw it as a possible means of escaping the financial crisis.[6] The regime had always built its power on its domination of the state apparatus and the public sector of the economy, and the enormous inflow of oil revenues during the 1970s and early 1980s was the backbone of this ideological stand. Therefore the private sector was always weakened and restricted to a limited domain of small industries, retailing, and transportation, whereas the state sector expanded to far larger and wider areas of the economy.

The destruction of Iraq's economy under sanctions did not spare the private sector. It was severely hit by inflation and the devaluation of the Iraqi currency. Following the imposition of sanctions, and as a result of increased unemployment and a decline in public sector wages, many small production and service enterprises, mainly family-owned, sprang up to boost the private sector. However, the insignificant private sector of the economy had always relied on male workers.

The findings of the survey showed that only nine respondents were employed in the private sector; 5 women out of 15 working women from Area III, and 4 women out of 84 working women from Area I, while none of the respondents from Area II was working in the private sector. As private sector employees, these women were receiving a formal wage. Despite the low number of surveyed women in the private

sector, it is essential to give some idea of their income earnings and their views of
employment in the private sector.

Table 3.4 Occupations and income status of respondents
as private sector employees

Occupation	No.	Area I	Area II	Area III	Average income, ID/month
Worker (Manufacturing sector)	2	2	–	–	15,000
Day care centre (kindergarten)	1	1	–	–	20,000
Retail shop sales person	6	1	–	5	30,000
Total/Average	9	4	–	5	20–30,000

It is notable that the average monthly salary of respondents in the private sector was
far higher (ID 20–30,000) than that of the respondents in the public sector. However,
the table above also shows that the average monthly salary income of respondents
from Area I was relatively lower (ID 20,000) compared with that of respondents from
Area III (ID 30.000). The absence of any of the surveyed women from Area II (which
is mostly inhibited by middle and highly educated middle-class people) possibly
indicates that a high proportion of these women was either unemployed or had jobs
in the public sector.

Obstacles to Women's Work in the Private Sector
The state's withdrawal from the economy and society had wide-scale and catastrophic
consequences, but these affected women in a particularly unique way. The role of the
weakened state in the economy and society had increasingly fostered more regressive
images of women as 'weak' and in need of protection, and control by the family and
by males represented further moves towards dominating women's lives.

However, obstacles to Iraqi women working in the private sector increased, as a
result of various challenges rooted in the economic and social conditions arising from
sanctions. In addition to diminishing job opportunities under sanctions, it became
apparent that, due to an 'unfriendly' private sector environment as well as to
'undesirable' working conditions, increasing numbers of educated middle-class
women were being dissuaded from seeking jobs in the private sector. Many women
and their families defined 'suitable' private sector employment in terms of the
prevalence of female workers, the type of occupation, and proximity to the home.
However, a more comprehensive view of obstacles to Iraqi women's work in any other
surroundings than the public sector showed that, in addition to the scarcity of

opportunities available to them in the private sector, women were also increasingly facing social constraints at the household level as well as from private sector employers.

Many respondents spoke about the 'dilemma' they faced; should they be fortunate enough to have the opportunity of a job in the private sector, many domestic and society restrictions and obstacles would promptly appear. Raja (aged 35, from Area III) was a sales manager in a private enterprise in which she was also a shareholder. She considered that the low percentage of females in the private sector was due to the increased social harassment of women. She describes her situation:

> It is extremely difficult for a woman to work in the private sector. My family and other people are constantly asking me about the owner of the company I work for; whether the manager is married; whether he is young, and whether he behaves decently! I am aware about the hidden doubts of such kind of questions. Society is questioning my behaviour, not the man's. It is all about the kind of a job I do.

When the protection provided by the state was undermined by the economic crisis, women were essentially left susceptible to the protection of other forces (family, the community and society). As in the case of Sana (aged 38, divorced, from Area III), work in a shop implied a great sacrifice. She said:

> I am a graduate of the Academy of Art. Before the sanctions I had a well-paid job in the National Theatre, but the theatre was financially affected and many employees had to leave. I had a 'husband as well' [cynically]. But everything was turned upside down. My husband left us [her and three children] for a better opportunity outside the country, but he has ended up with another wife in Jordan. My family is still blaming me, 'not him' for the breakdown of our marriage. I was left alone to face the insecurity. I know that working in a shop is not approved of by society or by my family. But it provides me with an income, which eventually, I could not manage without. Honestly, I don't really care whether people accept me as I am or not.

Her statement suggests that while women's employment opportunities in the public sector shrank, the problems associated with generating income by doing other types of jobs increased significantly (see more details on the status of divorced and widowed women in Chapter Five).

Mona (aged 42, from Area I) was working in a small grocery store (mini market) in which she was also a shareholder. She believed that women avoided jobs in the private sector due to social constraints. She said:

> It is not because women do not have the time or energy to take up the challenge of work in the private sector, but it is the society that portrays women as weak, less responsible, and needing the protection of a man. In this way, society

assigns us to domestic responsibilities, or at best, to working for the lowest wages.

This statement suggests that some women are becoming more ready to take up the challenge towards a new role in the society, although if this is true, it might be limited only to women who have material resources. In the absence of an adequate environment for a positive development of human resources, especially for women, it is impossible to build up a discussion about this issue. It is also incorrect to generalize the experience of a few respondents, especially women with financial ability in the form of capital, shares, or ownership of an enterprise, to a wider context. The need for an income, especially on the part of single women driven by their status as divorced or deserted wives to face the burdens of life on their own, leaves them sinking into ever deeper crisis. The experiences of the largest proportion of the women surveyed revealed that, in such humiliating circumstances, it was difficult for them to speak about such extravagances.

Private Employers' Attitudes
On the side of the private employers in Iraq, as in other parts of the Middle East, women are often perceived as less suitable employees than men. This attitude often reinforces the claim that women are less useful than men as workers, due to higher turnover and absenteeism rates; their higher likelihood of dropping out of the labour force upon marriage; and their relative unwillingness to work long hours.[7]

The labour market under sanctions increased women's disadvantageous position as a potential labour force, especially in the private sector. In the absence of state control under sanctions, such perceptions heightened the attitude that relegates women in the labour market to a disadvantaged position as unskilled production workers. It is therefore hardly surprising that Iraqi women, who were ready to challenge opportunities for better-paid jobs in the private sector, had to faced further rejection and reluctance by private employers. As one respondent remarked 'If a woman does not care what people may say about her working in private business, the private employer does'.

Homa (aged 31, from Area II), who had a diploma in English-French-Arabic translation in addition to a university degree in engineering, blamed private employers for escalating restrictions on women and perpetuating the weak position of women:

My father is a very sick man but he still goes to work every day from early morning to late at night. I am the oldest child and the only university graduate in my family. We are desperate for extra income. So, I took the initiative to search for a job in the private sector. It took me more than six months before I lost hope about finding anything worthwhile. I was faced with rejections and on many occasions, private employers complained that because of the deteriorating economic situation and the fluctuation of the exchange rate of the dinar, it was not going well for their businesses. However, it was the answer I received from one man [private employer] that really made me give up on my attempts and put an end to my wasted efforts. A travel agency owner told me that he personally had no objection to giving me a job, especially because I would be the only university graduate with computer and languages skills in his company. But, he said, he was hesitant about employing me because I was a woman. He claimed that having a woman in the agency would harm his reputation, and he would not be able to protect my own. Imagine!

Another respondent who was illiterate gave a similar account. Hamida (aged 54, from Area I) was trying to go back to her job in a small textile factory, which had been sold to a private owner. She said:

Poverty and the need for some support made me go back to the factory where I had been working for more than twelve years before the 1991 war. I was asking for a job as cleaner. The new owner told me that he was not willing to employ women in his factory. He added that a woman, especially one who was illiterate, was not what he was looking for.

The impression these statements give is that, while opportunities for an improvement in the economic situation of Iraqi women in the public sector were diminishing, women elsewhere were increasingly perceived as less qualified than men who were better at coping with the new working circumstances.

Respondents' Occupational and Income Status in Family Enterprises
There were only five women in the sample engaged in family enterprises, all from the rich area (Area III). Their occupations were as follows: a medical doctor in a consultancy clinic; an optician in a family enterprise consisting of a pharmacy, a laboratory, and an X-ray centre; a sales manager in a furniture house; a manager of a beauty clinic; and the manager of a health centre. In spite of the low number of respondents in such enterprises, the average monthly salary generated by these economic activities indicates that family enterprises had acquired a significant role under sanctions. Indeed, it is believed that real earnings in family enterprises were far higher than the average stated by the respondents (as indicated in Table 3.5 - below). It is also important to stress that family enterprises were owned and managed by people who had the capital and the skills through which they were able to keep pace with the economic crisis.

Experience from other developing societies, especially in poor economies, shows that a family-owned enterprise is significant because it protects its owners from economic insecurity, especially in a rapidly deteriorating macro-economy.[8] Under sanctions, the importance of family-owned businesses, both formal and informal, increased, particularly as means of control over the financial resources of individual families. Under the chaotic situation, family enterprises become a good source of primary or secondary earnings for family members. Most notably, the government had relaxed its grip on such types of economic activities since it was also relying on small businesses to break the sanctions.

Table 3.5 Occupations and income status of respondents
in family enterprises

Occupation	No.	Area I	Area II	Area III	Average income, ID/month
Medical doctor/Dentist	1	–	–	1	250,000
Optician/Pharmacy	1	–	–	1	300,000
Shop owner (sales and services)	1	–	–	1	500,000
Beautician/hair dresser	2	–	–	2	500,000
Total/Average	5	–	–	5	250,000–600,000

It is difficult to provide a precise figure as to the size of family enterprises in the economy, especially in the absence of statistics on this aspect. Nevertheless, it is apparent that the emergence of a wide range of enterprises, owned, operated, and staffed by family members, acquired great significance, both for the owners and for the objectives of the market.

Respondents' Attitudes towards Employment in Family Enterprises

In spite of the low number of respondents employed in family enterprises, their professional expertise appeared crucial for these kinds of economic activities. They were all professionally qualified workers. Aida (aged 32) was a health and beauty specialist, married and has two children. She explains her situation:

> We went through a very difficult situation when I was a full-time housewife and had to rely primarily on my husband's income [engineer, public sector employee], since it was insufficient for a family of four. My husband was trying to get a better-paid job elsewhere but he could not find one. Initially we did not have the capital to start this business, but a proposal from my father came just in time to save my family from splitting up, because my husband was seriously thinking of leaving Iraq to look for a job abroad. My father suggested that we could borrow money from him in return for shared profits with my youngest brother. I thought about a health and beauty studio, firstly because I have the skills and secondly because there is a market now for this sort of business in Iraq. My earnings are good. I can confidently say that we have succeeded in overcoming the crisis.

It was obvious that not everybody in Iraq under sanctions was poor and in desperate need of an income. Aida said that her clients were rich or well-off women who could afford time and money to spend on such luxuries.

Rouba (aged 41) who was a pharmacist similarly confirmed that without her family business she and her family would have run the risk of relying on low public sector salaries:

> We have run this business since the 1970s. My father was a pharmacist, and many members of my family are in the medical and health professions. We are grateful to our father for establishing this business, without which we could be crushed by the catastrophic situation that has turned the majority of middle-income people towards poverty and desperation.

However, the statement by Sumeia (aged 38), divorced with three children, revealed different insights into the situation of women in family businesses. Sumeia was employed as a beautician in a business owned by her sister. She described her situation:

> My family went through an extremely difficult time because we were relying only on my husband's low income [public sector employee]. We sold everything that could have a value in the market. First we sold my gold, then our furniture, and we ended up by selling our house. I decided to buy this business together with my sister who is a professional beautician. My husband felt it was a disgrace to let me work in a beauty salon, but I insisted. Then he decided to divorce me. I am doing fine. I am managing to take good care of my children. My husband left Iraq with his new wife.

Regardless of the codification of law – whether personal status or family laws – the patriarchal system in Iraq always implies that a woman should obtain permission from her father, brother, or husband if she decides to seek employment, apply for a loan, or start up a business. Although the right of Iraqi women to seek employment and generate income is codified in law, men are still the 'main' breadwinners, according to 'ideal' Islam and traditions. Paradoxically, however, while sanctions increased the insecurity of the male's role as breadwinner, patriarchal control of women continued to exist, and was particularly revealed through the strengthening constraints over women (for more details see Chapter Five).

Under sanctions, Iraqi women who were willing to conduct their own business had little chance of applying for bank credit or taking training courses. These and many other obstacles limited their opportunities, even if their businesses were confined to the supposedly culturally and socially appropriate (such as women-run day-care centres, nursery schools, and kindergartens). This issue was articulated mainly by young respondents, who had some brilliant ideas about the use of their time and expertise.

Informal Economic Activities and Self-Employment
Definition of Informal Economic Activities
Informal work is the activities of the working poor – those who are very hard working but who are not recognized, recorded, protected or regulated by the public authorities. In general, the informal sector is made up of small business 'units' with

limited capital and few employees, unregistered and unreported to tax officials.[9] The informal sector has always existed in Iraq, but was confined to the lower-income classes and the poor communities of low-educated and mainly rural migrants.[10] Under sanctions, informal economic activities as means of generating income became a phenomenon. These activities range from manufacturing, such as the production of households goods and consumer goods (clothes, shoes, food furniture, etc), to trade, and community and personal services. The significance of informal economic activities under sanctions was emphasized not only through the value of the goods and services produced, but most importantly, as the means of providing a basic income for numbers of lower and middle class urban and rural families.[11]

However, on the level of the survey, it was difficult to provide a precise and accurate number of respondents in informal and self-managed economic activities, and the type of income that these provided (primary or secondary). The information acquired from the survey revealed that around 60 unemployed women were either self-employed or engaged in informal income generation. However, further examination (by open-ended interviews and case-studies) revealed that these economic activities also provided a secondary income source for about 23 women who were 'officially' employed in the public sector. The respondents in informal and self-managed economic activities were exclusively from the poor and middle class areas (Area I and Area II).

As far as income generated from these activities is concerned, respondents' statements revealed that their earnings fluctuated considerably, following demand for their services as well as the currency exchange rates. It should be specifically emphasized that market fluctuations follow the political climate; when there are attempts to relieve the economic situation, people tend to feel more secure and this is often reflected in increased spending on goods and services. On the other hand, continuing tensions in the political climate often mean a deterioration of the economic and the psychological situation of the market.

As for the educational background of women in these types of activities, the survey showed that in this regard there was no classification. The educational level of respondents varied from university graduates to illiterate respondents. However, there was an obvious class categorization. All women involved in informal economic activities were from middle- and lower-middle class backgrounds. In the face of a desperate need for some basic essentials and an absence of other opportunities under sanctions, many Iraqi women found relief by generating a little income through carrying out informal activities. An attempt was made to understand women's attitudes towards this type of employment, in particular by examining the source of income (primary or secondary) it provided.

Informal Network Activities as the Primary Source of Income

It was clear that a large number of respondents, forced by the need for an income, were engaged in self-employment activities for the first time in their lives. Other respondents were engaged in informal network economic activities, mainly in agricultural work, clothing factories, or production of household goods. The informal network often relies on family members and neighbours for labour. Women engaged in this type of activity often expressed frustration about the working conditions and the responsibilities they encountered, especially the double burden of household work and production responsibility. There were also complaints about the instability of earnings from these activities. However, women also confirmed that their work was indispensable because they needed the income so badly. Fatima (aged 38, from Area I), married with five children, was generating income from agricultural work on a neighbouring farm. She complained about the situation:

> My husband [outlaid manufacturing worker] has been moving from one job to another every second or third day. He hasn't been able to find a permanent job since he was discharged from the army in 1992. My children have suffered because we could not give them much. Now we are working on the neighbouring farm. I do agricultural work and my husband peddles the goods at different selling points. In return, I get a small daily wage and some vegetables. My husband gets a daily wage based on the amount of goods sold. I am very exhausted and torn between home responsibilities and doing this work.

Hassna (aged 27, from Area II), a high school graduate, had looked for a formal job (in the private or public sector) but ended up working in a textile firm located in a private house in return for a tiny daily wage. Her husband had casual work as a mechanic. She complained about the tremendous amount of work she had to do. She said:

> All the workers are women. The conditions at work are bad but we are not supposed to complain because we'll be thrown out of work on the spot. Sometimes we have to work twelve hours a day without any extra allowance. We are not allowed to take breaks, except for half an hour for lunch.

Other women in jobs of this kind remarked on the amount of stress they encountered due to their double responsibilities as workers and as wives and mothers. Some admitted that the wages they received were not worth the pressures they were enduring on a daily basis.

Kamila (aged 45, from Area I), a widow since Iraq-Iran War, had two children and had been laid off from her job in a military industry. After a long search she had found a job in a small clothing factory. She said that she did not mind the bad conditions at work, but travelling for three hours every day (because she had moved house) was forcing her to reconsider her job in spite of the desperate need for an income. She explained:

> Sometimes I think I must put an end to this humiliation but at the same time, the consequences of losing my income scare me. I will certainly go begging in the streets if I give up this job. I am the only breadwinner for these people

[pointing to her children and her mother-in-law]. Knowing that I cannot make them happy either way turns me to ashes every single day. If I had ever known that they [her children] would be exposed to this suffering, I would not have brought them into this 'unfair' world.

Within the human development paradigm, poverty is defined as a 'deprivation of human capability, of essential opportunities and of choices needed for the well-being of an individual, a household or a community'.[12] As these statements show, the harmful effects of the economic crisis were directly translated into hardship for women whose only choice for earning an income was to take informal jobs.

Self-Employment as the Primary Source of Income

A self-employed person is 'a person who, during the reference period, performs some work for profit or family gain in cash or in kind, as in paid employment'.[13] Typically, self-employment relies upon limited capital investment, self-exploitation, and common skills such as petty trade, production of simple consumer goods, clothes or food production.[14]

Under sanctions, in an attempt to generate income many Iraqi women were forced to do jobs they would never have contemplated under 'normal' economic circumstances. Zubaida (aged 54, from Area II) had been a widow since 1993 and had three daughters, all of whom were students at medical school. She had previously been a primary school teacher, but left teaching in 1991 because of its 'worthless' salary (ID 3,000 / US$1.50 per month), and the family had lived on her husband's income as a taxi driver. Zubaida, an extremely proud and strong woman, had carried her family responsibilities alone, but did not hide the fact that she was exhausted and looking forward to being paid back by her eldest daughter who was about to graduate as a medical doctor. Zubaida managed to carry with life by supplying ready-made food to different shops, and occasionally by preparing party food for other people from her home. She said:

When my husband died, I became both the father and the mother for my children, but I also realized that I had to do something in order to keep them alive. It did not require much cleverness to find out that, under these circumstances, there were not many things a woman like me could do. First, I started to sew clothes for women and children, but there were not so many people who wanted hand sewn clothes. So, making food was the second best option. Now, I make food for people, sometimes in large quantities. My neighbours and my three daughters help me by spreading the good reputation of my food to their friends and colleagues.

Nawal (aged 42, from Area I) was the mother of five children. Her husband received a monthly pension of US$1.50 (previous income in 1989 was ID 75, equal toUS$240). She spoke of the misery that had beset the lives of her family after sanctions: 'We have sold everything that could be of value. We do not know what to do'. She voiced her feelings:

> The embargo is 'evil'. It took everything from us. It has battered our lives
> mercilessly. Before, I would never have thought of cleaning other people's
> houses in order to bring food to my family. Now, I have no alternative. I have
> even become used to enduring the humiliation and the constant pain that are
> always part of me. This situation has left no space for us to think.

The experiences of these women reveal that the economic shock had caused deep suffering to Iraqi women from poor and lower-middle class income backgrounds. Prior to sanctions many of them had had better incomes and living standards. Under the chaotic economic situation, the lack of income was not the only problem, but the absence of other economic choices also rendered them completely helpless. These statements reveal that it is not absolutely correct to attribute the sum of total human deprivation to the absence of income. The impoverishment of these women was multidimensional, and the lack of income was just one aspect of this. The situations of these respondents, often as sole breadwinners and insecure financially and in terms of health, all represent forms of human deprivation.

Self-Employment as a Secondary Source of Income

Many Iraqi women were involved in self-employment as a secondary source of income, in addition to a primary job that was often in the public sector. However, it is not possible to provide a precise account or numbers of Iraqi women in these activities, since a large number of respondents overlooked the question in the survey about this issue. Indeed, it was hardly a glorious matter for a professional (educated) Iraqi woman to reveal that she was generating additional income by, for example, making palm leaf brooms or sweets for wedding parties, and so on. Further investigation indicated that many highly educated respondents were engaged in secondary income generation.

The statements of some respondents confirmed that they and many of their colleagues were either interested in, or directly engaged in a secondary source of employment. Given the amount of financial pressure on Iraqi households, especially those relying primarily on public sector wages, it was not surprising that many educated Iraqi women were taking on a secondary income source. Luma (aged 29, from Area II), a university graduate and a bank assistant, received a monthly salary of ID 3,000 (US$1.5). She described her life as 'exhausting' and commented that the 'fight for survival seems endless'. Luma and her youngest sister (a student) sewed clothes for money. She said:

> I and many of my colleagues try to do whatever work we can to ease the
> pressure on our families. My family cannot afford 'now' to buy clothes, so I
> make my family's clothes and other things at home. I also sew clothes for my
> colleagues and my neighbours for money. It is exhausting work but the
> additional income from my sewing helps us to carry on.

In another case, Soha (aged 36, from Area II), who was an employee at the GFIW, was generating secondary income through petty trading among her colleagues at work and around the neighbourhood, which involved selling various household articles, clothes, and cosmetics. It should be noted that prior to sanctions, employees of the GFIW, both Iraqis and Arabs, were paid lucrative salaries plus other extra benefits, in an attempt to encourage women to remain close to the government. Prior to sanctions (July 1990) Soha's monthly salary had reached ID 100 (US$320) per month, as compared with her 'current' salary of ID 7,000 (US$3.5 per month). However, employment at the GFIW has always been limited to Ba'thist women only. Soha's statement indicates the scale of sanctions-induced change and how, in terms of material benefits, it was permeating the lives of even the most privileged women. As Soha explained:

> I am not proud to speak about it but I think it is important to tell you that the situation has also changed at the GFIW. 'Now' there are a few women who gain from being employees here, while the rest get nothing. I admit that before the sanctions, women of the GFIW received good salaries and many other advantages. 'We' were the most privileged of any other women in Iraq, whereas now the few women who have remained privileged get nothing less than millions (ID), in addition to valuable gifts from the delegations who make frequent visits. In order to manage the difficulties of life I sell things and get some commission. My brother works as a bus driver between Baghdad and Amman. He buys things from Jordan and I sell them for commission. The income I generate helps me to buy things for my children. The state is not taking care of all the Ba'thists, as you can imagine!

Indeed, not all Ba'thist women remained close 'Comrades' or 'friends' and 'sisters' of the leader (as Saddam Hussain always liked to call the GFIW women). At the GFIW headquarters in Baghdad, the assistant to Manal Younis Al-Alousi, the Secretary-General of the GFIW, was deliberately leaking information about her 'boss'. She disclosed that Al-Alousi, with her few 'favourite' colleagues, was keeping 'a close eye' on cargoes of humanitarian aid that were often delivered by visiting delegations. These profitable spoils were often plundered from the Iraqi people and distributed in various lots among the government elites, according to their degree of friendship with the leader. The assistant complained that she was excluded from Al-Alousi's privileged clique, which meant that she was deprived of a share of the lucrative spoils. While this observation reveals the situation of those who were mostly 'advantaged' Ba'thist women, it may also reflect the scale of the pressures endured by ordinary (non-Ba'thist) women in the deteriorating economic situation under sanctions.

Iraqi women with very high educational levels are not spared from the desperate need for an additional income. The survey and interviews with a number of female students showed that many university lecturers and tutors were offering personal tuition in return for money. The students revealed that the average charge for eight individual lessons per month was far higher than the official monthly income of a university teacher. It was also profitable for many women with medical expertise, such as graduate nurses and public health specialists, to sell their skills privately after official working hours.

Respondents' Previous and Current Employment Status
First Group: Unemployed (previously employed) Respondents
The survey showed that 80 respondents had given up their formal jobs after the imposition of sanctions. The highest proportion (39 women) were from the previously identified middle-class area (Area II), 22 were from the rich area (Area III), and 19 women were from the poorest area (Area I). There were also 6 retired respondents.

Interviews with a number of women in this group revealed that the decision to leave work was either taken by women willingly or was due to pressure from their families. This suggests that the lack of material incentives was not the main reason for leaving work, but rather was one of many obstacles that significantly affected women's professional careers. Laila (aged 38, from Area II) articulated this situation:

It was my dream to become a successful electronic engineer. I studied hard and I graduated in 1987 with distinction. A month after my graduation I got a job with a good salary [ID 92, equal to US$296, per month]. Later, I got married and my salary got even higher after the birth of our first son in 1989. I stood by my husband and bore the financial responsibilities of the family equally with him. After the 'nightmare' [the sanctions] had befallen our lives, things changed. Stress invaded our lives. My job turned out to be an additional burden for my family. My husband started to complain about my safety and the environment at my work, claiming that I was surrounded by men colleagues. One day, he ordered me to leave my work. First, I protested and cried but that changed nothing. Now, five years have passed since I left my profession. I am sitting at home just like any housewife. I have forgotten everything about engineering.

This statement reveals that, when the material benefits of women's employment decline, social and cultural obstacles come to the fore in overshadowing the value of women's careers.

Iraqi women's access to employment and various types of occupation under the effects of sanctions increasingly revolved around notions of female protection that confined women either to the home or to 'culturally' accepted types of jobs. The result of this change was the growing differences in the symbolic meaning of occupations for different sexes within households. This was also clearly reflected in the statement of one respondent, Hanna (aged 46, from Area III), who decided to leave her job in the Iraqi Ministry of Planning after 23 years of service. She said:

I am a university graduated economist. My job in the Ministry was a good one [ID 120 equal to US$400, per month], and respectable. I had the blessing of my husband and my closest relatives. Imagine; my husband even had no objection to my participating in deputations outside the country. In the 'good times' the Ministry used to send employees for training and as delegates abroad. After few months of sanctions, my job became a permanent issue in confrontations at home. My husband could see no point in my leaving home for a job that was worth nothing [ID 9,000 equal to US$4.5 per month]. When I resisted, he started to put pressure on me, demanding that I should cover my hair and wear long flowing clothes, and so on. Our lives turned to a living hell because of my job. In the end I gave up. Now I am a full-time housewife. However, I don't blame him at all. He works day and night in order to provide for the family. What could I do with my little salary?

The statements of these respondents reveal that attitudes confining women to the home are somehow more influential in the lives of educated women who belonged to the previously-identified middle income/class, whereas these notions were less envisaged in the lives of respondents with lower levels of education, especially respondents from the lower middle-income/class. Interviews held with poor or lower middle class, less-educated respondents revealed that they suffered the same consequences of the economic crisis as most of the respondents from the middle-class. However, for some of them (both young and old) it was much more acceptable to give up their jobs in the public sector in order to have better earnings from petty trade or from agricultural jobs, or an income from informal jobs.

For example, Fawziah (aged 49, from Area I) did not face much social awkwardness when she decided to carry on a petty trade after giving up her job as public sector employee. It was also possible to follow her case in detail through a visit to the location of her work on a street corner in Baghdad. She was standing in front of a small desk with strikingly distinct and simple items, such as spoons, make-up, two pair of shoes, some small mirrors, etc. She said:

I was working as a school-assistant before I became 'like this' [she points to her desk]. I am the only breadwinner in my family [her husband is seriously ill]. I did not want to become a beggar but what you call this? However, though I do accept alms, I personally would never ask for it. It is very difficult for me to believe that there is no hope left for us, the poor people.

In reply to a question about whether she found this trade better than working in the school, emphasizing the latest promise by the government to increase the wages of public sector employees, she answered:

For the time being, this trade is better [very cynical]. Before sanctions, my income in the school was good [ID 65 equal to US$200, per month] but 'the United Nations has punished me without reason'. Everything has turned upside down since then. Seventeen years ago, I become the proud owner of my house [state housing]. Thank God I have this house now. Otherwise, we could end up living in the street. Life changed dramatically and it has become very difficult to survive. With this poor trade I go home every day with food. This would not be possible with an income of ID 3000 [US$1.5] per month [salary from her previous job, under sanctions].

Obviously, Fawzia preferred not to say anything about the part of the survey question on the government's initiative to raise the salaries of public sector employees. However, it was understandable. Nobody in Iraq was willing to comment on something that related directly or even indirectly to the government. It can be assumed that her comment about the UN implied that it was not the Iraqi people who were behind this crisis, but rather some other 'entity' that she would not name. She probably meant that the political agenda of the government and the UN were responsible for her unfortunate situation. The cynicism expressed by her statement and by the gleam in her eyes revealed a great insecurity.

Some of the respondents revealed that the deteriorating conditions at work had driven them out of their jobs. Haifa (aged 42, from Area III) had been an ultrasound technician at a major hospital in Baghdad, but decided, in the aftermath of the Gulf War in 1991, to leave her work. She revealed the scale of devastation which had befallen the health sector as a result of sanctions and war, and explained the trauma that had made her job unbearable:

It was not in my mind to leave my work, despite the deterioration in the value of my salary compared with market prices. I tried to keep going to work, but I found that nearly all my colleagues had given up. Nothing was functioning. It was a terrifying situation. I decided to leave my job. We [her family] are managing with my husband's work in a private family business.

More than one respondent from the three residential areas expressed their feeling that the economic crisis had made their jobs worthless, and that this had persuaded them to become economically dependent on the income of male family members.

In the same context, one should specifically mention the difficulties relating to proper childcare, such as nurseries and kindergartens, which has represented a huge obstacle to the employment of women with small children. Prior to sanctions, this was one of the essential securities ensured by the state for all working women with small children for a symbolic charge. The deterioration of these services after the imposition of sanctions was a major worry for working mothers. A large number of unemployed women in the sample were mothers of small children. Sarab (aged 38, from Area II) had left her job as a physician at the Medical School for six years in order to bring up her child. At the time of the survey, she was considering returning to work on a part-time basis. She said:

I am happy that I can go to work now, even in a part-time job. We could not afford to put my daughter in a kindergarten. But I still have a problem with the times of school vacations and holidays. I think I have no other option than to take her with me to work, but it is worrying me a great deal because of the increasing risks of contagious diseases at the hospital.

It should also be noted that not all the women in this group had left their jobs unwillingly, or for that matter, because of the low wages. Some respondents said that work was no longer necessary for them after they had married. For some, work had put immense pressure on them after they had become mothers.

However, the case of Iman (aged 38, from Area III) reflects another dimension of the advantageous aspect of sanctions for a small segment of Iraqi society, namely government officials and those who had the upper hand in the Oil-For-Food contracts, and oil smugglers. Iman met her husband in 1984. They were both students at the Institute of Business Administration. After graduation, Iman (who is one of the three cases illustrated in Chapter Five below) had a job in one of the ministries, before the transformation of her husband in 1997 from a government sector employee to a wealthy businessman. The change encouraged her to leave her waged employment. Iman openly expressed her opinion about the situation. She said:

Why I should bother any more? Things have changed for the worse for women who care for their careers. I have better and much more valuable things to care for. My husband and my children need me more than any job outside the home, especially as everyone is facing increasing uncertainty about the future. I am now more contented without my job. My husband provides me with absolutely everything a woman could dream of.

On my comment that many people were negatively affected by the economic sanctions, she immediately responded:

I mean the embargo and the threat of war. But honestly, I should tell you that those who complain about sanctions are weak people and they don't like to work to improve their economic situation. They are lazy people, because they were always used to being fed by the state. When this was not available anymore, they started to complain. I really believe that sanctions have provided them with a legitimate cause to venture in the street begging. Personally, I think that sanctions have been much more of a blessing than a problem to my family.

In general, there was an overwhelming sentiment of comforting for economic sanctions among the newly enriched and the sanctions profiteers. However, the statement above reveals that despite their advantages, these people were living with a great deal of insecurity and uncertainty about the sustainability of their advantageous situation.

Second Group: Unemployed (never employed) Respondents
This group consisted of 53 women, of whom 21 came from the poorest area (Area I), 11 came from the middle-class area (Area II), while 21 were from the richest area

(Area III). Most notable was the fact that the majority of these women were young (aged between 15 and 30 years), and were recently educated.

Latifa (aged 23, from Area II) was unmarried, and had graduated from commercial vocational high school in 1999. At the time of the survey, she was living with her oldest brother and her youngest sister. She had lost her father in the Iraq-Iran war, and her mother had died in 1998 after a serious illness. Latifa and her sister lived on her brother's limited income. When asked if she would like to join the labour force, she answered:

> I wish I could work. We need an additional income because my brother's income is not enough even for basic needs. We could not afford to buy the medicine for my late mother. I have discussed this issue with my brother several times. He said that for the little income that I could get, it was not worth taking the risks of the harassment and crimes that are increasingly being seen in Iraqi society.

Even though women's labour participation had become severely hampered by a range of economic and social obstacles, a new dimension in women's attitudes towards themselves and their roles in the society was very noticeable. Many young women and a large number of the highly educated among them had refrained from thinking about work/careers, because their only dream was to grab the opportunity of marriage to Iraqi/Arab men living abroad. Latifa was one of these women. She had been promised in marriage to a man who lived abroad and who had ordered her to stay at home. The 'promising' man was commanding Latifa's life and she was obviously living a dream that was far more lucrative when compared with the hassle of job seeking and related matters.

However, it must be emphasized that not all women in this group were keen to join the labour force or were feeling uncomfortable as full-time housewives. On the contrary, some women were demonstrating the comfort of being economically and emotionally dependent on a male, especially a husband. This was an attitude expressed exclusively by a few women who were wives of rich husbands, sanctions profiteers, or government officials.

Conclusion

Iraqi women's labour participation and their income earnings were greatly affected by the sanctions-induced economic crisis, through growing rates of unemployment, a decline in wages and per capita incomes, and high rates of inflation. Consequently, while more women began to seek jobs out of the need for an income, and as unemployment surged, more women had fallen out of the labour market. It is clear that Iraqi working women were adversely affected by the down-sizing of the state's role in the economy, and women's position in the labour market was undermined when the public sector was squeezed and its resources were reduced.

In general, Iraqi women's economic participation in relation to their status under sanctions witnessed contradictory tendencies: while households headed by women had increased, female dependency on male providers had also increased, just as productivity among women had declined. This situation had resulted in further marginalization of Iraqi women from productive employment and increased their poverty.

It is important to note that the considerable body of Iraqi laws and regulations specifically addressing women's position in the labour market, as either active or as passive players, remained unchanged during the period of sanctions. However, to a large extent the economic crisis had invalidated the active implementation of these laws, and Iraqi women were left to face the direct impact of market forces and their sharp fluctuations under sanctions without the positive intervention and mitigating policies of the state. The economic crisis had directly transferred into a negative impact on the demand for women's labour, the types of employment open to them, and the conditions under which they worked.

The survey revealed that the impact of sanctions on women's labour participation was differentiated following women's needs, opportunities, qualifications, and personal familial conditions. It showed that the burden of the economic crisis had fallen in particular on the shoulders of the urban poor and middle-class women. Prior to sanctions, most of these women had held good jobs and enjoyed respectable income levels, which made them responsible for household budgeting and maintenance. Sanctions had rendered their jobs worthless and left them to cope with the extra burden of high prices and living costs.

Moreover, and due to the socio-cultural binary that governs the lives of individuals from these backgrounds, educated Iraqi women from the previously identified middle-class had increasingly become unfamiliar with the labour market under sanctions. Women from this socio-economic background saw employment under sanctions as below their social position and degrading. The decline in the economic and social returns of employment under sanctions had pushed a large proportion of these women back into the home, and had made them become fully dependent on male providers. Some, however, had seen informal earnings as an alternative. As such, in contrast to the situation in the 1970s and 1980s, when women's work was considered as a path towards independence, self-actualization, equality and participation in society, the social price of the economic decline under sanctions had been to increase gender and class inequalities in the Iraqi society. While opportunities for decent income earnings were shrinking in both the public and private sectors, social restrictions and increased labour market segregation had exacerbated the problems. The marginalization of women in the labour market was seen through an increased inclination towards ascribed roles of women in the society, and an increased dependency ratio of women.

In general, the compounded effects of high unemployment rates and the diminishing incentives of work meant the loss of human capital resources, especially the educated, the economically active, and people with high professional expertise. Sanctions had a discriminatory impact on people, not only according to sex, and their social, and economic backgrounds, but also according to their educational or professional backgrounds. The situation particularly affected the high professional educated cadres, both men and women, who became captives isolated from global technological development and exposed to increased psychological pressure.

The economic crisis created an enormous burden on lower middle-class, poor and women-headed households. These women had to compensate for the withdrawal of subsidies and for the cutbacks in social expenditures. The situation increased workloads within the home and pressured such women to seek incomes outside the home, often in informal situations and under inadequate social and health conditions.

While these were some of the grim sights that were emerging in Iraq, it appears that the other by-product of the sanctions was the evolution of the sanctions profiteers. Supported by its favourable position vis-à-vis Saddam's regime, this tiny segment snatched the opportunities provided by the economic crisis. This grouping differed significantly from the broad majority of the Iraqi people, since its members had managed to grow rich on the despair of the majority of the Iraqi people.

4

THE CRISIS OF FEMALE EDUCATION UNDER THE UN SANCTIONS

Introduction

The deteriorating condition of education under sanctions in Iraq was mentioned by the Arab Human Development (AHD) Reports of 2002 and 2003 as well as several UN-commissioned studies. However, these reports were concerned more with statistical aggregates than with providing a detailed analysis about the impact of UN economic sanctions as having contributed to this deterioration. Moreover, they largely overlooked a gendered dimension of the impact of sanctions on education in Iraq.

The intention in this chapter is to provide a realistic assessment of the impact of sanctions on female education in Iraq. The analysis of this issue is based on findings from the student survey (50 female students), and from the follow-up of a number of the students after graduation, in addition to data obtained through the main survey (277 women).

The first part of the chapter takes into account the situation of female education in Iraq in the 1970s and 1980s, as a contrast to the situation of female education in Iraq under sanctions, and relies mainly on Iraq's official statistics on female education, as well as data from other sources such as UNICEF and UNECSO. The second part provides an assessment of the impact of sanctions on female education by exploring the sanctions-induced constraints on various aspects of education in Iraq. The third section is intended to shed light on the implications of sanctions for female education, through an interpretation of the situation of female education with regard to its effect on public health, and social values and attitudes towards women.

Recasting the Development of Female Education in Iraq

Education in Iraq was proclaimed as an exclusive function of the state that must be secured for all citizens on an equal basis.[1] Accordingly, the state was entrusted to raise the standard of education in Iraq. Special emphasis was given to female education. Towards the realization of the state's vision for education, the first step was the adoption of the Compulsory Education Law No. 118 in 1976. This law required that both sexes should attend school through the six years of the primary level, from ages six until twelve. The law made education at all levels free of charge, including fees, books and all other requirements, and foreign and private educational institutions were abolished. The law obliged the state, as a key player in the economy, to set up special policies and programmes, with measurable results and monitoring techniques.

Accordingly, the Iraqi government invested heavily in education, and public expenditure on education in the 1970s and 1980s was introduced as a main component of the national development plans. Some believe that improving education was the second most important strategic issue for the Iraqi government after defence.[2] Iraq's allocation to education rose from 3 to 6 percent of gross national product (GNP),[3] and in 1979, for example, Iraq's spending on education averaged 4 percent of GNP and 15 percent of total government spending.[4] In 1988/9, the budget for education mounted to ID 690 million (or US$2.2 billion at an official exchange rate of ID 1: US$3.2).[5] These levels of spending were above those of comparable developing countries, and were on a par with those of high-performing Asian economies.[6]

In addition to paying special attention to both quality and equality in education, the state's key policy was also directed towards ensuring that education would be more accessible to low-income families and rural populations. These and many other developments of the 1970s and 1980s made education more accessible to all citizens, thus transforming education from a privilege into an entitlement. Female education in particular was one of Iraq's major achievements. As the statistics and analysis show, education was considered by many Iraqi women as a major route to personal achievement and fulfilment, and it is evident that there was a steady decline in gender inequality of female enrolment in all levels of education during the 1970s and 1980s. The Arab Human Development Report for 2002 referred to Iraq's education system as one of the most advanced in the Arab region in the 1970s and 1980s, especially where quality and gender equality were concerned, noting that the focus of education in Iraq was especially directed toward building human capabilities through its emphasis on training and acquisition of knowledge.

It is believed that the education system in Iraq in the 1970s and 1980s achieved tangible results, and had it continued under normal economic conditions, it could well have been one of the most significant successes in the Middle East region. Unfortunately however, Iraq's education system was severely hit by sanctions, and the sanctions-induced economic and political crisis was particularly felt in this very effective socio-economic sector.

After the imposition of sanctions in 1990 and until mid-1997, there were no official allocations for education at all. Official allocations for the education sector began under the Oil-For-Food Programme but these were limited to US$12 million per six months, for the first three phases up to June 1998.[7] When the ceiling on oil sales was eventually increased and revenues expanded, the resulting allocations for the education sector rose considerably, e.g., to US$180 million in Phase VIII.[8] Up to 2003, the total OFF allocation for educational supplies to Centre/South was US$1.5 billion, or an aggregated average of 3.6 percent of all the available resources of OFF.[9]

However, the tightened and detailed verification procedures that accompanied each delivery of contracted aid that was required by the Sanctions Committee had hampered the efficient rehabilitation of this viable sector. By March 2003, the total amount that Iraq had accessed for the rehabilitation of the education sector and related supplies in the Centre/South had reached roughly US$489 million.[10] It is undeniable that the state attempted to mitigate the deteriorating conditions of education under sanctions, but the critical shortages in this sector remained largely unalleviated. For example, the state continued to build new educational institutions, but as more buildings went up, less money went into them.[11] Therefore, any analysis of the gender-specific impact of sanctions on female education has to extend from simple rates of female enrolment and graduates to an exploration of the impact of sanctions on the quality of education, and its economic and social return for Iraqi females.

However, the following is to provide an idea about rates of female enrolment in the different educational levels under sanctions and during the 1970s and 1980s, as a comparison with the situation after the imposition of sanctions. Iraq's formal education enrolment categories,[12] as provided, are based on the General Population Census of 1977.

The Education of Females: Statistical Aggregates
Illiteracy Eradication
The first step towards eradication of illiteracy in Iraq was taken in 1971 by the adoption of the Illiteracy Eradication Law, which was followed by further legislation – the Comprehensive Illiteracy Eradication Law No. 92 of 1978 and its amendment in 1979 – and the establishment of a detailed programme of action (campaign) through a High Committee of Illiteracy Eradication.[13]

The 1978 Campaign was initially designed for a period of 36 months within the period 1978–87, and all illiterate adults aged from 15 to 45 years were required to participate. The programme was designed to be carried out at three levels – basic, 'popular schools', and follow-up classes; these classes consisted of an integration programme in which students aged 15 to 25 were transferred to normal schools or into professional training.[14] Logistically the plan involved the mobilization of a huge number of staff, including teachers and university students, and the opening of schools and centres all over the country.

The degree to which the law of illiteracy eradication was enforced is unclear. Official Iraqi statistics for 1977 indicate that, prior to the campaign, 70.7 percent of the illiterate population in the age group 15 to 45 years was female (i.e., a rate of 64.4 percent of the total female population of this age group in Iraq).[15] Another official source estimated that 75 percent of Iraqi females had become literate by the end of 1987.[16] As a reward for its efforts in eradicating illiteracy, Iraq received the UNESCO prize nominated for this purpose in 1987. However, these figures seem unrealistic or overstated, especially bearing in mind that the campaign had had to be terminated due to the Iraq-Iran War, which was ongoing during the period 1980 to 1988.[17] In fact, the Ninth Regional Conference of the Ba'th Party in 1982 openly admitted the limited success of the programme, though it did not reveal any figures.[18] It ascribed the programme's limited success to the priority required by 'the National Duty' – the war with Iran – and promised to resume the work.[19] The programme was duly restarted in 1986, but was limited to those aged 15 to 25 who had been unable to finish the first programme, in addition to children aged 11–14 years.[20]

By the year 2000, under sanctions, illiteracy rates among adults (over 15 years) in Iraq were far higher than they had been in the 1970s, before the illiteracy eradication programme got under way (see Appendix Table 4.1). The rate of illiteracy among females (aged over 15 years) had jumped to 77 percent, or 5,070,000 women.[21] These figures were shocking, not only on the level of Iraq but also because they were the highest among all Middle East and North Africa (MENA) countries (See Appendix Table 4.1).[22] However, the most appalling figures were those concerning illiteracy rates among young females in the 15–24 age group, since they accounted for no less than 71 percent of the female population of this age, or 1,593,000 women.

It should be noted that the MENA countries have the highest rates of illiteracy compared with other developing countries, especially countries with comparable or lower per capita incomes.[23] It is estimated that there are over 75 million illiterate adults in the MENA region, over half of whom live in Egypt, Iraq, and Morocco, with around a third of them living in Iraq. Given that Iraq is a middle-populated country (22.7 million in 2000) as compared with Egypt and Morocco (70.5 million and 30.1 million respectively in 2000), this means that the situation of illiteracy in Iraq has reached a catastrophic level.

Female Enrolment in Primary Schools

With the adoption of the Compulsory Education Law of 1976, female enrolment in primary school increased from 30 percent in the mid 1970s, to 43 percent in the 1978/9 academic year,[24] and by the academic year 1989/90, the rate of female enrolment in primary school had reached 44.3 percent of the total enrolment at this level (see Appendix Table 4.2).

The improvement of female-male ratios at the primary school level was significantly associated not only with the compulsory primary education law, but also with the economic situation. During the 1970s and 1980s, primary education in Iraq received 47 percent of the total public expenditures on education.[25] This included teachers' salaries, and the textbooks and educational materials (such as stationery, notebooks, pencils, geometry sets, and school uniforms) that were provided for all children throughout Iraq.[26]

Under sanctions, statistics may reveal the gender disparity in female enrolment in primary schools (see Appendix Tables 4.2 and 4.3). Iraq's official statistics (Appendix Table 4.2) shows that, in the academic year 2000/01 a rate of 44 percent or 1,776,212 girls enrolled at primary school level. However, the real number of Iraqi females who were not officially enrolled in primary education is appalling. Based on the total female population aged 5 to 14 in the year 2000, over one and a half million Iraqi girls who were eligible for primary school enrolment were out of education.[27] Paradoxically, however, Iraq's law of Compulsory Education remained in effect during the sanctions era, although its implementation seems to have been less important, given the weakened economy and the state's control over all aspects of the welfare of the population.

Private primary schools also began to emerge after the imposition of sanctions. Nevertheless, for the vast majority of Iraqi people, public schools remained the overwhelming option. Public primary school enrolment remained largely free of charge, but by mid-2000, the state had begun to impose 'symbolic' registration fees. These ranged from ID 2,000 (US$1) per year for primary school to ID 25,000 (US$12) per year for university, and parents were often asked to purchase scarce educational supplies, such as chalk.[28] Moreover, following the imposition of sanctions, other benefits previously provided by the state had to be shouldered by Iraqi families. Many families could not afford the purchase of basic necessities such food and medicine, let alone school requirements for their children, and such families were often under pressure to let their children simply drop out of school prematurely or to send them out to work in order to generate income by petty work or begging.

Female Enrolment in Secondary Schools
Iraqi female enrolment at secondary level (intermediate and high school) has always been lower than that of males. However, following the imposition of sanctions, female numbers in secondary school decreased further. UNESCO statistics show that in the academic year 1989/90, the Gross Enrolment Ratio (GER) of females in secondary school was 36 percent, and in the year 1995/6 GER had declined to 32 percent, in spite of the high population growth (see Appendix Table 4.4). By the academic year 1999/00, the rate of female enrolment in secondary education had increased to 38.5 percent before it fell to 29 percent in the school year 2002/3, which was less than that of the 1970s (see Appendix Table 4.5).[29]

Obviously, gender inequality – as the main dependent variable for the status of women – begins to be significantly associated with female enrolment in all educational levels above the primary school level.[30] The low and declining rates of female enrolment in secondary school, as indicated above, disclose the fact that the gender inequality of female enrolment in secondary school has been exacerbated under sanctions.

Female Enrolment in Vocational Education
The same trend could be observed with regard to female enrolment in vocational high schools. Female enrolment in technical and agricultural vocational schools began only in the mid-1970s, whereas females had previously been allowed only in commercial and domestic arts vocational schools. The urgent need for a middle-qualified cadre for production and administrative jobs was reflected in the growing number of vocational schools and in female enrolment in different streams in qualifying schools (see Appendix Table 4.6). In the academic year 1978/9, there were 102 vocational schools in which female enrolment amounted to 12,569 girls. By 1987/8, the number of vocational schools had increased to 248 establishments, and the number of girls enrolled had reached 40,313. Iraq's official statistics for the 1970s and 1980s show that female enrolment in vocational schools took place specifically in urban areas,

indicating that increased urbanization and economic activity had had a positive effect on social and cultural attitudes toward women's employment and types of occupation. It also indicated a decrease in gender inequality of female enrolment in vocational schools.

Under sanctions, female enrolment in vocational schools witnessed an unprecedented collapse. By the academic year 1999/00, the number of vocational establishments had declined to 234 schools, and female enrolment in all types of vocational schools had fallen enormously, to 8,840 girls (see Appendix Table 4.6). The cessation of economic development and the collapse of the labour market due to sanctions seem to have had a direct effect women's motivation to acquire these types of qualifications. It also suggests that under sanctions the socio-economic climate had negatively affected social attitudes towards female enrolment in these types of qualifying schools.

Female Enrolment in Higher Education

Although middle- and upper-class Iraqi women had been attending university since the 1920s, rural women and girls had been largely uneducated until higher education was made free of charge by the Compulsory Law of 1976. During the 1970s and 1980s, there was an increase in the numbers of new higher educational establishments in Iraq, and increasing numbers of female students in all kinds of disciplines. Female enrolment rose from 8,045 students in the academic year 1969/70 to 61,204 students in the academic year 1989/90, or 34 percent of the total enrolment in higher education (see Appendix Table 4.7).

However, the progress of female enrolment in higher education achieved during the 1970s and 1980s must not be understood solely in terms of 'numbers'. State-sponsored education and state policies concerning Iraqi women, as witnessed in the pre-sanctions period, should also be considered as a 'quality' change towards minimizing gender inequality in formal education. Even though female enrolment in higher education has been lower than that of males, there has been a steady increase in female student numbers, especially in atypical disciplines such as technology and engineering, economics and management sciences, and agricultural sciences.[31] In addition to the increased demand for highly-educated labour, it was also prestigious for middle-class Iraqi women to acquire a university degree.

Under sanctions, female enrolment in high-education did not decline, but nor did it show any potential increase. By the academic year 1999/00, the rate of female enrolment in the state-sponsored higher education sector had increased by only 0.7 percent to reach 34.7 percent (from 34 percent in 1989/90) (see Appendix Table 4.7).

Private education began to venture into the general field of education and thus became caught up in the complex economic situation under sanctions.[32] Although private universities have existed since 1989, they were limited in scale and types of profession. In the 1990s, private universities became 'fashionable', especially among privileged groups and those who could afford to obtain a university degree with 'less effort'. The problems associated with private education in Iraq do not end with its high expenses – it is also important to mention that generally speaking, a degree from a private university is less appreciated compared with one from a state-sponsored university. This is because admission to private universities and colleges requires lower grade averages in high school final exams than the high grade averages needed for admission to state-sponsored universities. (Numbers of females enrolled in private universities are shown in Appendix Table 4.7).

Female Enrolment in Postgraduate Education

With regard to postgraduate studies, it should be noted that postgraduate education first became available in Iraq in the mid-1970s, but in a limited number of disciplines only.[33] Prior to sanctions, nearly all postgraduate studies were carried out abroad. Iraqi postgraduate students were privileged to have all the expenses of their education abroad covered by the state, including education fees and living expenses. Even so, statistics for the 1970s and 1980s shows a steady increase in the numbers of women who opted for postgraduate studies inside Iraq (see Appendix Table 4.8).

Notably, however, female numbers in postgraduate studies in the academic year 1999/00 had increased to 4,883 students against a background of only 700 women students in the academic year 1989/90 (see Appendix Table 4.8). Obviously, while job opportunities were declining, many Iraqi women saw postgraduate studies as an alternative that might be advantageous in the future. Interviews with some professors and female postgraduate students at Baghdad University revealed that the vast majority of female postgraduate students had previously been part of the formal labour force. In addition, many of the highly educated women, especially those who could afford to avoid the tiresome aspects of low-paid jobs, had opted for postgraduate studies as an alternative to socializing with others.

Female Enrolment in Teacher-Training Institutes

Iraqi women have always constituted the overwhelming majority of students in teacher-training institutes (see Appendix Tables 4.9, 4.10 and 4.11). By 1986, some of the teacher-training colleges had been re-graded into Institutes for Teacher Training; these provided a college degree (diploma) after five years. The number of college also increased from 29 to 44 entities.[34]

Under sanctions the collapse in wages was especially felt in the education sector. Teachers' salaries fell dramatically, from pre-sanctions levels that corresponded to some US$500–1000 per month, to around US$3–5 per month for primary and secondary teachers, and around US$20–40 per month for university teachers.[35] Surprisingly however, female enrolment in teacher-training institutes continued to increase, even though teaching (official) ranked among the lowest paid-jobs under sanctions (see Appendix Table 4.10).

Obviously, the continued high rates of female enrolment in teacher training, especially as teachers at primary, secondary and vocational school levels, reflects the strengthening social attitudes that channel women into 'socially' accepted, but relatively low-paid work positions. In Iraq as in many other parts of the Middle East, school teaching is considered one of the most respectable occupations for women. As noted earlier, the high unemployment rate among women was also attributed to the further strengthening of social attitudes that tended to confine women to 'traditional' types of jobs – the lowest paid.

Quality of Education under Sanctions: An Assessment

A measure of the quality of education can be ascertained by observing such indicators as average number of students per class or per teacher, and rates of failure and dropouts.[36] It is also maintained that a good student/teacher ratio requires the building of more schools and the creating of new educational projects, in order to improve the quality of education as the population increases, and in particular to avoid the problems of congestion and to stop double or triple shifts in the use of school buildings. Due to the non-availability of precise statistical data on the issue, it is not possible to initiate a discussion of the implications of sanctions for these indicators.

However, an examination of the impact of the UN sanctions on female education is offered by exploring the interrelations between the shortage of finance and social constraints that are the most obvious determinants for education under sanctions in general, and for female education, in particular.

Destruction of Educational Establishments

At the time of the survey, well over a decade had passed since the Gulf War of 1991, but the after-effects could still be felt, perpetuated by the consequences of the economic crisis. It is well-known that Iraq's education sector was exposed to extensive damage as a result of the 1991 Gulf War, especially because the United States and its allies believed that Saddam was hiding his weapons in these facilities. As a result of the destruction of buildings, equipment, laboratories, records, furniture, books, and other fundamental requisites, it was estimated that the rebuilding of this viable sector would require an amount of US$3.4 billion.[37] Following the Gulf War of 1991, According to UNESCO's estimate of the priority needs for damaged schools in the South/Centre after the 1991 Gulf War, around 12,567 schools (more than one third of all schools in these regions) needed urgent maintenance and partial reconstruction.[38] The estimated total cost for the replacement or repair of 4,157 severely damaged schools was US$645 million. A further 84 percent of all schools also needed rehabilitation.[39] The crisis did severe physical damage to educational institutions in Iraq, which was difficult to alleviate because of the financial constraints of sanctions.

By 2003, only US$22.4 million-worth (4 percent) of critically-needed rehabilitation funding was being spent on Iraq's education infrastructure.[40] This means that the condition of the majority of school buildings in the Centre/South had deteriorated considerably under sanctions. Realistically, therefore, a rehabilitation plan was unlikely to achieve any improvement in expenditure for the education sector either under sanctions or the Oil-for-Food programme. A primary school teacher described her school as being in 'ruins'. She said:

The whole building was seriously damaged during the bombing in 1991. A large part of the school, including many classrooms and bathrooms, was turned into wreckage. The classroom doors and student desks and chairs had disappeared [looted]. People wanted these things for firewood, because, for more than six months after the war, we lived without electricity and fuel. The school was closed for three months. We needed every bit of effort in order to pick up the pieces and resume teaching, so the children would not lose the year. We had to put two or three class groups together in one room. Most of the children had to sit on the floor. They were freezing because it was winter. Now (2001) however, we have had the windows repaired but we still have to wait for the rebuilding of the rest of the classrooms that were totally destroyed.

Economic sanctions have created a serious shortage of materials necessary for reconstruction and building, and this has led to the postponement or total stoppage of new educational projects, including the building of new schools all over the country. Such projects had been planned to meet the natural growth in student numbers in the coming years.[41]

In 2002, as Iraq was heading into another devastating stage of its everlasting cycle of war, occupation and terrorism, the crisis situation created by the Gulf War in 1991 was still intact. It continued to be reported that about 31 percent of the Centre/South primary schools had experienced a severe shortage of drinking water due to the deterioration of school plumbing and frequent interruptions of the external water supply.[42] In addition, 52 percent of toilets did not meet basic standards of hygiene. Only 26 percent of the schools had rubbish collection bins in their compound, and in the remaining schools, rubbish was scattered around corridors and across the school compound.[43]

Shortage of Material and Human Resources

The education system in Iraq under sanctions was not only directly affected by the wide-scale damage inflicted upon the country's socio-economic viability, but damage had extended to a whole generation of students, teachers and academic institutions. It was noticeable that the sanctions-induced isolation of Iraq from knowledge of global information and technology systems had caused dual shortages of schooling requirements and (qualified) teaching staff for the acquisition of scientific know-how and educational efficiency. Iraqi libraries were suffering a serious shortage of modern scientific reference books and periodicals. Students complained about this problem and were aware of the consequences. This particular problem affected female students differently from their male colleagues.

Due to the economic situation, women and girls in particular have been subjected to increasing restrictions that, in many instances, undermine their careers, whether in waged work or education. The difficulties encountered as a result of the deterioration in education quality often turn out to be a problem for female students, who have less freedom of mobility, compared with male students, to seek other alternatives as regards reading materials and reading-groups, or assistance by private tutors. The problem has been exacerbated because of the diminishing economic benefits of education, particularly with regard to employment opportunities and wage earning. Many respondents spoke of the dilemma of trying to hold things together. Maha (aged 24), a student of electronics engineering, and the daughter of highly educated parents, expressed this problem:

> In spite of being in the final year in engineering and with only few months remaining before I graduate as an engineer, I still have to convince my family about the meaning of my education. Ironically, I sometimes also doubt myself. Electronics is one of the applied sciences and to become a good practitioner in such a profession you need a great deal of laboratory practice and up-to-date knowledge and equipment. At the university, we suffer serious shortages of equipment, books and periodicals about new innovations, which are absolutely essential for our knowledge as electronic engineers. Therefore, it's no wonder that my family tries to protect me and keep me away from all this hassle!

According to Maha, lab supplies had dwindled, broken equipment could not be replaced, and printing presses had ceased operation. Entire classrooms of science students would gather around one piece of equipment.

Clearly the impact of sanctions has expanded beyond the physical destruction of schools and educational establishments to affect the education system's performance quality and efficiency. The other face of the crisis was portrayed through the shortage of teaching staff, particularly qualified staff members. For example, it was reported that by the end of June 1994 the number of permanent teachers dropping out of the service had reached 2,918 individuals, resulting in 1769 vacant hours/classes daily.[44] Further estimates suggest that 2,000 professors – usually the most qualified – fled from Iraq's twenty major universities between 1995 and 2000.[45] This is also confirmed by Iraq's official statistics (Appendix Table 4.11).

The dramatic decline in teachers' salaries, along with the severe constraints on activities such as teacher training and curriculum development, was behind the decision of many teachers to leave the profession.[46] According to statements by some professors in Iraq, the majority had, out of necessity, taken on second or even third jobs in order to make a living. Apart from a few top Ba'thist professors and administrators who, because of their support for the regime, could expect to receive special privileges and high salaries, the majority of teachers and professors had in effect been turned into an impoverished segment of Iraqi society under sanctions. University professors often worked as private tutors or in other types of businesses, but some – usually the most qualified – left the country for better opportunities in neighbouring countries or in Europe and America. During the 1990s, as increasing numbers of academics and teachers departed, the government prohibited foreign travel and refused to issue graduation certificates and other documents needed to apply for jobs abroad. Nevertheless, many escaped by bribing people in the passport office. Their disappearance always upset their departments and could be considered as a permanent loss to the universities. Many respondents commented that weeks might pass before they discovered that their professor(s) had escaped.

For many female students this problem also became their own. Lamia (aged 21), a Political Science student at Baghdad University explained:

> To reach my university I have to cross half of Baghdad City. Our effort, money, and time are wasted nearly every day, because classes are often cancelled due to the absence of our teacher(s). Last year, we had to postpone one of our majors to a later semester because the teacher had left the university very suddenly. I had to hide this from my family because it might have encouraged my brother, who is opposed to my daily trips outside the home. He has threatened me several times to prevent me going to the university.

In order to avoid the extra pressure of confrontation with her family, Lamia admitted that she had to hide the difficulties she was facing with her education. While problems such as teacher absences, shortage of books, or the long distances to the university were obstacles that were normally beyond the student's control, they were nevertheless seen as reasons for families to increase pressure on female students to give up their education. This situation affected women differently from men. While many male students deliberately failed their exams in an attempt to avoid compulsory military service, education's weakened conditions often increased the vulnerability of females to family and patriarchal domination.

By 1998, in an attempt to mitigate the troubled education sector, the state had initiated certain measures, including raising teacher's salaries and encouraging enrolment in teacher training institutes, and permitting private colleges to offer teacher training. However, education's alarming situation remained largely unchanged. Corruption entered university life in the 1990s. Professors blackmailed students, who in turn bribed professors. The intensifying pressures inflicted on people damaged the culture of education that Iraq had been so proud of for so long, and this was reflected in the behaviour of students and teaching staff. Even so, and notwithstanding the widespread rumours about the bribing of teachers in return for 'passing' exams, it was impossible to find a student who would personally admit that she/he had 'bought' their exams. However, one student did refer to the phenomenon on behalf of her friend:

> My friends said that last year's exams had cost her ID 405,000 [US$203]. She considers herself lucky because one of her teachers 'costs' a lot more. She said; she had to bargain with him (in the parking area at the university), and in return, she promised that she would not tell other students about the discount that she'd negotiated!

Emergence of Private Education

The deteriorated conditions of schools and the shortage of teaching staff have thrown up a problem exacerbated by the phenomenon of widespread private tuition. Private tutors have become indispensable, especially for high school finals, for obtaining high grades in the public qualifying examinations for enrolment in higher education. The AHD Report for 2002 worried about this phenomenon, which has found way into all MENA countries in recent years. It is believed that if the situation continues, education systems may split into two tiers, with high quality education available only to the wealthy minority who can afford private tutors, and low quality public education as the sole option for most citizens.[47] Such a trend would turn education into a 'means of perpetuating social stratification and poverty' rather than being a means of increasing social equality.[48]

In Iraq, it is striking that in recent years admissions requirements for universities have demanded extremely high averages in the state high school exams. These are often very difficult to achieve, especially given the deteriorated conditions and quality of education.[49] The average requirements for university admission vary from one discipline to another. However the observations on the ground suggest that is very difficult to obtain an average that would allow admission to a state university without the assistance of private tutors. This situation means that admission to universities, especially the state-sponsored, could become the exclusive preserve of financially privileged groups who can afford private tutors/lessons. While admission to private universities and colleges is not strictly limited to high-grade averages, it is strictly limited to those who can afford the fees.[50]

One respondent mentioned the problem of her friend who had interrupted her education at one of the private universities because she could not afford to pay the tuition costs. She said:

> My friend was in the third year when her father got sick and wasn't able to work any more. She couldn't pay the second semester's tuition fees, but she attended the final exams. While she was in the exam hall, the manager came in and asked her to leave, without even letting her finish. She was very embarrassed. She had to leave the place forever.

It is believed that the demand for high averages by state-sponsored universities is a deliberate policy by the state, aimed at slowing down the numbers of university entrants, especially as shortages of material and professional cadres limits educational capacity. Moreover, as increasing numbers of young males fail to enter universities a larger number of them will end up doing military service. At the same time, high unemployment rates, meagre job opportunities, and deteriorating living standards due to the economic crisis have limited the alternatives for female high school graduates. Suad (aged 21, from Area II) was newly married and had finished high school a year earlier. She described her situation:

> I always dreamt of marrying after I had finished a university degree, but

unfortunately, and despite doing my best, I could not score a good enough average to qualify me for admission to higher education. I think it is so unfair that admission to higher education has been increased so strictly to such a very high average, especially as the state exams were unbelievably difficult in contrast to the teaching standards at high schools. Many of my colleagues could not make it to university. There were only few girls who scored high grades because they could afford private tutors. Some of them had more than five private tutors. Those girls, like me, who could not pay for private teachers, have to do something else with their lives.

About the significance of private lessons for high school students, she said:

It was extremely necessary. During the final year in the high school, four teachers had left very suddenly, and we were left without any teaching for a long time during that year. Therefore, it was absolutely important to have private tutors in order to be able to complete the curriculums for many of the subjects. For subjects such as physics, mathematics and English, it would be impossible to learn them alone.

Statistics shows that female enrolment in the private universities and colleges has been extremely low since the establishment of these educational institutions. The 1995 Arab Human Development Report showed that the annual growth rate of female attainment in the period 1990/1 to 1994/5 was 20.6 percent, whereas it was 24.4 percent for males.[51] Female enrolment in private universities in 1998/9 was 21.5 percent and it decreased further to 19 percent in 1999/00.[52]

Under sanctions, gender inequality of female enrolment in private higher education was further influenced by the financial constraints on Iraqi families, whose limited resources were evident through the increased preferential treatment given to males at the expense of females. Families with restricted funds would rather spend money on educating their boys than girls. This is because under an increasingly restrictive social and economic environment, males would probably have more and better job opportunities compared with females. Nada's statement may give some idea about this particular and unprecedented problem. Nada (aged 23) was a first year student of English literature and was quite bitter about her experience. She said:

My family made it clear that if I opted for a university degree, it would have to be in a state-sponsored university. My parents were very worried about my younger brother's education because of the military service. At the same time, they could not afford to pay private college fees for both of us. However, for me, it was much more difficult because I had to achieve the grade averages for admission to a state-sponsored university, and these are much higher than the averages required at private colleges, I had to repeat the final year of high school three times. But I am happy now, even though I will be graduating two years after my younger brother, who is studying English Literature at a private college. I am proud I finally made it.

Drop-Out and Failure Problems

The 1995 Arab Human Development Report (UNDP) and the 2002 Report of the Arab Fund for Economic and Social Development (AFESD) warned of the alarming rise in Iraqi education's failure and dropout rates.[53] UNESCO's 2000 Report revealed that failures and repeat rates in all educational levels in Iraq ranged between 17.7 and 27 percent.[54] This figure was higher than the earlier statistics in the 1970s and 1980s, at 16 and 20 percent respectively.[55] Certain types of education, such as teacher training and vocational schools, witnessed the highest levels of failures and dropouts, during the 1990s (see Appendix Table 4.12).[56]

However, failure and repetition rates were consistently higher for males than for females in all levels of higher education (undergraduate level). Although, it is widely believed that Iraqi boys fail on purpose, in order to delay military service, it is also true that a large proportion of males failed because, in addition to their schooling, they often had to work. Due to the financial inability of families to send their children to school, especially as the economic return of education has declined or diminished, it is expected that rates of failures and dropouts will increase. Indeed, when the whole community is under immense economic and political pressure, the crisis is reflected upon all aspects of life, of which education become a less attractive option for parents and young people.

As for female students, there is another dimension behind the increased rate of female failures and dropouts. While males were going out of education in order to generate income, females were dropping out of education to stay at home.[57] More often, females were required to share in income generating, particularly by engaging in informal economic activities. However, the consequences of this situation are often grave. Indeed, countless incidents were observed of immature girls being pushed into humiliating situations in order to earn their living. It was striking that small girls of school age often wandered in rich neighbourhoods, begging or banging on doors to ask for work (cleaning), often in extremely unsafe conditions.

Material Incentive of Female Education under Sanctions

Education is considered as one of the most important 'human capital' variables and has proved to be influential on the degree of female labour force participation, and the position of female labour at work.[58] Sociological studies confirm that increased secondary school enrolment among girls is often associated with increases in women's participation in the labour force, and with increases in their contribution to household and national incomes.[59] It is also believed that education becomes distinctively important for women, specifically in societies where gender roles are strongly enforced and where men are more likely to have direct access to wage employment as well as control over wealth.[60] However, it might be true that female education contributes to an improvement of gender equality and women's empowerment, but improvement to gender equality can only be realised if female education is associated with a rise in women's participation in the labour force, and an increase in their contributions to household income and national income.

As noted in Chapter Three of this book, as job opportunities under sanctions were diminishing in the public and the private sectors both for men and women, Iraqi women continued to make up more than 40 percent of the total labour force, but this was in the lowest-paid sector, the public sector (see Appendix Tables 3.1 and 3.2). While large numbers of males have left low-waged public sector jobs for other occupations in the private sector or in petty trade, or have simply escaped from the country, Iraqi women were bound to stay in the lowest-paid jobs in the public sector. Indeed, as the value of real wages declines, it is expected that this will be reflected upon rates of educational output and upon the value of education, particularly for the majority of young/economically active women. All these problems are reflected in education, which sanctions had turned into a less attractive investment option for families and for their female members.

Chapter Three also revealed the increasing disparity between the educational status of the surveyed women and their status in the labour market. In addition to the high concentration of women in the lowest paid jobs, there was a high prevalence of unemployment among the highly educated respondents. The impact of this situation was very obvious since a large number of the women surveyed seemed not to have hesitated about giving up their education for other options such as marriage and/or travelling abroad. Maria (aged 24) was a university graduate (Political Science). She spoke about a gloomy future:

> I live on my dreams. I regret the hard work for more than four years of my study at the university. At the end, I cannot find a job. I do not what to do! I am sitting at home all the time. However, sometimes I think positively. I say, one day everything will be OK for the Iraqi people, and then it would be better for me with a degree.

Although schooling has taken on a different meaning for some of the women interviewed, the respondents' statements generally revealed that educated women feared the limited choices concerning their future careers. In some cases, this issue was a cause for deep disappointment. Almost all the women who took part in the student survey expressed their frustration about the future after graduation. Huda (23 years) was a final-year Psychology student. As she explained:

> It is a lost time in my life. I seriously doubt that it will be better for me after graduation. I wonder about my future. I know it is very difficult to find a job. However, why I should bother? The salary wouldn't even pay my daily transport expenses. I think it is better to be a housewife and forget about psychology – however, marriage is another hopeless issue!

The inability or the failure of the job market to meet the output from education has left negative traces on the young Iraqi generation who pursue education supposedly to find adequate job opportunities and incomes. It is striking that, although a large proportion of the young respondents would rather speak about marriage and going abroad, they also stressed the importance of education as a useful asset for women, if not under sanctions, then certainly for the future.

Female Education: Continuity and Change

Many respondents remarked cynically that the 'only' benefit of education was the opportunity it offered to socialize with others outside the home. Sausan (aged 24) was a fourth year Humanities student. In reply to a question about her plans for the future, she answered sadly that she was expecting 'a black future': 'I have no plans, none whatsoever'. For a little while she looked gloomily at the floor without speaking before she remarked:

> I think my life as a student is far better than what is waiting for me after graduation. Coming to university every day is the only life I have. Here I meet some people, but after I finish my studies, I will be imprisoned at home. There is no chance of getting a job. Many of my friends among last year's graduates are still unemployed – the men have either become taxi drivers or have fled the country. Personally, I wish I was less conscious about life than I am now. It might have helped me to carry on but unfortunately there is no escape into the past.

It may well seem depressing, but this statement explains the reality of the young generation of Iraqi women. Many respondents revealed the same opinion. Paradoxical as it may seem, such a phenomenon also indicates that, in spite of the negative implications of sanctions for education, socially, female education remains 'largely' respected. This attitude was particularly observed among Iraqi women and families from the previously-identified middle class. This also explains the reason behind the continuing enrolment of large numbers of females in higher education, in spite of the meagre job opportunities and the low wages. Typically, a middle-class Iraqi family may oppose the idea of a female member leaving home to work outside in order to earn an income, especially under such inadequate economic circumstances, but may not reject the idea of a female member going outside the home to pursue an education.

At the beginning of the 2001 academic year, at the library of one of the main universities (*maktabat al-wazeriya*), it was striking to see a crowd of Iraqi women of different ages queuing behind the loans desk with lists of recommended literature, anxious to get a chance to borrow some books. In the reading rooms, long lines of women surrounded the tables, occupying most of the space. Some of them were sharing one reading source. It was possible to exchange some words with Zoha and her colleague about the crowd of women and about themselves. Zoha said:

> I am a physician. From 1989I was working in a medical centre [state-owned but recently I decided to leave my job. I felt I was not doing the things I had

learned. Due to shortages of equipment and of most of the essential treatment materials, we could not solve the most basic problems. It was distressing to see so many desperately sick people when you were not able to help them. My salary also was disastrous. It was not worth going through all that hassle. We had eight physicians at the centre, six women and two men. The men left for better jobs abroad, and five of the women, including myself and Faten [the woman with her] have given up work to become fulltime housewives. However, you start to feel lazy and worthless being at home all the time. Later, we decided to use our time and knowledge in a more constructive way, especially as the opportunity for postgraduate studies is available now. Faten and I made a pact to become specialists. May be the future will make better use of us!

Wafa (aged 33) had BA in Social Science, and was unmarried. She made a similar point:

After I was made redundant from my job three years ago (1997), my life changed dramatically. Now I regard finishing a master's degree as a good opportunity. For me, it is not just a degree; rather it is a new chance to go outside the walls of my home.

It was obvious that mounting social pressures and increasing restrictions on Iraqi women's participation in the labour force as a result of diminished incentives to work were encouraging many bright women to challenge the remaining opportunities. In spite of the economic and social upheavals caused by sanctions, a large number of Iraqi women, especially from middle class backgrounds, seized the opportunity of female education being socially acceptable to pursue their postgraduate studies.

The Crisis in Education: A Crisis of Many Faces
The Turning Point and Change of Values
While female education was still commonly considered as socially acceptable, especially among the previously identified middle class, it had gradually became an unaffordable privilege for the wider majority of poor and impoverished Iraqi families. A large number of Iraqi females from poor families were categorically denied access to education.

During the 1990s, Iraq's enrolment rates at all educational levels and its illiteracy rates were the worst among the MENA countries, as seen in relation to population and economic resources. As the tables show (see Appendix Tables 4.1, 4.4, 4.3, and 4.5), illiteracy and school enrolment among females in Iraq were lower than, or similar to, those of the poorest highly populated countries in the MENA region. These figures are particularly regressive, compared with the previous records of the 1970s and 1980s. It is obvious that, while education reform policies in other MENA countries are directed towards achieving equity and a better quality in education, sanctions in Iraq reversed the progress that the country had achieved in education during the 1970s and 1980s.

However, it is not only Iraq's official statistics that showed the deteriorated conditions of education under sanctions. Observation on the ground revealed the alarming and unprecedented phenomenon of street children (girls and boys) in Iraq. With the rapid rises in living costs, females from impoverished families were pressured to drop out of school, either to take on household responsibilities or to engage in informal income earning. Under sanctions, it was shocking to see large numbers of small girls venturing into the streets and darting between cars at traffic lights, often holding hands or carrying smaller children and begging for some cash. By 2000 and 2001, Iraqis seem to have become used to these sights, remarking that the number of street children had been far higher in the first 7 or 8 years of sanctions. The numbers did indeed start to decline, not because the situation had improved, but because the police took action against the children by arresting them. Many people said they were organized 'mafia', or 'professional thieves', and some believed that professional gangs were behind this disturbing phenomenon, stealing children from other parts of Iraq and bringing them to Baghdad to make money by begging and prostitution. These and many other disturbing sights of deprived, weakened and vulnerable people were totally new and shocking in a rich country such as Iraq with the second largest oil reserves in the world.

Another phenomenon could also be glimpsed because of the economic hardship. It is unusual for Iraqi people to complain about the 'burden' of having female children. It is not a social taboo, but in general, Iraqi people are proud of their children, regardless of their sex. The issue was brought up by many respondents, but Shokria (Um Hussain, aged 45) was able to uncover particular aspects that others were hesitant about discussing. Shokria was a widow and mother of six children (four girls and two boys). The family lived in two-roomed house in the poorest area (Area I). She said:

> My eldest daughter (Fatima, aged 14) dropped out of school to get married. I thought it was better for her to marry, even as a second wife [unofficial marriage or *zawaj urfi*]. We can't afford the 'dream' of education. She and her husband (who visits Fatima twice weekly) live with me, but they give me rent and help me with living expenses. We couldn't afford the expenses of the school. I wouldn't hesitate to give up the other three daughters for polygamous marriage, if there was no other option to hand. Any marriage is better than begging or exposure to evil rumours. They [her daughters] would do better to forget about education. These are different times now. Before the sanctions, people had decent lives. Now, it is impossible, especially for a widow like me to feed all these children! What can schools do for me?

The desperate economic situation and the absence of effective state controls on society have led to countless unrestrained forms of abuse of young females, such as 'selling' juvenile girls into unofficial polygamous marriage, prostitution, and other brutal methods of earning informal incomes. In disorderly times, an opportunity for early marriage (official or unofficial) may seem the best of the worst, but the common denominator between all these methods of exploitation is the gloomy future of the girls, who have no prospects for personal development.

According to Iraqi law, the marriage of juveniles (under 15 years of age) is not prohibited, but is conditional on the consent of many parties, including in particular consent by a state-authorized judge as well as official registration of the marriage in the courts (Law of Personal Status, 1978). Under sanctions, cases like that of Fatima, above, seemed to have spread in Iraqi society, especially among its poorest and most despairing segments, nor were people reluctant or afraid to speak about it. It was noticeable, however, that the state, known for its iron grip over the society, was now turning a blind eye to these and many other forms of abuse, and that it was most markedly ignoring these violations as long as they did not directly threaten the political system. In the vast disorder that had befallen the country under sanctions, women's rights were the easiest to sacrifice.

Fertility and Public Health

As previously mentioned, not only is education one of the most important instruments for social and economic development, but it is also the major determining factor for the position of women in the family and society. The benefits of female education for women's empowerment and gender equality are huge. In addition to the fact that education increases women's earning capacity, female education, among other things, improves fertility and the growth of a 'healthy' population, especially as infant and child mortality declines and child nutrition improves.[61]

Many surveys emphasize education as the single most important determinant of both age at marriage and age at first birth in MENA countries, since women in the region tend to give birth soon after marriage (see Appendix Table 4.5).[62] The findings of studies on female education in MENA region reveal that highly educated women generally want smaller families and make better use of reproductive health and family planning information and services in achieving their desired family size.[63]

As for Iraq, the total average fertility rate by the year 2003 was 5.4 births, which is comparable to the world's highest rate (5.5 births). However, the most disastrous issue in this context was the serious rates of mortality among children, especially under the age of five.[64] Increased child morbidity and mortality was an alarming trend brought about by international sanctions against Iraq (see details in Chapter Six). It is doubtful whether the scale of the damages inflicted upon Iraq's health system, including public health education and awareness can be completely alleviated in the near future. The deterioration in public health education and increasing illiteracy, especially among women, has led to increased risks of diseases due to contamination of water and the collapse of sanitation systems and health services.

The impact of the situation on the poor population of Iraq is hard to describe. It is not only the data on morbidities and mortalities that tells the story – equally important are the crippling effects of deteriorated public health education and the increased lack of knowledge among young mothers about these morbidities. Before sanctions, Iraq's health and educations systems enjoyed a special resource allocation (both material and human) for educating women about basic health and sanitation, while a health policy promoted reproductive health through improvement of antenatal and postnatal services.[65] The impact of the hardship and suffering was illustrated in the malnourished faces of countless numbers of young women and girls around the streets, begging for food or for money for medicine. Indeed, these sights were unprecedented: they would never have been seen in Iraqi society prior to sanctions, but became a common sight of Iraq under sanctions.

Conclusion

Recasting female education in Iraq for the period of the 1970s and 1980s shows that the state, through its commitment to improving women's educational status, had encouraged a remarkable and positive change in the status of Iraqi women. Laws, regulations, and follow-up programmes were put in place to reflect the state's pledge towards this end. Through its work towards realising educational output, the state also became a key player in organizing the labour market. New graduates, both female and male, were centrally distributed across the country's widespread state sector.[66]

Iraqi women were prime beneficiaries of this policy. Even though the overwhelming majority of students were males, a social and economic conceptualization of the growing rates of female enrolment in different levels of education – especially at primary level, in vocational schools and in higher education – revealed that a positive change in the status of women was in progress. The statistics show that the progress achieved in female education during the 1970s seemed have been sustained during the 1980s, although statistics also show that while education was still limited it had been extended to many more women than employment had been. Still, it is hard to avoid the conclusion that the education of females and women's labour force participation were both greatly affected, not just by state laws and state-sponsored development but also, and simultaneously, by gender consciousness in the wider society and in the family.

Sociological studies about the impact of education on women's status in developing countries suggest that expansion of schooling for girls has probably had an even greater impact on families in developing countries than it had in the West.[67] It is argued that education destroys the 'corporate identity of the family, especially for those members previously most submissive and most wholly contained by the family: children and women'.[68]

It is strongly believed that, education for men and women in MENA countries is highly valued as one of the driving forces behind progressive social change. In particular, state-sponsored education in MENA countries has, in a rapid and revolutionary fashion, affected the status of women since it has an immediate impact on women's perceptions of themselves as well as on their social mobility and expectations.[69] In the specific case of Iraq, female education was particularly encouraged by the government, not only due to labour force shortages, but because the regime also supported female education as part of a deliberate policy to weaken tribal influence.[70] The move was considered a challenge to the traditional patriarchal system and its control of women.

Sanctions have affected Iraq's education system, which was once known as the best in the whole Middle East. School enrolment of females in all education levels has declined. The results are most evident in the dramatic increase in female illiteracy. However, even though many girls have been excluded from, or have dropped out of education, many have continued to receive less rigorous teaching, due to shortages of educational necessities and a severe shortage of teachers and professors. In the meantime, sanctions have given a boost to private education. Bearing in mind the image and the quality of private education in Iraq, this increase should be understood as an element that threatens the scientific correctness and the ethics of education.

The effect of sanctions on female education was closely associated with the deterioration in the labour market situation and in job opportunities generally. The increasing disparity between women's educational status and the needs of the labour market affected males and females differently. The decline in the economic and social returns of education undermined the status of educated people, both males and females. While males were more likely to have access to waged employment and to control over material resources, whether within or outside Iraq, women were becoming increasingly dependent economically on male providers, thereby increasing their vulnerability. The withdrawal of any positive intervention by the state severely limited women's social and economic options to resist traditional family controls. In female students, this could also be seen in their increasing dependency on the family. For example, the special allowance made by the state to all students had been seized under sanctions,[71] although non-Iraqi students continued to receive these privileges, in addition to free education (i.e. with no charge for tuition). This in no way suggests that male educational status and their enrolment in education were less affected by sanctions. A large number of males dropped out of education in order to generate income, being often engaged in petty trade or taxi driving, or simply left the country in search of other opportunities abroad.

The impact of sanctions on female education was seen not only through increased restrictions on women's economic mobility but, more importantly, through the effect of sanctions on social attitudes toward female education. Even though sanctions failed to diminish people's respect for female education, sanctions had some serious implications for the social culture of Iraqi society. There was a growing tendency to regard the 'uselessness' of education for both sexes, but particularly for females. Unprecedentedly, work and education became widely perceived as a potential risk to women's security and morals (see Chapter Five and Chapter Six).[72]

Thus, the implications of sanctions for the education of Iraqi women and girls should be seen through the impact of sanctions on social attitudes towards the role of women in society, the economy and the polity. Once the social and economic returns of education had been systematically degraded under sanctions, more women and young girls were taken from schools and universities and for preference were encouraged into early or premature marriage.

Due to their essential roles as mothers, women were particularly affected by the deterioration in public expenditure on public health education. The result was seen in the dramatic increase in mortality rates of children under five years and infants. A more specific analysis of this issue is introduced in Chapter Six.

5

THE IMPACT OF ECONOMIC SANCTIONS ON GENDER RELATIONS INSIDE THE FAMILY

Introduction

Knowing that societies, as physical and socio-cultural environments, are continually changing it is therefore inevitable that people will adjust, or at least attempt to do so. Social change always comes about through economic change, class conflicts, political actions, and political conflicts. Therefore, an understanding of social change must be placed in relations to economic processes, political dynamics, and cultural practices, over a period of time.

Social change also necessitates alterations in values, personal habits, and kinship, and creates new social classes with new characteristics and patterns of life.[1] As such, socio-economic changes are often associated with important changes in prevailing choices and behaviour of social actors, and imply a rapid change in roles of institutions, including the state, the family and kinship.[2]

As previously discussed in this book, it is the interrelated and interdependent social behaviour, cultural outlook and economic infrastructures of Iraqi society, that simultaneously affect and reinforce each other, and as a result of one another. We have seen how economic and political change/upheavals during different historical configurations have influenced the core stratification relations (gender and gender relations) in the public realm (employment and education).

Iraqi women are one group in the society whose varying social positions (or 'women's status'), as traditionally ascribed to them, are also expected to have been highly affected by the economic and social upheavals due to sanctions. This chapter explores the impact of sanctions on gender relations in the private realm (the household), including their impact on the roles, structure and relational features of the Iraqi family. It introduces three case studies of Iraqi women who were surveyed over a period of two years.

The selection of these cases was based on their diversity in terms of social and economic contexts on one hand, and on their similarity in reflecting the situation experienced by the majority of Iraqi women under sanctions on the other. The chapter sheds light on some aspects of social relations in the Iraqi society and the family that have been affected by the economic crisis due to sanctions.

Case Studies
The First Case: Halimah (Um Zamen, 'the Mother of Time')

Halimah was standing in front of a popular food shop called Mr Milk (*saied al-Haleeb*) in the commercial part of Al-Mansur city (Area III), one of the finest residential areas of Baghdad. The name of the shop was an unusual and rather funny name for an Iraqi shop. However, the story about the shop was not at all funny. Saied al-Haleeb had initially become famous during the first six years of sanctions – in other words before the Oil-for-Food agreement – because the owner sold milk. During the years of economic hardship, the Mr Milk shop became a meeting point for those who enjoyed comfortable living standards and those who were less privileged including poor beggars. One respondent said:

> If you had been here at the time when "Saied al-Haleeb" first existed you would certainly have obtained many stories about the suffering of Iraqi people under sanctions. When milk was as valuable as life for many children, Saied al-Haleeb had the milk. It was expensive but the well-off people could afford to buy it for their children. But outside the shop, many poor women stood with their tiny malnourished children begging for some milk. It was prestigious to shop at Saied al-Haleeb, and I expect it is the same now, because it means that despite everything, some people can still afford to eat well.

Halimah was dressed entirely in black but did not look as if she was a beggar. Rather, her appearance suggested that she was waiting for somebody as she seemed uncomfortable and impatient. It was evident that she was suffering from pain in her legs since she kept changing her position and from time to time shifted from one leg to the other. She was looking at the street but occasionally she glanced at the people around her.

Initially she was unwilling to exchange conversation, but on the following day, it seemed we had become closer to each other. We had a long 'chat' and I agreed to meet Halimah at the same place so we could go together to her house. The neighbourhood was one of the extremely impoverished state housing residential areas in Baghdad. When we approached one of the compounds in the area, the taxi driver refused to drive along the tiny muddy roads inside the compound, so we had to leave the car and walk for a quite long distance to her house. On our way, many people greeted Halimah respectfully and many were curious to know about her guest. However, to avoid revealing more information about me she tactfully avoided having any prolonged conversation with them.

We eventually turned into a tiny road with parallel lines of small houses. We went into one, with a long narrow passageway that led into a medium-sized room, simply furnished with a rug and two mattress covered with blankets. The place was rather empty and very tidy and it was clear that the room was designated for guests. Halimah called to her 17-year-old daughter, Zamen, and asked her to make some tea and bring her grandmother to the room. Zamen means 'Time', and is rather an unusual name. A tall slender young girl with white scarf covering her hair came into the room holding the hand of her grandmother who could scarcely walk, and Halimah introduced me to her family. While the old woman welcomed me without hesitation and with customary Iraqi hospitality, Zamen looked at me thoughtfully and somewhat doubtfully. Understandably she was used to treating strangers with some caution. Zamen appeared resentful towards strangers because she was trying to protect her mother from any unnecessary trouble. She explained: 'life has taught me to be careful with strangers'.

Halimah's Story
Halimah married at the age of 17, immediately after finishing intermediate level school. Six months later, she was employed as a control officer in a girls' high school in Baghdad City. Her husband was a skilled worker in one of the biggest state-owned industrial factories, and with two income-earning partners, the family enjoyed the life of an average middle-income household. She recalls:

> Our incomes was not big but was enough to cover simple living expenses. However, we were ambitious to build up a good standard of living. I was excited about my job at the nearby school. We agreed to delay having a child for some time because we were so in love with each other. We were young and trusted that life was ahead of us.

Two years after their marriage, her husband had to return to military service because of the Iraq-Iran War. She described the war as 'the black cloud that hung over our heads'. When her husband left for the army, the couple's families disapproved of Halimah staying in the house on her own, and suggested that she should stay with her family or with her in-laws until her husband returned. However, both Halimah and her husband rejected this suggestion and instead found a compromise solution, that Halimah's mother was welcome to stay with Halimah. She said:

> My husband did not want other people to interfere in our lives. He was different from other men. When our families opposed the idea of my working outside the home, he did not listen to them. He used to say that it would be enough for two to make a good family.

Halimah was able to meet her husband during his leave periods every two or three months. Like so many other Iraqi women, she hoped that an early end to the war would bring her life back to normal, but this did not happen. In 1983, when she was five months pregnant Halimah heard that her husband had been killed in the war. She was devastated and suffered severe psychological damage. She spoke of her pain, saying:

> I did not have time to think about my dreams, nor did I ever have time to dream again because I found myself fully responsible for the life of this girl. I accepted my destiny and believed that I had to replace her father. I promised

Zamen to work hard and take care of her until she had finished her education and had become the wife of a decent man.

Halimah had inherited the house from her late husband, ownership of these state houses has having been granted to the occupants who were mostly migrant workers from different parts of Iraq. Halimah spoke passionately about the life she had had with her late husband and said repeatedly that she had had a happy marriage although it was short.

Following her husband's death Halimah rearranged her life that her mother could take care of Zamen while she went on with her job at the school. She mentioned that she had been hoping to get compensation from the state for the death of her husband but that after long deliberation, her right to compensation was denied. During the Iraq-Iran war, it was customary for the state to give a sum of money or a new car to the families of soldiers who had been killed (martyrs). However, Halimah was excluded from these grants on the grounds that her husband had lost his life in a non-combat situation. She said: 'The report stated that a grenade had hit him as he was fetching water from a nearby river'.

Halimah, now aged 20, functioned as the main provider for her family, depending on her own income and her husband's pension. As a single bread-winner, she was promoted at work, and was entitled to full child benefit. Her monthly income was sufficient, especially as she did not have to pay rent or school expenses for her daughter. She said proudly:

> In addition to buying good food, I could save some money from my salary every month. I was able to buy some household equipment such as a washing machine, an electric cooker, and some furniture. Although life had taken a different course, it seemed that everything was going well. It was not 'heaven' but it was manageable.

Though she was a young widow, remarriage was not an issue for her. 'I did not marry again, not only because I couldn't think about another man but also because nobody had asked to marry me'. In order to protect her reputation as a young widowed woman, Halimah had to arrange her life in a different way. She started to wear Islamic dress and rearranged her contacts with other people in order to keep her relationships within the confines of her family who did not interfere with her life.

After the end of the Iraq-Iran War and several years of hard work, Halimah's dream for a better future for herself and Zamen was revived. However, this was to be for a brief time only, before life once again took a completely different path as over-powering and dramatic changes took place. Within two months of the imposition of sanctions, Halimah's monthly income had become insufficient to buy basic food for her family. She described her life thus:

> I felt as though the earth was shaking under my feet. Things were getting out of hand so suddenly. I started to realize that there was nothing that could help me through this again. My work at the school had become worthless. When

there is no value in the work you do, it becomes a burden on you. However, I still hoped that the world would not let us down. First, I did not believe that more than thirty countries would bomb us, but it happened! Then, I did not want to believe that the sanctions would last for very long, but this has also happened! I realized that nothing is a history except our dreams for better lives.

It is clear that the shocking events that took place left Halimah wondering whether she was still capable of taking care of her little family. During the 45 days of allied bombing of Iraq, she was completely shattered, especially as one of the attacks happened close to her house, which was near a military zone. Her daughter was also seriously shaken by the noise of the attack and became ill for some time. The situation was so bad that Halimah was unable to pretend that she could manage alone. Instead she decided to take Zamen and her mother and go to the house of her brother who lived in a town near Baghdad. After the war had ended she decided to return to her house but arrived to find that it had been completely looted. She said:

The thieves did not even spare us a mattress to sleep on. I blamed myself for this. I also realised I had not been in a normal state of mind when I decided to leave my house. I was unaware of what I was doing. I only wanted to save my child and my mother.

Halimah went home to a devastated neighbourhood. Many families had been traumatized by the loss of beloved family members in the notorious attack on the Al-Ameriyya shelter in which more than 800 women and children from the area were killed. Shattered houses and looted homes were seen as a relatively minor loss compared with the tragedy that had befallen the neighbourhood. She said:

My share in the casualties of this war was insignificant. I know how it feels when you lose a dear person from your family, but when I saw the pain of others who had lost more than one family member, I could see that the damage I had incurred was minimal.

Halimah was unable to pick up where she had left off, including her job at the school. Life went quiet for more than two months after the end of the 1991 war but eventually she understood that the school had been shut down indefinitely – because of the severe damage it would not be possible for it to reopen until 1998. Some of the school staff were transferred to another location, and the rest, including Halimah, were made redundant. After some months of searching frantically for a job, Halimah realized that her life has begun a 'brand new' and difficult phase. The possibilities for employment were few and the salaries offered were insufficient for a household with a single breadwinner. Eventually she found a job as a housekeeper at a private kindergarten on the other side of the city which meant travelling daily for around two hours in each direction and having to stay at work until late. However, following the closure of the kindergarten eight months later, Halimah again became jobless.

She went back to job hunting, but without any positive results. She explained at some length the horrendous difficulties she and her family had encountered by having to rely mainly on the state monthly ration. She said:

> For many months we survived on bread and dates. Thank God, there are plenty of date palms in Iraq. We were entitled to rations for three people every month. These included rice, flour, tea, lentils, beans, cooking oil, sugar, soap, washing power, and sometimes some milk powder. We thought we could divert part of the rations to sell on the 'black' market for some cash. We desperately needed to buy candles for lighting and some oil for heating. However, by the last days of every month, we were literally starving. The most painful thing was to see my child withering away in front me.

Seeing the miserable state of Halimah's neighbourhood ten years after the imposition of sanctions, it was obvious that the majority of these people were living in similar circumstances and therefore could not expect any generosity from each other. Speaking of her neighbourhood, Halimah said:

> They are all extremely poor. Everybody is exhausted and disappointed with the world. We feel we have been abandoned and that nobody can help us. We know we are forgotten; maybe also by our own families whose conditions are better. People are shocked and it is difficult to make sense of what is happening!

Deprivation eventually drove Halimah to swallow her remaining pride and decide to plead for help from her family in-law, but it appeared that, after long years of separation, they were not willing to take care of their late son's family. And although Halimah's own family of three sisters and a brother were much closer to her than her husband's family, nor were they any better disposed towards her. She said:

> My three sisters and my brother are married and their living standards are far better than mine. They all have children old enough to provide additional incomes. I approached them all for some help, but I was turned away. They gave a little charity in recognition of the fact that I was human being but basically they treated me as a stranger. They did not like my situation as a widowed single woman and their hostility extended to include my daughter, who was growing up. The aggressive attitudes of my brother and my brother in law towards us became a daily burden for Zamen because they wanted her to leave school and just sit at home. I found their demands were simply unacceptable, so I decided to resist the pressure.

Describing her brother's image of her, Halimah said:

> It was shocking. I had no idea that my brother had stored up all his anger towards me for so many years. My desperate need for help from my family

actually uncovered his real feelings towards me. He accused me of being a 'disobedient', 'dishonoured' and 'degenerate' woman. When I tried to discover what it was that made him think of me like this, he simply said it was because I could not manage to get a 'decent' man, to marry me after the death of my husband. But, when I asked him why, if he was angry with me because of this matter, he had kept quiet about it for so many years he replied that previously they had been spared from my troubles, but now they were not.

After having been economically independent for a long time, Halimah's desperate need for help from her brother had become a negotiating ground for different issues. Despite the fact that her brother was economically far better off than the rest of the family because he was working as chauffeur for the United Nation convoys, he refused to stand beside Halimah during the hardest time of her life. He also put conditions on any help that might come from his side by giving himself the right to interfere in her life. His orders extended from banning Halimah from leaving her house to preventing Zamen from attending school and suggesting her early marriage to his eldest son who suffered from a chronic mental illness. Above all, he was also bargaining with Halimah's desperate need for help. He suggested that she could sell him her house and either live with his family or move to a rented place instead. However, as soon he understood that the deal was unacceptable for Halimah he insulted her and decided to exclude her totally from his life. Later she learned that he and his family had left Iraq and settled in Europe as refugees. She spoke of her disappointment:

> I cannot understand what has happened in this world. If even my own brother was negotiating with me about the price of my food and his mother's food, no wonder that other people steal from you or blackmail you for money. We didn't know about this ugly face of life before. However, this situation has taught me that something very wrong is taking place in our lives, something that is pushing us to a dangerous end. We cannot stop it or control it.

Halimah faced the same sort of rejection from her sisters. They claimed that they could not help her because their husbands did not approve of her situation. As a reaction to her vulnerable situation, Halimah became over-protective of her and Zamen's reputations.

Halimah was experiencing the pain of the turmoil that had fallen on the whole of Iraq. She worked as a petty trader. She had sold whatever she owned, including two doors from her house, and she had ended up begging in the street. However, she had kept her 'occupation' as a beggar secret from her family and neighbours, and pretended that she was working as housekeeper in a kindergarten. Before she agreed to respond to my questions she made it a condition that this would remain a secret between us. Halimah undertook 'her work' nearly every day. About her daily trips she said privately to me:

> I try to protect my child from any harm through knowing that her mother is begging out in the streets. Zamen is proud of me and I do my utmost to see that she will also become proud of herself. I know the value of education and being independent. Therefore, I hope I can protect her until she finishes her education and then, I hope she gets a decent man to make her own family. In spite of the weakness in my legs I stand for hours in the street until I have gathered enough food for the day. I thank God I don't have to pay rent.

The Second Case: Hanan and Rafah

Hanan was 38 years old, unmarried, and employed as accountant at the Central Bank in Baghdad. She had finished a degree in accountancy in June 1990 and had become formally engaged to Ahmad, one of her colleagues, when they were third year university students. They planned to marry after they had graduated and received their job appointments. It should be noted that prior to sanctions nearly all employment for university graduates was dealt with centrally. The graduate candidate would complete various job applications, indicating the three most desired positions. The final allocation of posts was usually decided centrally according to the employment requirements of public and governmental institutions.

Two months after they graduated, Iraqi troops had invaded Kuwait and the second Gulf crisis began. Hanan and Ahmad's plans for the future took a different course. Ahmad, who had to serve in the army, was sent to the front in the southern part of Iraq, while Hanan was unable to find a job because the government had postponed the assignment of all the new graduates. It proved impossible to contain the crisis and some months later the Gulf War was raging. Iraq witnessed the systematic destruction of its infrastructure and the death of thousands of its citizens. Ahmad was one of the casualties. He was severely injured but managed some months later to get himself smuggled to one of the European countries where he obtained refugee status. Under the impact of these chaotic changes, Ahmad and Hanan had to adjust themselves accordingly. Ahmad promised to arrange Hanan's visa and her travel outside Iraq as soon he had settled in the West. Hanan said sadly: 'I remember that day as if it was just yesterday. We had hoped to endure the crisis, but our dream was snatched away from us'.

Ahmad was unable to settle for two and half years after his departure from Iraq. Contact between the couple was hampered because of the difficulties of communication, both by telephone and by letters. Even so, Hanan tried even harder than Ahmad to maintain the contact, despite of incurring considerable expense.

While she was waiting for Ahmad's promise to be fulfilled, the situation at home was deteriorating. Hanan, her youngest sister, Rafah, and her mother were sharing a house with her oldest brother, his wife and his six children. Since the father's death in 1987, her brother had moved the rest of the family in with him and he was financially responsible for them all. In addition to the late father's pension, the family depended primarily on the income of the brother who was a mechanical engineer in one of the state-owned enterprises. The mother was hoping that the burden on her son would be reduced when her daughters get married. However, life had taken a different path taking no heed of many people's wishes and plans.

Hanan's marriage plans had been postponed indefinitely. She was employed in a bank with a salary of ID 3000 (around US$1.50–$2.00 per month), which was insufficient to cover her basic expenses. She had hoped to find a better-paid job in a private firm, but in spite of exhaustive attempts had not been able to find a better alternative, and told me that her chances did not look encouraging. The government decided in 2001 to give all civil servants a quarterly sum of money as an addition to their monthly salary. Accordingly, Hanan was receiving about ID 25,000 (equal to US$12) in state grants every three months.

The collapse of public sector wages had pushed Hanan's brother to move from one job to another in search of better pay. He ended up working for a private firm as a car mechanic. One day the family had to face the horrifying news that an accident at work had left him paralysed and unfit to work anywhere. Nor was it possible to get compensation for his injuries. Since 1993, the whole family had been put into an extremely vulnerable situation because of the accident. Hanan's family was in desperate need of some cash in order to manage their day-to-day living. After long discussions with the car firm's owner, the family embarked on a deal whereby they sold their own house and moved instead to a smaller one belonging to the owner, for which they paid a minimal rent. However, two years later, the money had been consumed and Hanan's family was unable to pay the rent of the house.

The family had to confront another crisis. This time, they had to bargain for a very dangerous deal with the man who had been responsible for Hanan's brother's disability. The owner of the car company, a 55 year-old businessman, offered to let the family stay in his house and to give them some cash for living costs in exchange for Rafah as a young wife. Rafah, aged 21 and a university graduate, had to become the man's second, junior, wife. Since Rafah's marriage in 1996, Hanan had been unable to pull herself out of a depression brought on by seeing the end of her little sister's dreams and her struggle with a strange environment.

On one visit to Hanan's home it was possible to meet with Rafah, who was eight months pregnant with her third child. Whereas Hanan was talking about her sister's disadvantageous situation, Rafah herself was rather unwilling to reveal any personal feelings about her life. However, she was extremely interested in my research and asked specifically about the part that concerned the lives of young students. She said:

> I finished a university degree in History. More than anything, I was interested in academic life but I had no chance to fulfil my dream. The days pass very heavily for me, not because of my pregnancy [she smilingly indicated her swollen belly] but because my real life has nothing to do with my dreams. It

does not relate to any of them. I am unable to reconcile these two things. This is why I feel great unease.

While all these events were taking place, Ahmad had distanced himself further from Hanan. She said:

> First he used to call me once a week, then once every two weeks. Then I was receiving a call once in a while. I did not want to give up. I used to borrow some money and call him from a public telephone. He was less and less enthusiastic about hearing about my situation. My friends kept encouraging me to speak to him openly about his promise, especially as we were 'officially' engaged, but I felt it was humiliating. But I did try.

It seems that Hanan's brother's accident was 'the straw that broke the camel's back'. In one of their telephone conversations, Ahmad put an end to Hanan's prolonged waiting, telling her that she should consider herself 'a free woman', and that she had to envisage her life with a different man since he was going to annul their marriage certificate. Hanan said sadly:

> I was extremely upset when I first become certain that I would never have a life with the man I had loved for more than ten years. However, after that shock I believed that nothing could hurt me any more. I was waiting for him for many years and all that time I lived in denial while he had started a new life. I am not bitter because he went back on his promise. It is our destiny. However, I expected him to remain as a friend, but he did not. Ahmad knew I needed his support but he has never offered a hand for help.

At home, Hanan was acting as a mother to her brother's children. Everyday after work she had to pass by the market to buy food for the family. She was now the single breadwinner for a family of nine members, and was an excellent household manager. In the middle of her crowded life, Hanan was extremely concerned about the future of her nieces and nephews, and especially about their education. It was amazing how she used to call the older nephew (aged 17) 'the doctor', and her niece Shahed (aged 15) 'the engineer'. Hanan also appeared to have maintained a good relationship with her sister-in-law to whom she was very grateful because of her sister-in-law's devoted treatment of her disabled husband. Hanan said proudly:

> I look after them as if they are my own. They all very good at school and they take care of their father and their grandmother. Although they are still young they know very well what sacrifices I have made in order to secure at least the basic things for them.

It was a bit difficult to explore the nature of the relationship between Hanan and her brother because she was feeling extremely sad and emotional about him. However, she repeatedly mentioned that her brother's psychological condition, due to the accident and the marriage of Rafah to the 'awful' man, had been deteriorating. Hanan said:

> My brother used to be a strong and clever man. Since the accident he has become isolated and very bored at home. Also giving Rafah as a wife to that 'dishonest' man broke my brother's back for a second time. He felt very depressed and hopeless. Therefore, he has begun involving himself in every tiny thing at home and gives non-stop orders. Sometimes, it is difficult to please him.

Her brother was in his late forties and appeared to be well cared for. He used to sit by himself in his wheelchair in a room facing the main door of the house. It was not possible to meet him because he seemed to be angry most of the time. It seemed that he was always calling loudly to his wife or his children who were usually either studying or watching TV in the other room. He was also angry because Hanan was working while he could not do so. Even though Hanan's income was the only source of livelihood for his own family, he was unhappy about Hanan's work outside the home, and especially about her coming home late because of working overtime. Hanan seemed very understanding of her brother's situation. She sorrowfully explained:

> Although he is severely damaged physically and mentally, he would never do anything to harm his family or us. He is an exceptionally kind, loving and caring person in spite of his disappointments. He has a tremendous respect for me and my work because he had experience of this in the past. Now, I am paying back some of what I owe to him. I always try to side with and support him, simply because it would be so unfair if I was to turn against him too.

A year later, I went back to meet Hanan at her work place, but she was not at work. Her colleagues said that she had not been feeling well for some time, and had taken a long leave from work, so I went to her home. She appeared to have become much older. The state of her house was much more miserable than it had been the previous year. The few pieces of furniture were all either broken or worn out, and her brother had lost a lot of weight. Hanan's eyes looked tired and weak, as if they were clouded with distressing thoughts that had been unrevealed for a long time. It was clear how sensitive this strong woman was to her surroundings, and realised that the entire family was concerned about Hanan's health. She explained:

> Some time ago I suddenly felt extremely weak. Apart from a headache I don't complain about any physical pain. I decided to take some time off to try to recover, but I am going back to work as soon as I can next week.

Hanan had felt sick after an unexpected visitor at her work place some months previously, when she found herself face to face with Ahmad who was on visit to Iraq and had paid her a visit too. She told me: 'Ahmad came to tell me how happy he was with his wife and his three kids'. Ahmad's brief visit had been the trigger that brought back some of the pain of the past. It seemed that Hanan's suffering had been accumulating for years but had she had kept silent because it was simply unacceptable to reveal it. Her injured pride had also been deeply hidden inside her but in a moment of truth she was able to refer to things that had burdened her for so long.

Hanan was able to resume work a week later. At work, she appeared with her new outfit: a black Islamic dress and had even covered her hands with a pair of black gloves. She seemed comfortable with the new situation, and commented ironically:

> I've grown older. I have to adopt an 'appropriate' appearance for an old woman. This outfit is necessary in order for me to manage my responsibilities. It gives me some sort of freedom. I have to convert myself into what is accepted as reputable and proper for a 'good woman'.

The issue of an increased tendency among Iraqi women towards veiling/Islamic dress will be discussed in more detail in Chapter Six on the psychological impacts of sanctions on Iraqi women.

The Third Case: Iman

Iman was 38 years old, married and the mother of three children. This case was also followed over a 2-year period, 2000–01. The family was living in a big house in Al-Mansur city (Area III). At first, Iman was resentful about speaking to me, and refused to answer the questionnaire. However, as soon she understood that this research was connected to a foreign institution, specifically in the United Kingdom, she changed her mind and became willing to cooperate. All interviews took place at Iman's home. She also explained the reasons for her initial rejection:

> I dislike speaking about my life with local people because they are 'envious' and I am afraid of being struck with the 'evil eye', especially because a growing number of people are now envious of other people's property.

She could also read the silent question: What made her think that I would not strike her with the 'evil eye'? She quickly responded: 'You are different. I am sure that you are a materially content person' (meaning that I would not be a threat to her prosperity like those deprived Iraqis). She explained that she was happy to inform the 'outside' world that criticism of sanctions was always exaggerated.

About the sanctions Iman said:

> Those who claim that the embargo on Iraq is the reason for their poverty are not telling the truth. These are lazy people. They have taken life for granted and now they try to blame the sanctions for their personal failure. These people have always been a burden, either on the state or on their own

relatives. Now, because things have actually changed, they don't want to make any effort – they just want to wander in the street begging. Sanctions have uncovered the way these people are being dependent on one another, or on the government.

She was concerned about disclosing the 'truth' about sanctions, i.e., that sanctions were not 'evil', especially for those who could take advantage of the situation, and put forward her own situation as an example. She openly revealed that without the chance provided by the sanctions, she and her family would not have been able to achieve the 'high-quality' life they now enjoyed.

Iman's house was the family's first ever 'nuclear' home. The family had bought the house during the worst of the economic turmoil during the sanctions period in Iraq, i.e., before the Oil-For-Food agreement. Iman proudly revealed that her husband had paid a very low price for it because the previous occupants, due to some 'emergency', had had to leave the country. She did not explain what sort of pressure had driven them to depart from their dazzling house and their country 'in an emergency situation'.

Iman was the wife of an increasingly wealthy businessman. She and her husband belonged to the lower-middle income class. She was a qualified primary school teacher, and had taught for two years before being employed in a government institution for four years. Until the end of 1990, the family had survived on their limited income. In the course of her conversation about the upturn in her life after the imposition of sanctions, Iman stressed that their incomes had been adequate to support the family because they were also sharing a house with her husband's extended family. The turning point in her life happened in 1992 when her husband moved from working as a government employee to being a businessman and she left her job to become a fulltime housewife. In that year, the family had moved from their home city in southern Iraq to live in Baghdad. Since then, her husband had become one of the highest-ranking figures in the trade in foodstuffs and other important materials and was known for his close contacts with government officials, especially with Uday, the oldest son of the overthrown dictator, Saddam Hussain. Iman's husband was one of the newly emerged elites responsible for managing oil smuggling operations from Iraq to neighbouring countries.

While she characterized the earlier period of her life as an 'average', 'normal', and 'quiet' time, Iman described her present life as:

A dream I am always afraid I will lose one day. As for the money, I feel such improvement would not have taken place without a 'golden opportunity' and the hard work of my husband.

However, Iman was less excited about discussing her marital situation. Her resentment was not all about the 'evil eye', but rather that the sudden and unexpected material security that she found herself enjoying was not altogether without its price. Her voice fell and she became less confident as she started to spell out her deep insecurity regarding her husband's loyalty towards her. She said: 'It is a secret I keep in my heart. I am afraid to hear my own words talking about it'.

She revealed that her husband's attitude towards her had changed along with his growing material enrichment. Since his involvement in business life, he had distanced himself from Iman and from his home, often justifying this as the result of his demanding job and his frequent trips outside Iraq. She said:

> I began to feel that he was less attracted to me. Initially, I thought it was only my imagination, but later he began to indicate that my appearance was not appropriate for the wife for a businessman like him. I tried to become more attractive. I lost some weight and dyed my hair, but there was obviously something else that had changed him.

Her husband's criticisms and complaints did not stop at this level. Iman also found that their 'new' lifestyle compelled her to reassess her connection with her 'simple and poor' relatives. The demands of the new life had created a restrictive environment that had led to Iman becoming distanced from her own family. She told me:

> Every time I had a member of my family to visit, my husband became very angry, until I could not put up with his complaints any longer and decided to tell my family about it. Since that time, and it's now more than three years, nobody from my family has come to visit me.

However, confided Iman, even while he was restricting her contacts with her family, he was putting pressure on her to keep up with his own family members. His two married brothers and a brother in-law worked in the same line of business, and had recently left their native city to move to Baghdad.

A year later, Iman was keen to speak about all the developments. She appeared to have grown ten years older, had lost a lot of weight, and did not look happy. She was wearing rather youthfully styled clothes, a size or two too small for her, and had dyed her hair in an exaggeratedly blonde colour. It was obvious that her emotional insecurity had been causing her a lot of suffering. The persistent doubts about her husband's behaviour had finally been confirmed when he revealed that his material assets had enabled him to acquire a second wife. Becoming tearful, she said:

> He has enough money to find a second wife, a fresh one, at least twenty years younger than him. I am appalled that he could turn his face against the woman who accompanied him through the hardest part of the journey. I remember very well the times when I shared the responsibilities of the house and our children with him. Now, he thinks it's time to get rid of those memories. Now, he has enough money to buy new things, a wife and a house, who knows what else!

This time, she was less paranoid about her house and the evil eye. She ordered her two housekeepers to prepare an 'Iraqi lunch', while complaining about her laziness; that her 'clever' housekeepers were turning her to a princess 'but without a prince'. An arrangement had been reached whereby her husband came two days every week to her house, and spent five days a week with his new wife who was living in a newly-bought house in the same area.

Despite Iman's somewhat confused state of mind at this time, it was remarkable to observe the change in her attitude towards herself and the situation. Instead of blaming people in general for the miserable economic situation, she was able to articulate the situation in a different way, once again, but under different circumstances, offering her own situation as an example. Evidently, the shock of losing her husband to another woman had prompted her to grasp the impact of the shocking economic changes. She demonstrated an increasing awareness about the situation, and continually drew on the circumstances of her previous life before the deluge of wealth. She said:

> Honestly, I long for the old times, and wonder what has befallen our lives? Yes, money was scarce but at least we were looking forward to making it better, to working together for that aim. But nothing will make those times return, even if we wished them to. How I can be the loving wife again after what has happened to me? How can I forget what he put me through? How can I expect the love and support of my family after I threw them away in response to his demands? Certainly, they are asking questions in the same way that I do. We have all become embittered and corrupted.

It was obvious that Iman was going through a process of reconciliation with the self. Unfortunately however, because of the absence of any motivating opportunity in her life, she seemed to have become trapped by the comforts provided by money, and haunted by thoughts of losing her looks as she grew older.

The Iraqi Family in Tradition and Contemporary Contexts

Before proceeding to analysis of the cases, it is essential to shed some light on the nature of the Iraqi family, both in traditional and most contemporary contexts, and to look at the main features of the family as the basic unit of social organization, including its roles, structures, and relational constructs.

The functions of the classical Iraqi family, and in a wider context, the Arab family lies in the fact of its being the basic socio-economic unit of production at the centre of Arab social organization and socio-economic activities.[3] However, as a result of structural change at the level of socio-economic production and social organization, the Arab family has been undergoing significant changes. These changes have been supported and reinforced by encounters with the challenge of the state/nation-state, specifically by increased employment and education and, more recently, by globalization of the economy, and the diffusion of science and technology. Political upheavals and wars are also influencing changes in the Arab family.

The Iraqi family is placed within this context. Until the mid 20th century, the Iraqi family was the determinant social institution which undertook diverse tasks and responsibilities, including education, socialization, training, defence, welfare, and religious upbringing.[4] Most importantly, the classical Iraqi family was the basic unit through which persons and groups received security and support in times of individual and societal stress. As such, relations inside the traditional Iraqi family were so intertwined that the success or failure of an individual member became that of the family as whole.

However, from the 1970s and 1980s a basic alteration took place in the Iraqi family, which increased its vulnerability to the state. This happened when Iraq's predominantly agricultural economy began to shift to being a mixed industrial (oil) economy. The centrality of the Iraqi family in the lives of its members was increasingly challenged by the state and by related social institutions.

Instead of the family, state structures began to be in control of the economy, education, and socio-cultural life. The state became the biggest, if not the sole employer in Iraq. Young men and women sought education and careers away from their parents in towns and cities both inside and outside Iraq. These structural changes, including legislation concerning labour force, education, and family law, and especially stipulations concerning the position of women, were directed towards undermining the classical roles and value orientations of the Iraqi family. These and many other factors led to a new construct of relationships in the society, on the level both of individuals and the family and of family-state relationships.

In addition to socio-economic policies, the state's intervention in family affairs was also seen through the role the General Federation of Iraqi Women during the 1970s and 1980s. The branches of the GFIW throughout Iraq (in both rural and urban areas) attempted, by organising seminars and campaigns and the use of the media, to share certain responsibilities with the family, while at the same time played a key role in marketing state policies concerning women.

As previously mentioned in this book (Chapter Two), the GFIW was actively involved in encouraging Iraqi women's participation in the labour force whenever this was needed by the state, but it was also the first organization to advocate the state policy for increasing the birth rate, through which Iraqi women were encouraged to leave their jobs. On the level of health, the GFIW was involved in organizing campaigns to make vaccinations available to more children, especially in rural areas, and was, moreover, actively involved in campaigning against illiteracy and advocating the importance of girls' education through seminars and follow-up activities with citizens in their residential areas or through local schools. The GFIW was also engaged in combating violence against women, although this was limited to raising awareness and advocacy assistance, and was available only to women who turned to the organization for help.

The structure of the classical Iraqi family is the other main feature that should be mentioned. The classical Iraqi family, as with other Arab families, is patriarchal, extended and hierarchal, particularly with respect to sex and age.[5] Patriarchies are central to the social organization of almost all Middle Eastern sub-national and national communities where citizenship is not premised on equality among individuals, but rather on the dominance of male elders over kin groups. Based on this order, patriarchal societies entail a clear separation between the public and the private spheres of life where men in both spheres dominate women, and where women are organized and addressed in the context of their positions within patriarchal structures, often as minors and subordinates.[6]

The patriarchal structure of the traditional Iraqi family has also seen considerable changes since the emergence of the nation-state in Iraq. The regime's support for Iraqi women's rights in the 1970s, although intended to win loyalty of women (more than half of the Iraqi population), was also a deliberate policy to weaken tribal influence on the society and polity. State intervention in the family through social policy and legislation was particularly considered a challenge to the traditional patriarchal system in Iraq and to its control over women.

Perhaps this was most clearly indicated by the Code of Personal Status of 1978, which brought about the most important changes in the social role of women in Iraq. The Code's rationale rested in the fact that whenever traditional male rights over women weakened or were abolished, the state adopted this role, specifically acting 'on behalf of' women. Nevertheless, the state was ambivalent towards women's roles in the society as determined by economic and political exigencies. This was particularly clear through state's frequent and contradictory regulations concerning Iraqi women's productive and reproductive roles (Chapter Two).

The other main feature of the Iraqi family, both classical and contemporary, is being connective and relational.[7] In spite of the state interventions in family roles and structure during the 1970s and 1980s, the traditional extended family retained its role, particularly as a source of emotional support for its members. It is believed that the increased tendency towards nuclear family creation that was motivated by the new modes of production and state legislation did not affect the relational construct of the Iraqi family. Iraqi men and women have largely continued to view themselves in a connective and gendered contexts. It is believed that the economic conditions of individuals and of the nuclear family have always played an influential role in determining the fine lines that separate emotional connective from dominant (patriarchal) familial relationships.

In other words, the rewards of economic security in the 1970s and 1980s, in the form of jobs, education, and health security, were crucial for defining an individual's position in relation to the other, including the family. However, while socio-economic security was provided outside the realm of the family, it did not imply the complete separation of the individual from the family and kinship, and it was not achieved on the account of connectivity within the family.

The Iraqi Family under Sanctions

During the thirteen years of UN sanctions the Iraqi family was exposed to varying degrees of economic and social crisis. The initial impact of sanctions and the aftermath of the Gulf War of 1991 had obviously brought everything to a halt, but most people thought that the situation would not last for long.

The first two cases reveal that the disturbing social changes in the first few years of the crisis, when neither state nor society was prepared to endure the shock, put the Iraqi family under immense pressure and made women an easy target for different forms of abuse. Whether in nuclear or extended form, families were placed under great stress as a result of the economic crisis under UN sanctions, and suffered unprecedented consequences. It is, of course, natural in times of crisis that people who are struggling to adapt to new economic and social conditions will be most in need of the support of their family members. One of the paradoxes of the impact of sanctions on Iraqi society was that while kinship and family were becoming very much the focus of everyday life, it was becoming increasingly difficult to offer the same forms of support, whether financial and/or emotional, to its members.

However, Iraqi society was unable to adapt to the new circumstances, even some years after sanctions had been imposed, and getting on with life under sanctions continued at the cost of considerable sacrifice. As the case studies show, while the first stage of sanctions brought confusion and despair, the later years left society in a state of extreme insecurity, humiliation, and emotional deprivation. Iraqi women were suffering, regardless of their social and economic background. Due to their vulnerable economic and social situation women are highly dependent on familial, communal, and institutional support. However, with the society unable to preserve the old patterns of familial and communal relations, it was increasingly difficult to acquire institutional or other remedial support.

While Halimah lost her job, was unable to find an income, and eventually ended up begging in the streets, Hanan had to grow up fast and sacrifice her dreams in order to deal with the tremendous responsibilities she had to face. And although Iman's situation seemed better than that of the first two cases, the personal damage she suffered went deeper, causing her a permanent lack of self-esteem, emotional insecurity, and total dependence on her husband.

One important implication of sanctions for the Iraqi family was that, under the pressure of the need for some cash, many middle class families who were mainly public sector employees, sold their houses and moved, either renting or buying cheaper places in less expensive or poor neighbourhoods. Unable to preserve the same pattern of their lives, most middle class Iraqi people became preoccupied with their own survival, while traditionally strong familial connectivity weakened. The case studies reveal that despite people's physical proximity based on kinship, family, and neighbourhood, the complex economic turmoil caused by sanctions had undermined support networks and expectation from one another.

Halimah's case shows how the relationship of demands and compliance, implied by the connective patriarchal relationships between brother and sister that was one of the characteristic features of Iraqi society, were changed into different, 'impersonalized' patriarchal forms of relationships. For the majority of nuclear families, while relationships with extended families were forced to become more impersonal, nothing replaced the extended family and kinship as sources of support and alliance.

New Forms of Patriarchy

The case studies, as well as the statements of many of the respondents, uncovered an unprecedented level of social and patriarchal control over women that had been happening since the beginning of the 1990s. It was striking however, that the decline in economic and social support networks between members of a particular family had not coincided with a decline in patriarchal relations, as is always assumed. It is obvious that while the Iraqi society was witnessing a decreasing incidence of the extended family, society in general remained closely locked into a kind of relationship that left limited room for women's independence and privacy.

Iraqi women's participation in the labour force and income earning under sanctions seem not to have undermined patriarchal hold and control over women. The cases of Hanan and Halimah, as well as those of many other respondents who were working and generating income (through formal or informal jobs), were subjected to an intensified form of patriarchal control both in the home and at work.

Hanan's case reveals the oddity of women's professional lives under sanctions. While unemployment rates were soaring, many young people resented the burden of public sector jobs because most were seen as thankless and ill paid. Even though Hanan was the head of a big family and the only breadwinner, she had to obey the dominance and control of her brother. In the case of Halimah, she had to put up with her brother's domineering and abusive attitude while he turned a deaf ear to her appeals for his help. However, analysis of the third case reveals that in this situation, women living within a nuclear family might well have experienced a more oppressive form of patriarchy than that of the extended family or kinship type. Obviously, with the perpetuation of the economic crisis and the diminished support network offered by the extended family, the nuclear patriarchy, more than ever, became an integral part of Iraqi women's lives.

It is important to point out that physical proximity, which is usually provided by the extended family and the local community, may hinder a positive development of women's status under 'good' economic circumstances, but that in a 'bad' economic situation it may afford women a sense of security and a measure of protection. However, the absence of support from the extended family and from the state might eventually lead to a woman's high dependency ratio on a single male provider, thus perpetuating her subordination to that particular male.

As in Halimah's case, it would seem that the patriarchal order embodied in the Middle Eastern sister-brother relationship was first settled on the grounds of her economic independence and income earnings. Halimah's experience shows that, even after the death of her husband, she was able to run her own life, relying primarily on her own income earnings. Nevertheless, she was able to preserve fairly good relationships with her brother, and the rest of her family. The fact that she was economically independent did not necessarily mean that she was less integrated into her family or community, nor that she expected fewer demands from or compliance with others. However, the absence of any independent source of support or income under sanctions not only increased Halimah's vulnerability and subordination to her brother/sisters, but the weakened connectivity within the family also rendered her emotionally helpless.

Furthermore, the situation of despair and insecurity also intensified the various forms of 'street patriarchy' that were to be observed everywhere in public, in the streets, public transport, food markets, etc. Increasingly the public sphere became a hostile place for women, and was generally dominated by men. It was noticeable how the public environment had changed, compared with that of the 1970s. While women, whether divorcees or widows, were increasingly becoming the sole providers for their families (Halimah's case), they were more than ever exposed to control by their families and society. This is also illustrated in many ways, such as the increasing condescension shown towards women in public areas, and especially through images of women as weak and a potential threat to public morals.[8] In order to put up with the mounting pressures in public and in the home and to minimise the risks of sexual and other forms of gender harassments outside the home, Islamic outfits and shapeless garments became increasingly popular among large numbers of young Iraqi females.

Crisis in Marriage

Marriage is so highly valued in the Iraqi society that it is considered to be a main aim in life, especially for women, who are under immense pressure to marry. Meanwhile, sexual contact outside marriage, particularly for women, is scarcely possible and totally unacceptable. Young single women living on their own represent an uncommon and an ill-tolerated phenomenon in the Iraqi society. Regardless of whether or not she is economically independent or of professional status, an Iraqi woman is usually judged according to whether or not she has achieved the status of wife and mother.

The economic crisis intensified the chronic dilemma of finding a partner by increasing an already overwhelming burden. The frequent wars of recent times were the reason for the deaths or the physical and mental impairment of many of the young men who would have been eligible for marriage, while huge numbers of Iraqi men escaped from the country in search of a better life abroad. Additionally, the problem of marriage under sanctions is portrayed in the fact that the state was no longer able to provide the facilities previously given to marriage candidates,[9] while the majority of Iraqi men had either become unemployed or were surviving on such low incomes that they were unable to support themselves, let alone a new family.

A social science professor[10] mentioned in an interview that while the economic situation was in constant state of deterioration for the majority of the Iraqi population of both sexes, many young Iraqi women were increasingly reverting to the 'traditional' image of the husband as sole provider. He also emphasized that while large number of males were pressured to give up their education in order to generate income, large numbers of highly educated middle-class women held on to the requirement that a suitable marriage candidate should be of a corresponding or higher educational status. The result of this situation was a growing number of unmarried women and a simultaneous increase in social pressure on them. The implications of sanctions for marriage are seen through conflicting tendencies in both the demands and the actual reality of life under sanctions. The crisis in marriage in Iraq can be described as reflecting the interrelated economic and social aspects of marriage under sanctions.

The impact of the economic crisis on marriage is illustrated by the difficulty of being able to afford the dower (*mahr*). In Iraq, as in many other Middle Eastern societies, the bridegroom has to give *mahr* to his bride or to her guardian, prior to marriage. Traditionally, a dower is handed over when marriage is accepted. Dowry consists of two parts. The first part is a sum of money that should be given in advance (*al-muqaddam*) and ideally is paid to the bride when the marriage certificate is signed.[11] The second, deferred part (*al-mu'khkhar*) is a stated amount of money to be paid to the wife if the husband files for divorce. In addition to the dower, the man should give his fiancée some sort of valuable gift soon after the marriage agreement is concluded; traditionally this is in the form of some gold jewellery.

It is pertinent to mention the findings of a study undertaken in 1996 by the University of Baghdad, based on random sample of 4200 women aged 19 to 30 years.[12] In general, the study found that while the economic situation had deteriorated enormously, attitudes among the majority of Iraqi women towards the importance/value of dower remained largely unchanged. From this it was concluded that Iraqi society had witnessed a growing materialistic tendency along with a constant increase in the amounts of dower during the 1990s.

This situation also affected married women, but in different ways according to the material status of their husbands. A married woman, whether or not she is a professional and/or earning an income, tends to identify herself through her husband's occupational and income status. Society, too, looks more than ever at married and unmarried women through the status of their husband and family.

As Iman's case illustrated, her husband's unexpected opportunity to acquire wealth had robbed her of a conventional home base, and led her to cling to an unusual degree to her relationship with her husband. While she was gradually separated from the outside world, in the form of her job, her own family, and her close friends and relatives, she had become totally dependent – economically, socially, and emotionally – on her husband. Iman's pre-eminent credentials as a 'wife' had prevented the integration of personal preferences into her own life, and had also subjected her to an increased vulnerability to, and dependency on her husband.

This case reveals also that, the lack of self-determination for decisive and effective action had prevented Iman from dealing with her life and her family problems. The absence of other alternatives for personal fulfilment simply aggravated the conscience-based stereotype of internalised morality that glorifies women's submissiveness to the male provider. The contradictions of life under sanctions have undeniably amplified the arrival of the societal norm that acclaims material possessions and material respectability over the free pursuit of happiness in the fulfilment of personal desire. For Iman and other women in the same situation it has become, more than ever, acceptable to compromise integrity and indulge in hypocrisy for the sake of the economic security and social respectability provided by marriage.

'Wanted: Rich Husband and Rich Wife!'

The statements of many of my respondents revealed a growing tendency towards changing criteria for determining the degree of prestige of a specific family. Rather than basing this on social status – often related to honourable reputation and/or the bride's level of education and her beauty – there seemed to be rather more concern with a family's material possessions and its connections to the powerful political elites. The effects of the economic situation and the types of income division under sanctions – a poor majority and a rich minority – seem to have implanted a sense of insecurity that was reflected in people's attitudes towards marriage. Hanan's statement suggested her awareness of the phenomenon. She said:

> People have changed. These days, nobody thinks of marrying a poor woman, regardless of her other qualities, such as being young, beautiful, highly educated, and from a 'good' family. A poor man strives to find a better-off woman, and the rich man likes to get a wealthier wife regardless of any other criteria. True, marriage is the dream of every woman. I would love to have a husband and children. But as every day passes, the possibility of realising this dream is reduced. There is not much hope left for me.

Hanan described herself and many Iraqi women in her situation as resembling 'desert flowers that flourish, open up, age, and die, alone'. It is clear the desperate situation had forced her and many other young women in Iraq to take up positions for which nothing in their lives had prepared them. Given that the difficulties presented by the fact of marriage represented a very 'personal' issue, especially for unmarried women, most women hesitated about openly revealing an interest in marriage. It was not easy to break through the reticence imposed on these women by the harsh and extremely restricted situation.

It was very noticeable that, during the one-year time lapse between the two phases of my fieldwork, there had been a significant change in the attitudes and self-conceptions of a large number of respondents. This was especially evident among respondents who were unmarried. During the first phase, it was obvious that the question of marriage was one of the disheartening issues for most of the respondents even though many were optimistic that they would get married sooner or later. Hanan was ready to share her thoughts about this problem only after I had had several meetings with her. In spite of the disappointment with Ahmad, she was able to disclose some more hopeful insights about another opportunity with another man. She was (probably) thinking of another chance that would eventually change her life. She said:

Although I am still very shocked about what happened with Ahmad, I can't deny there has been a hope hanging above my head for years. However, as time passes, part of that hope passes with it. For example, three or four years ago, I strongly believed that I would get married to a man who I would care for no less than I did for Ahmad. As for now, I still hope to get married, but I honestly doubt that I can carry on dreaming so foolishly in this way.

However, a year later Hanan seemed to have grown older than might have been expected. Expressions of anger and anxiety about the future had almost disappeared. She seemed to be certain that the 'failures' and 'disappointments' of life would no longer hurt her – she said there 'wasn't any more hope'. Rather, she was attempting to accommodate the loss by withdrawing into another world, notably by means of religion. This was evident through the way she had changed her style of dress in public and through her frequent use of pious expressions, such as 'our destiny has been written and decided by God thus we will accept it', and 'you may dislike something where the divine good has been hidden for you'.

The same observation could be repeated with regard to some other unmarried respondents, particularly some of the final year university students. Feelings of uncertainty and insecurity about the future were common among these women, but at the same time, it was also recognised that education would probably increase their chances of marriage. However, a year later, only one woman out of the student sample of 50 women had become engaged – to a man she had never seen because he was living abroad!

Many women, particularly students, openly expressed a wish to find a suitor who would be an Iraqi man living abroad. They also revealed that they would prefer marriage to an older, financially secure man rather than a young, impoverished university colleague. Asia, a 23 year-old female student was extremely hesitant before she opened up to ask for a favour. She shyly asked:

I really don't know how to put my words together because I am aware that the thing I am about to ask you is difficult, but because I trust you, I think you can help me. The story is that an Iraqi man who is 53 years old, living in London, has asked his family in Iraq to find him a bride, a young woman. They have proposed to me. My family is pressuring me to accept the offer regardless of his age and the fact that I, and we, know nothing at all about him. My family thinks he is fine only because he lives abroad. So, they believe it is a gift from heaven sent to remedy our miserable economic situation. But, I am hesitant. I am afraid. When I saw you, I thought you might be able to help, to find some information about this man. For example, his morals, his life, whether he was married before, or has children, whether he is sick, etc. Can you take his details and his picture? Can you help me?

Unfortunately, it was not possible to be of help to this woman. However, this observation indicated that the economic crisis had led to a change of marriage patterns in Iraq. Iraqi society was previously widely known for its high degree of endogamous marriage.[13] Traditionally, although the bridegroom's material condition was important for many Iraqi people, it had never been the most important criterion. Sound family and personal reputations, social background, political alliance, and physical proximity (relatives) were always much more significant criteria than material considerations. These latter were less essential in endogamous marriages in which the closer the kin, the lower the dowry, and the further the kin, the higher the dowry.

Under sanctions, it had apparently become very popular for Iraqi woman to get a chance of marriage to an Iraqi man living abroad. A man who lives abroad, regardless of anything else, is a man with money, not any old money but hard currency, and with a home abroad. Men of this kind have also become popular among families who are trying to have their female member(s) married. This phenomenon reveals a change in attitude among Iraqi people towards physical proximity and social alliance. It seems to have become less of a problem for people to compromise their other values in favour of more material possessions. It is believed that the deteriorated living standards of most middle class people underlie the generalization about this particular attitude.

Polygamy

Along with the other unprecedented trends that pervaded Iraqi society under sanctions, the increase in polygamous marriages had also become a phenomenon, and there are many Iraqi (local) studies confirming that polygamy had increased since the imposition of sanctions. Some of the pre-sanctions studies showed that polygamous marriages had declined remarkably since the issuing of the 1978 Code of Personal Status and the family law.[14] Al-Jenabi's study cited official statistics for 1980 concerning families in Baghdad City, which showed that in 1940, out of 100 married men, 8 percent had more than one wife. This percentage had been reduced to 2 percent by 1980.[15] In reality, however, polygamous marriages were rare in Iraqi society. Although polygamy was legal for many decades, it was not widely practised and was more or less restricted to a few tribal communities and to childless marriages. Having multiple wives was also disapproved of by the society, despite state encouragement, and especially during the eight years war with Iran.[16]

The 1978 Personal Status Code did not prohibit polygamous marriage but its conditions laid down that consent to polygamy should be given by the first wife and a state-authorised judge.[17] Such consent could only be given if the man was capable of providing for more than one wife; if the second marriage was based the mutual interests/consent of both the husband and the first wife; and where polygamy provided grounds for divorce. According to this, a woman could initiate divorce but could not expect to receive the deferred part of the dowry (*al-mu'hkhkar*), whereas a man who initiated a divorce was required to pay the woman the full amount of the dowry.

The family law reviewed here incorporated major elements of *shari'a* law as well as of modern legislation.[18] The Iraqi family law of 1978 was considered as reformist in nature, or where *shari'a* law had been interpreted in reformist ways. It did not, however, seek to establish new relations between men and women.

It is important to mention that there were no major new amendments to the laws regulating polygamy in Iraq after 1978, and nothing very much during the sanctions era. Thus, the increase in polygamy in Iraqi society under sanctions was influenced far more by social and economic factors rather than by legislative factors. This phenomenon can be partly interpreted as an attempt at adjustment, where the society seeks to cope with the gender imbalance. It appears that society has begun to adopt polygamy as a solution to the limited choices for marriage that currently exist in Iraq. According to the UN's Department of Humanitarian Affairs, four million people, or 20 per cent of Iraq's population, were living in extreme poverty in 1998.[19] In the context of these statistics alone, it is undoubtedly true that, in order to assure their future as mothers, as well as to gain some degree of economic security, a large number of Iraqi women and their families had become less hesitant about polygamous marriages.

As demonstrated by the second case study above, Rafah was 21 years old and newly graduated from university when her family (who had no history of polygamous marriage) decided to give her into a polygamous marriage to a 52 year-old man with five children. Undoubtedly it was the collapse in the living standards of this middle-class family, whose survival depended primarily on public sector salaries or/and state pensions, that was behind a 'deal' of this kind; and such deals are, in most instances, unhappy deals. Rafah spoke of her reactions:

> First, I thought I would rather kill myself than marry this man. Then I thought, killing myself would only save me but by marrying him, all my family would be saved. I learned to forget about myself. It was the only option that could save my whole family from imminent starvation, especially as Hanan was still hoping to travel abroad. There was no space for me to think twice.

With the increased economic insecurity, polygamous marriage has become a means of economic and social security, not only for the woman but probably also for her family. The social stigma of polygamy appeared to have been widely compromised by the growth of social pressure, particularly as the numbers of unmarried Iraqi women were constantly increasing.

The seclusion of women from public life is another factor that encouraged the spread of polygamous marriages under sanctions. The meagre opportunities for women's participation in the wage labour force and the deteriorated value of education had largely limited women's socio-economic space for personal development. Depriving women of the opportunity for income earning, unemployment had also had other devastating impacts, particularly through curtailing opportunities for social interaction with others. The consequences of this situation not only narrowed a woman's chances of choosing a marriage partner but also reduced her ability to refuse to be a second wife.

Iman's case illustrates another aspect of the terrifying reality. A divorced Iraqi woman living on her own is unusual and badly tolerated in the Iraqi society. The weakened options for an economically independent life have perpetuated this phenomenon. The absence of other alternatives for economic and social security have reinforced and strengthened the internalized social values that emphasise marriage as a necessary condition for women's recognition and acceptability in the society. Indeed, Iman and many women in the same situation would have dealt differently with the problems concerning their marriage if there had been an adequate environment that enabled them to realise the self. Worth mentioning in this context is the opportunities for women to re-qualify themselves for the job market and through education. These options are undoubtedly essential in challenging attitudes that identify women primarily as wives.

Finally, the other face of this problem is that, while marriage chances diminish, it has also become increasingly difficult for divorced or widowed women to have a second chance for marriage. This problem constitutes an additional pressure on women, both married and unmarried. In addition it accounts for the existence of many unhappy marriages and unhappy women trying to keep their marriages alive. Thus it is important to provide some idea of the status of divorced women under such circumstances.

The Status of Widowed and Divorced Women

There are no specific statistics as to the number of widows in Iraq, but it is estimated that after Iraq-Iran War and the Gulf War of 1991, over 20 percent of young Iraqi women had lost their husbands. This group of Iraqi women became the most vulnerable under sanctions, as they no longer received the benefits that had previously been given by the state.[20] Single women breadwinners were the worst affected by the increasing despair of the Iraqi society under sanctions. Not only had they lost the formal support provided by the state, but the economic crisis had also shrunk the degree of support previously provided by the extended family.

While the effects of sanctions were leaving most of Iraq's viable sectors damaged and ineffective, the government was gradually withdrawing from the social arena and becoming increasingly preoccupied with its own survival. Women like Halimah who were widowed and single breadwinners were dramatically affected by the state shifting priorities. The 'bread for blood' scheme was an example of a policy designed by the regime in an attempt to mitigate the lost lives of valuable young men during the Iraq-Iran War, particularly during the first five years of the war. Most wives/mothers of 'martyrs', Iraqi soldiers who were killed in the battle, received special privileges in forms in of money or brand new cars, and their children were given concessions, e.g., for university admission, and so on, although, as in Halimah's case, not all widows of martyrs were able to obtain compensation. A condition for compensation required the soldier killed to have been in a combat situation, but Halimah's husband was not considered a martyr because he had been fetching water for the brigade when he was killed. However, Halimah was able to become the owner of her house (state housing), and received other benefits in forms of a salary allowance for being widow of a soldier and a single mother.

However, during the last years of the Iraq-Iran war, the state also conducted a policy of encouraging the marriage of war widows by giving special grants to men who were prepared to marry them. This particular issue suggests that, generally speaking, widows had acquired relatively better status than divorced women. It was believed to have been God's will that their husbands died, whereas divorced women were/are always blamed for their marriage break-down. Divorce is allowed in Islam but is considered the most hated lawful practice (*abgadh al-halal 'ende allah al-talaq*), so that, regardless of the fact that Islam allows divorce, social attitudes towards divorced women are harsh. A divorced woman is considered 'liberated', but this liberation means sexual liberation, which is extremely restricted by society. In this context, a liberated woman is a potential treat to the honour and the reputation of her family and herself.[21]

Even under normal economic conditions, a divorced woman in Iraqi society is considered a risk for the reputation of her family. In spite of the positive legislation that supports divorced women, including the right of women to seek divorce,[22] divorce remains a social stigma especially for females. In such a culture, Iraqi women would rather put up with problematic marriages in order to avoid divorce. For women, the awful consequences of divorce do not end with economic insecurity; more significantly, divorced women have to endure social isolation from their families and society. For example, families do not approve of their female members being friendly with a divorced woman; and it is extremely difficult for a divorced woman to have a second marriage, not because of the meagre chances for marriage discussed above, but because the remarriage of a divorced woman is disapproved of socially. It is argued that the low status of divorced women is due to the extreme value placed on virginity at marriage, which automatically excludes previously married women from the ranks of 'desired' mates.[23]

The deteriorated economic and social conditions of life under sanctions perpetuated the 'low' status of divorced women in Iraq, and increased their vulnerability. In these altered conditions, it was to be expected that the ill-conceived image of the divorced woman would increased women's fear of divorce and its consequences. For example, Iman pointed out how taxing the situation was for her; notwithstanding the misery her husband caused her, she had to be very cautious when she communicated with him because it was always easy for him to threaten divorce. She said: 'I lost my family because he wanted me to expel them from my life. I am totally dependent on him. So, if he divorces me, who is going to support me?' She saw it as part of her duty to accept the situation, because she could not afford the consequences of her marriage collapsing.

Conclusion

The lives of Iraqi women have always been restricted by cultural conventions. This is where the state played its most essential role in the lives of women in Iraq. In the course of the state's role as a mediator between patriarchal kinship and its female members, women were allowed to become more active participants in changing their social position, especially by taking up the opportunities (work and education) that were available to them. The retreat of the state as a key player in the lives of women left open a space in which gender and kinship and the patriarchal structuring of kinship were brought together to become the sole power structuring the lives and the views of women. Indeed, this is the power that allows people to view individual woman in terms of her family, not as an autonomous human being.

However, the economic crisis under UN sanctions placed the Iraqi family, whether nuclear or extended, under considerable stress. While family and kinship were increasingly becoming the focus of everyday life, they were unable to provide the same form of support for their family members. This situation led in particular to the economic collapse of the broad middle class population, and put the middle income family under immense pressure.

Sanctions linked the status of Iraqi women into extremely conflicting patterns, and as overwhelming social and patriarchal demands were strengthened, Iraqi women were increasingly treated in individualistic patterns, especially with regard to material concerns. The relationally internalized system of demands and compliance implicit in connective patriarchal relationships that was one of the characteristic features of the Iraqi society was largely changed into a different form of impersonalized patriarchal relationships. In this state of despair, middle class and poor women, whether working or not working, were the prime victims. The loss of security, whether in the form of adequate income earnings or in the protection provided by extended family and kinship, subjected these women to intensified forms of patriarchal domination, in addition to the impersonal patriarchal influence that was increasingly to be found in the family and in public places.

The sanctions did tremendous damage to the social fabric of the Iraqi society. Marriage opportunities had witnessed unprecedented decline, while attitudes toward polygamous marriage (official and unofficial) had found strong ground in the Iraqi society. The increased economic insecurity of the wide majority urged people's struggle towards materialistic gains, with young women/girls seen as the bridge to a safe haven. The emergence of these attitudes has affected Iraqi women in a way that reinforces and strengthens the internalized social values that emphasise marriage, however ill-conceived, as the only option for women's recognition and acceptability in the society.

Among other categories of women, widowed and divorced women were disproportionately affected, not only through becoming targets for economic disempowerment, but also because their impoverishment was more socially and emotionally felt. This was portrayed in the strengthened social stigma against single women who were breadwinners, especially young divorced women, who were portrayed as a potential risk for their family's reputation and a threat to public morals. These and other fearful consequences of becoming targets for patronizing social humiliation mean that married women's options for identifying the self have been limited mainly to the material status of their husbands.

This pattern of attitudes has been perpetuated because of the lack of other alternatives (e.g., employment, close friends and relatives) available to women under sanctions.

The experience of Iraqi women reveals that a regressive change in women's status has been allowed to take place in people's consciousness and has been reflected in social images of women. The deteriorated economic situation has caused women to see themselves as lacking an autonomous existence and has weakened their control over what decides their mobility or their achieved social status.

THE PSYCHOLOGICAL IMPACT OF SANCTIONS ON IRAQI WOMEN

Introduction

Having introduced the impact of sanctions on Iraqi women's employment, female education, and family relations, it remains to see how Iraqi women felt when the entire community was directly affected by this economic and political upheaval. What did living under this crisis mean to Iraqi women and what happened to them when they become caught up in a crisis that concerned everyone and everything in the community?

It is widely known that the sense of insecurity that accompanies times of political strife, conflict and economic disturbance strongly reflects upon women. At such times, women often undertake huge responsibilities both in the home and at work, replacing the destroyed infrastructure. However, in the specific case of Iraq where women are 'traditionally' represented as custodians of the nation's cultural values, times of upheavals also constitute a huge additional pressure on them.

Under these circumstances, women are portrayed as weak and in need of protection. Hence, men may step up their effort to control women by trying to reinforce the boundaries that confine women to the domestic sphere and undermining their position to one of lesser beings in the custody of men. As discussed in the previous chapters of this book, Iraqi women normally possess less power unless the state takes action on their behalf. The withdrawal of the state from the economy and social arena has had serious consequences for Iraqi women's lives, not only widespread despair but also awareness of their subordination.

This chapter looks at some aspects of the psychological impact of sanctions on Iraqi women. It investigates the issue of violence against women by exploring some insights into women's experience in this regard, and also considers women's domestic responsibilities, and the pressure of the food and health crisis on Iraqi women.[1]

Violence against Women: Definitions

The 1993 Declaration on the Elimination of Violence against Women[2] defines violence against women and girls as:

Any act of gender-based violence that results in, or is likely to result in, physical, sexual, or mental harm or suffering to women, including threats of such acts, coercion or arbitrary deprivation of liberty, whether occurring in public or in private life.

There is no one single factor to account for violence that is perpetrated against women. It is believed that several complex and interconnected institutionalized social and cultural factors have kept women particularly vulnerable to the violence directed at them. These include socio-economic forces such as: the institution of the family where power relations are enforced; fear of, and control over, female sexuality; a belief in the inherent superiority of males, and legislation and cultural sanctions that have traditionally denied women and children an independent legal and social status. All of these constitute the manifestations of historically unequal power relations.

However, lack of economic resources remains the underpinning factor of women's vulnerability to violence and their difficulty in extricating themselves from a violent relationship. It is argued that the link between violence and lack of economic resources and dependence is circular. On the one hand, the threat and fear of violence keeps women from seeking employment, or, at best, compels them to accept low paid home-based exploitative labour. On the other hand, without economic independence, women have no power to escape from an abusive relationship.[3] This argument however, is challenged by the increased violence against women who are in fact economically independent of a male provider.[4] Evidently, this is particularly true when the male partner is unemployed, and feels his power in the household is undermined.

Sharp economic changes (economic liberalization and globalization) and growing class inequities have been linked to increasing levels of violence, particularly gender-based violence against women. This is confirmed by studies of women's experiences in many parts of the world, such as Latin America, Africa, Asia and the Middle East region.[5] Also, the transition period in countries of Central and Eastern Europe and the Former Soviet Union — with increases in poverty, unemployment, hardship, income inequality, stress, and other abuse — has led to increased violence in society in general, including violence against women by their partners.[6]

However, there is no reason to believe the stereotype that Middle Eastern Muslim women are any more victimized by violence than women in other parts of the world. Social and anthropological studies about gender, sexuality, and violence against women in Middle Eastern societies may confirm that, in many instances, religious and historical traditions in the region endorse the chastising and beating of women, particularly wives, sisters, daughters, etc.[7] Nevertheless, the physical punishment of female members of the family is particularly authorized under the notion of entitlement and ownership of women, which is more culturally oriented than religious.

Male control of family wealth inevitably places decision-making authority in male hands, leading to male dominance and proprietary rights over women and girls. In turn, the concept of ownership, which legitimises male control over women's lives and their sexuality, has been deemed essential in many law codes in the Middle East to ensure patrilineal inheritance. Women's sexuality is also tied to the concept of family honour in many societies. A form of violence against women that is characteristic of the Middle East region is the killing of women for illicit sexual contact out of marriage, or so-called 'honour crimes'. Traditional, not religious norms in these societies allow the killing of 'errant' daughters, sisters, cousins, and nieces suspected of defiling the honour of the family by indulging in illicit sex or, in many cases, marrying and divorcing without the consent of the family. Nevertheless, in all circumstances, violence against women is a manifestation of historically unequal power relations between men and women, which is portrayed in male control of material resources and the consequent physical and psychological domination of women by men.

Moreover, the isolation of women within their families and communities is known to contribute to increased violence, particularly if women have little access to family or local organizations.[8] Women's participation in social networks has been seen as a critical factor in lessening their vulnerability to violence and increasing their ability to resolve domestic violence. Social networks can be informal (family and neighbours) or formal (community organizations, women's self-help groups, or affiliated to political parties).

Finally, lack of legal protection, particularly within the sanctity of the home, is a strong factor in perpetuating violence against women. In many countries violence against women is exacerbated by legislation, law enforcement and judicial systems that do not recognize domestic violence as a crime. Violence against women committed in an intimate relationship is often tolerated as the norm than being prosecuted under the law.

Sanctions and Violence against Iraqi Women

In Iraq, as in any other society, gender-based violence against women has always existed, but the implications of the economic situation for this issue are complex. Ultimately, as a consequence of the deteriorated economic situation under sanctions, there has been a clear tendency towards an increase in women's vulnerability and to growing ill-treatment by their families as well as by society.

What follows is an attempt to explain the nature of the gender-based violence against women that results from the discriminatory impact of the economic situation on Iraqi women. An illustration of violence against women under sanctions will be provided on three levels: domestic-based violence, centralized forms of violence, and street or public violence.

Domestic Violence against Women

Domestic violence is a unique crime because it occurs between intimate partners of one family rather than strangers, and its victims may not involve the legal system for fear of more abuse. Women are the prime victims of domestic violence (more than men). In Iraq, domestic violence against women occurs but little is known about its extent, since such abuse was customarily addressed within the tightly-knit family structure. There is no public record or discussion of the subject. However, under Iraqi law, spousal violence is forbidden, and constitutes sufficient grounds for prompt divorce and may also lead to prosecution. There are other codifications as well, that regulate parents' relationships with their children in case of violence against minors.[9] However, cases brought on such charges are reportedly rare. Moreover, not all offences of domestic violence and sexual harassment against women are explicitly identified under penal law. In fact, under Penal Code No. 111 of 1990, Article 41 of the penal code authorizes husbands to beat their wives for 'educational purposes'.

However, the laws intended to protect Iraqi women against domestic violence are constantly being undermined by 'traditional' societal attitudes, which tend to view this kind of violence as normal or as a discrete family matter. It is widely accepted in Iraq that a husband, father, or brother has the right to chastise the female members of his family whenever he sees fit to do so. Long before the imposition of sanctions, all forms of gender violence, including rape, wife beating, attacks on women and the killing of women by male relatives, existed and were often endorsed according to prevailing codes of conduct. In general, an Iraqi woman would prefer to tell you about the experiences of other women and will deny that she herself might be a victim of domestic violence.

There were very few instances of women complaining that they were suffering from violent behaviour in the home, even from those whom, obviously, were being subjected to domestic harassment.

Fatima (aged 20, from Area I) was a housewife and mother of two small children. The family was living in a two-room extension from the family-in-law's house. During a meeting with Fatima and her mother-in-law ('Um 'Ali), she had a sad expression in her eyes. Fatima was avoiding any direct eye contact with me and was silent. 'Um 'Ali was in her mid-50s, a woman who appeared tense and overprotective. She was inclined to take the initiative to speak and make statements on behalf of her daughter-in-law, Fatima. At first it was unclear what kind of relationship existed between these women, but it certainly reflected a daughter-in-law's submissiveness and fear of the mother-in-law. A sad glance and a bowed head was Fatima's response to a question about her life. 'Um 'Ali, however, took the initiative to answer, saying protectively:

> Al-hamdu lil lah [Praise be to God], she is fine, happy, and has nothing to complain about. This is, of course, if she grows to be obedient and understands what is good for herself and for her children. However, she is still very young, and does not know what is right from wrong.

As 'Um 'Ali finished speaking, Fatima stared tearfully at the floor. 'Um 'Ali hastened to comment:

> Fatima is about to lose everything good in her life. My son is not working and has no income. She has a high school degree and is not working either. We are spending on them. We are hosting them in our house. Now, my son has an excellent opportunity to have a better life, and this will be also for Fatima and

the children. He will have his own shop and then it would be possible for Fatima to eat better and wear better clothes. She is unhappy, ha!

So, why Fatima was feeling miserable? It appeared that the difficult economic and domestic circumstances of Fatima's husband ('Ali) had encouraged his uncle to take advantage of the situation. The 'rich' uncle had offered his daughter (aged 39) to become a second wife to 'Ali, and in return, 'Ali would be given a grocery shop, which would become his own if he proved to be a 'good' husband. Apparently, Fatima, the daughter of an extremely poor family from the southern part of Iraq, was struggling to keep her little family together in an extremely hostile environment.

On another visit to the family, Fatima was not there. 'Um 'Ali said, 'she is not feeling well'. However, a little while later, Fatima came defiantly into the room. Her face was covered with bruises. 'Um 'Ali complained about Fatima's 'improper' behaviour: 'This is what she gets if she threatens to run away from home!' 'Um 'Ali was pointing at Fatima's face. Fatima was dissolving into tears, but was apparently determined to speak out about some of her grievances. This was the only time she could say something about herself. She said:

> I am not crying because I am going to lose Ali to another woman. I have never had him. I have had enough of this life. A life that has never treated me as human being. I would rather die than being treated worse than an animal. I have nothing to lose. My children are not mine. They are hers [she pointed at her mother in law]. What is on my face today [she raised her face to me] is what I get if I say a word in this house. Because of this problem or any other, I always get beaten, for any simple reason. I do not want this life ...

Fatima was obviously a victim of a two-fold form domestic violence. She was a victim of violence by her husband since this kind of violence against women typically increases in conjunction with economic hardship that threatens or destabilizes the male's traditional role as breadwinner.[10] But her case also involved another type of violence, as it was obvious that 'Um-'Ali had been implicated in the pattern of the physical violence and/or mental abuse against her daughter-in-law.

Fatima's case symbolizes the stake of women in the patriarchal gender-based violence against other women. It is argued that, in many cases, as long as women who are living within the system of patriarchy, do not challenge the patriarchal structures, they too might become implicated in it, particularly in violence against women.[11] In these circumstances, women may find more power by manipulating the system and gaining power both from and for the system.

In Iraq, this is particularly emphasized in relationships between young and older women, typically in the relation between wife and mother-in-law. Most importantly, this behaviour is linked to poverty since it is often observed within poor and low educated segments of the Iraqi society. It is explained that, within a woman's life cycle, an older woman who might have been oppressed at some time in her youth may think that she has arrived in a position where she has power to oppress another woman. Indeed, 'Um 'Ali's suppressive behaviour against Fatima also reflected the increasing incidence of older women's stake in the system of domination, especially with the diminishing of other economic choices available to young families.

It is believed that, under the increased economic insecurity, the Iraqi society has been witnessing a resurgence of this and other forms of domestic violence against women. However, this kind of violence is typically conceived as an intimate family mater, thus, little is known about it.

Honour Crimes

It appears that the concept of 'honour' often acquires a very special place in Middle Eastern societies.[12] In the specific case of Iraq, the concept of 'honour' seems to have a substantial role in the lives of both men and women. Many men see women as the weak link in the chain that threatens a family's dignity. To safeguard a family's honour, male kin believe they must keep a close watch on their female relatives, and do so through a strict and careful monitoring of the activities of female relatives.

In Iraq, fear of scandal occupies a major place in people's lives; hence upholding the honour of the family and protecting it from rumour is a vital responsibility. A woman's sexual contact outside marriage is considered the worst that could ever happen to injure her family's reputation. This attitude originated particularly from Bedouin tradition, according which, a woman who 'violated her honour', violated the honour of her kin, and thus deserved to die. Honour crimes always mean killing the woman for the 'crime of adultery'.[13] The killing of a female accused of an honour crime often happens secretly, but within the intimate circle of the family.[14] There are many instances where a woman is killed simply on suspicion of having committed adultery, and before any facts have been established or a medical testimony obtained. Because there are many restrictions surrounding this issue, there is no official data about victims of this crime. Nevertheless, every Iraqi woman knows the fearsome consequences of an 'unofficial' affair.

After a long period of being outlawed and punished according to law,[15] the tribal practice of killing women for 'honour crimes', or illicit sexual relations was reinforced and legitimated by Saddam Hussain's regime, prior to the Gulf Crisis of 1990.[16] The supporting legislation was promulgated in the context of the regime's efforts to gain the support of Iraq's tribal leaders and religious fundamentalists, in preparation for Saddam's next aggression against another neighbouring country, the invasion of Kuwait. In 2002, an assessment of the situation in Iraq carried out by the UN Commission on Human Rights noted that there had been a resurgence of the practice during the 1990s. It was reported that since the passage of the law, an estimated 4,000 women and girls had been victims of 'honour killings'.[17]

The Centralized Form of Violence against Women

The Saddam regime's record of human rights abuses against his political opponents, both men and women, is widely known. However, the point at issue addresses another form of centralized violence against Iraqi women – namely the killing of a large number of women allegedly accused by the regime of prostitution and/or soliciting.

Prostitution and pimping is illegal in Iraq. A decree issued by the Revolutionary Command Council (RCC) in 1988 stipulated that those who managed, pimped, or solicited for prostitution were to be punished by a maximum of seven years in prison.[18] In 1993 the RCC issued a new decree through which the government instituted the death penalty for pimping, soliciting, and many related categories.[19] There appear to be no statistics or sources of data about the number of people prosecuted or sentenced for this crime. Although this issue was mentioned briefly in many reports on the humanitarian conditions of the Iraqi people under sanctions, it was impossible to find precise data anywhere.

There were many incidents where respondents' concerns and worries were expressed with great caution that many Iraqi women have been driven by the great need for basic items such as food and medicine to concede the notion of honour and shame. However, it was evident that prostitution had become quite visible in Iraqi society during the years of sanctions. The phenomenon of pimping and brothels has always existed in Iraq but during the 1970s, it was extremely difficult to see a woman trying openly to sell sex in Baghdad or in other parts of Iraq. Prostitution was always restricted to designated places, either in the suburbs or in specific district in the cities. Apart from a very few specified locations, which were mostly either commercial areas or apartment buildings usually occupied by single men and inadequate for families, this particular 'business' was forbidden in residential areas.

However, in line with the deteriorated aspects of life under sanctions, this phenomenon also underwent some important changes. Prostitution and pimping became a widespread occurrence during the years of sanctions. Many luxurious villas and houses, mostly located in the finest residential areas of Baghdad city, were designated for leisure and sexual entertainment for men who could afford to buy these services. Rumours spread about the powerful men and women who managed these services, and who had direct connections to the upper echelons among the political elites.

In addition to the luxurious sex services, the intensifying conditions of pauperization were to be seen in relation to women who were forced to take up humiliating ways of earning money around the streets of Baghdad. The most familiar and shocking sight, however, was the increasing numbers of young women, hidden in the anonymity of the *abaya* (the traditional black garment enveloping the entire body) and begging at street corners. Indeed, degrading ways of earning income become the only option for many young women who had to provide for themselves and their families. For some other people, both men and women, the circumstances of sanctions made sex services as one of the few, and most lucrative options.

However, what happened on one morning in November 2000 may shed light on this phenomenon and the way in which it was tackled by the government. In one of the fine neighbourhoods in Baghdad, two women who were occupying two luxurious, newly-refurbished villas were executed in front of their houses. As noted earlier, as a result of the economic collapse, and the mounting pressure for cash, many Iraqis sold their expensive houses and either moved to smaller and cheaper areas or migrated to villages or home towns, or left the country altogether. Often, the new buyers were war/sanctions profiteers, political elites, merchants, and pimps. These two villas had been sold in the mid-1990s to new occupants who just happened to be organizers of prostitution and their women.

The closest neighbours were greatly disturbed every evening by parties that usually ended only in the early hours next day. However, apart from complaining to each other, nobody from the neighbourhood dared voice an official complaint about the situation. Everybody was terrified, but people were afraid to protest, even verbally, to these women or their visitors. The neighbours were sure that the women were strongly supported by various high-ranking officials or their sons, who were the prime beneficiaries of these luxurious sex services (and who had evidently been seen and were known by name).

On that morning, the whole neighbourhood was shocked by the news that two of the women were being publicly executed (beheaded). Nobody knew what had happened or why these executions had taken place in such a way. That day, all the neighbouring households were busy speculating, but at the same time everybody was in a state of shock. One respondent said:

This incident left the entire neighbourhood but particularly those who had witnessed the 'ceremony', in a shocked state. Some of the closest neighbours had seen the killing with their children because the incident had occurred at the time when many children were on their way to school.

Some days later, rumours had spread all over the country. Many people across the central and southern parts of Iraq had experienced similar horrors, since executions of a large number of prostitutes, pimps and agents, rumoured to number around 360 women and men had taken place in different locations that day. Later, in its 2003 report on human rights practices, the Bureau of Democracy, Human Rights and Labour (2004) said that Iraq's security forces had allegedly beheaded at least 130 women between June 2000 and April 2001, along with an additional number of men suspected of facilitating prostitution in November 2000. It stated: 'Security agents decapitated numerous women and men in front of their family members'.[20] According to Amnesty International (cited in the Bureau's Report on Human Rights, 2004), the victim's heads were displayed in front of their homes for several days.

Many Iraqi people saw this action as a desperate attempt by the government to demonstrate that it was still capable of maintaining a strong hold on society, especially its control over women. There is also no doubt that the action was an attempt by the government to gain the favour and support of the tribal and religious groups which were increasingly coming to the forefront of official politics in Iraq during the years of sanctions.

The action was allegedly motivated by the 'morals' of the Ba'th, according to claims by the Iraqi dictator.[21] However, whatever the motivation behind this action might have been, the killing left damaging scars on every Iraqi woman, and must have been particularly terrifying for those who might have engaged in prostitution out of despair and those who had no chance of stopping the injustices imposed on them.

Street Violence

Reports by the United Nations and other independent bodies about the humanitarian impact of the sanctions on Iraq's civilian population indicated increasing rates of crime in the Iraqi society under sanctions. Gangs of demobilized men roamed the street and many women were robbed raped, and murdered.[22] Iraqi women expressed great anxiety and often referred to the lawless situation with fear and distress. Manal, aged 23, who was a university student, said:

> After two young girls disappeared from my neighbourhood, my family and I no longer trust anybody. I travel to the university in a taxi, which I share with three female colleagues. If something happens so that the driver is not able to come to collect us, we stay in the university building until a male member from one or other of our families arrives to pick us up. On one occasion, the taxi driver didn't come and we were stuck inside the university building for hours. The telephones weren't working. We waited three hours till my brother arrived to fetch us.

Iraqi women also expressed fear and apprehension about their safety outside the house. They spoke about the phenomenon of female abduction, which had become a nightmare for every young woman in Iraq. Now, in an unprecedented development, women in public had always to show that they were there for a specific purpose and were not just out for a walk or wandering about, and it was also very unusual to see women outside their houses after nightfall.

Remembering how things were in the 1970s, it was extraordinary to observe the extremely dangerous and restrictive conditions of women in Iraq at the onset of the twenty-first century. One respondent explained her personal experiences in terms of these two periods. Batuol (aged 53, from Area III) was a social scientist and lecturer at Baghdad University. She had once been a victim of theft. It is interesting to quote her statement at length.

> If you had asked me twenty years ago about how I envisaged the conditions of Iraqi women at the onset of the twenty-first century, I would have given you a very bright and positive picture of them, a picture that it is difficult even to speak about now. Iraqi women are strong and willing to learn, and are open to life. I had no idea that we would be victimized in the way that we are now. Nowadays Iraqi women are victims of all kind of physical and psychological harassment. During the 1970s, we [women like her] were the elite women in Iraq. We studied at the universities side-by-side with men colleagues, and went out to work on an equal footing with men, but we were never subjected to the types of harassment that most of us are suffering from today. As the elite, we were aware; we had to cope with people who were not used to seeing women everywhere, participating in public life outside their homes. We believed that we were paving the way for our children, for our daughters, who would be grateful to the pioneers. Now, I feel that we are living in terrifying conditions

that are awful for all of us. Iraqi women are now living in fear for their lives and their security all the time, even when a woman is inside her home. The situation is especially dangerous for women who are fighting to keep pace with life or those who are under pressure to work outside the home. Rape, abduction, theft, and all forms of physical and psychological harassment have become common features in our society today. It's hardly surprising that economic deprivation and impoverishment have caused such wide-scale social distortion. The Iraqi society today is a masterpiece produced by the United Nations sanctions ... It's true that the whole society is suffering, but it is women who are the prime victims.

Women spoke of many incidences of violent thefts and young girls being kidnapped from the doorsteps of their homes. Suha, a political science student at Baghdad University, referred to an accident suffered by a female friend who had been the victim of such crime. She said:

In daylight, as my friend was arriving at her home by car, two masked men leapt in front of her car and ordered her to leave the car keys. When she resisted, the two men jumped inside the car, pushed her to the other seat and drove off. Three hundred metres further on, the men pushed her out of the car while it was being driven at speed. She suffered severe injuries and many broken bones, and was psychologically traumatized. She still hasn't recovered since the accident. She gave up the university and refuses to go one step outside her home.

Obviously, whether or not Iraqi women increasingly become direct victims of gender-based violence under sanctions, the denial of socio-economic rights for the majority of the population and for women in particular, left Iraqi women vulnerable to violence, harassment, intimidation, and economic dependence in their daily lives, inside and outside the family.

Opting for the Veil
Fear about the harassment that all young women risked encountering outside the home was reflected in the way they moved around and the sort of outfits they wore in public. Large numbers of young Iraqi women had either resorted to veiling, or alternatively wore shapeless garments and covered their heads with scarves. Alia (aged 24, from Area II) was a university graduate. She emphasized the psychological impact of the situation on Iraqi women:

Our lives have changed dramatically since the 1990s. Previously, Iraqi people used to sit outside in the gardens of their houses after sunset. I remember those nice times when we used to eat dinner and watch television in our front garden every day. We often entertained our guests in the garden as well. Now, this is impossible. Today, the only people who enjoy life in Iraq are those who have

enough money to be able to afford to hire private guards to stand outside the
doors of their houses. We, the poor, the majority, and especially women are now
spending our lives inside, behind closed doors. I feel as though I am in prison.

Over the course of one year between the phases of this empirical work, it was striking
how many respondents had changed their outfits to Islamic dress or wore a veil. Many
of them were young women who were also students. Nazik (aged 28) who worked at
the library of Al- Mustanseriya University, was one of them. About her new outfit,
she said:

> Nobody pressured me to cover my head, but I realized it was much more
> reassuring to appear in public with my hair covered and wearing long dresses.
> Last Ramadan, we agreed at work to cover our heads just for the month. I felt
> much freer when I was covered, which made me decide to keep my scarf. Other
> colleagues removed theirs.

Indeed, the issue of the Islamic dress and veil also involves personal choice as well as
an increased tendency among people generally to shift towards attitudes that are more
religious; on the part of women, this is seen in the adoption of an Islamic outfit.
However, it also seemed that Iraqi women intended to benefit by complying with the
demands of some of the society's more traditional or religious groups and taking up
the wearing of Islamic outfits. Through such compromises, Iraqi women were trying
to secure the real stakes they had in their lives within their families, communities,
and social and economic contexts. Apparently, many women might have had much
to lose if they failed to comply with this practice.

Obviously, by wearing an Islamic outfit or veil, Iraqi women were complying not
only because of potential male control or the existence of threats and risks to their
mobility if they failed to cover their heads (veil), but probably because there were also
some religious elements of this practice that women did genuinely want. This was
especially encouraged by the increased religious tendency in Iraqi society during
sanctions.

Women's Domestic Responsibility

Food Supply Responsibilities

The 'traditional' role of women in the Iraqi society confines them to domestic
responsibilities and nurturing the family. Many Iraqi studies on the impact of
industrial development on Iraqi women's roles and responsibilities during the 1970s
and 1980s stressed that even working women had to shoulder the full burden of
domestic responsibilities.

However, the wide scale destruction of Iraq's infrastructure (such as water supplies,
sanitation, electricity and fuel shortages) as a result of wars and sanctions created extra
domestic responsibilities for Iraqi women. Before sanctions and the Gulf War of
1991, almost all urban dwellers and 72 percent of rural residents had access to clean
water.[23] Iraq used to have supplies of pure water that satisfied the needs of over 90

percent of the population in Central and Southern Iraq, based on a network of 200 water treatment plans for urban areas, and around 1,200 small treatment plants in rural areas.[24] During the 1970s, Iraq had also built a modern sanitation and sewage disposal system that covered all major cities and most of the rural areas.

Since the early days of the 1991 Gulf war, and after more than 13 years of sanctions, water and electricity supplies to most Iraqi households, as well as sewage disposal, had still not been restored to their pre-crisis condition. UNICEF confirmed this in 2002, and reported that 'raw sewage was discharged into the river with no or minimal treatment'.[25] The destruction of electrical generating systems resulted in the total paralyzes of the water purification and supply network. Despite the gradual post-war restoration of electricity, most water pumping and water treatment facilities remained inoperable or function on a very irregular basis. This is because the electricity sector was also severely affected by the large number of contracts that were put on hold by the Sanctions Committee, which prevented the minimum rehabilitation of the sector.[26] In this way, the upgrading of the water and electricity sectors was also hindered because of lack of production of chemicals and spare parts, while importation of these was impossible.[27]

The deterioration in the water sector was mostly evident in the decreasing quantity and quality of potable water and inadequate sanitation for the population as a whole. This situation also contributed to a sharp increase in the incidence of water-born diseases throughout Iraq. Respondents from the poor areas in Baghdad City (Areas I and II) in particular, complained frequently about the water supply. Because piped water supplies were disrupted and erratic, fetching water from sources (usually big tanker lorries) outside their homes became an added responsibility for women in poor neighbourhoods, who had to carry large water containers and stand in line for hours before struggling to carry them back home.

Obtaining subsidized foods was another worrying responsibility for women in the poorest neighbourhoods in Baghdad City. It was a common scene to see huge crowds of men and women pushing and shoving in order to buy one or two subsidized chickens, or a kilo of powdered milk.[28]

While men were expected to go out to earn a living, women were left entirely responsible for the household and the children. However, single mothers had to bear the burden of both tasks. The deterioration in living conditions under sanctions placed another major responsibility on Iraqi single mothers. Women had to take on the task of receiving the family's food rations and planning so these would last for a whole month. They also had to be aware of market prices and what were the available cheapest foodstuffs. Many respondents 'proudly' said that they had cut meat items out of their daily or weekly food shopping, because they could not afford it. However, the prices of food, including other foodstuffs such as vegetables, fruit, grains and wheat, fluctuated constantly. In the food markets, one could observe the incredulous expressions on the faces of both men and women, as they stopped in front of food shops to look at the food or simply to ask about the prices, and then went on their way. There were many instances where women confronted the shopkeepers about the prices of foodstuffs. One woman complained agitatedly in a grocery shop, looking randomly at people's faces: 'This is unfair. How can they do this to us? I cannot manage. Can you? God, what shall I do? What to buy? The prices are going up in flames'. In the end, she bought a few onions and went muttering out of the shop.

Permanent Stress and Fatigue

There is also another dimension of the amount of pressure on Iraqi women due to the abnormal economic situation under sanctions. Women are traditionally expected to pick up the pieces when men are physically or/and psychologically unfit. Iraqi men, traumatized by wars and sanctions, found themselves unemployed or able only to generate unstable and scarce incomes. In such circumstances, women were expected to be at home to cope with the frustration, distress, and anger of their men folk. However, although women were counted on to manage the burden of domestic responsibilities, it was not possible for them to obtain any sort of practical or psychological help or support.

While men were expected to go out to earn a living, women were left entirely responsible for the household and the children. However, single mothers had to bear the burden of both tasks. Certain aspects of the lives of Iraqi women who became the breadwinners under sanctions are explored in the previous chapters of this book, but their deepening impoverishment was not limited to a single case or some few cases. These women were driven by poverty into begging. It was a common sight to see women, on their own or with their infants, begging in the streets. It would have been extremely difficult to count the numbers of pale malnourished Iraqi women wrapped in their rusty black *abayas* wandering under the harsh sun amongst the traffic, either begging and/or selling petty items. This is an unprecedented phenomenon in Iraq, never seen before sanctions. Denis Halliday, the UN Humanitarian Coordinator, who resigned in 1999 in protest about the OFF programme, on the poverty scenes under sanctions commented:

> In 1998, I used to bring food rather than money for children at stop light on my way home in the evenings so that the children involved, some so small they could not be seen below the car window, would get something to eat. Iraqi drivers and people walking past often were angered by the scene of children begging from a foreigner.[29]

The research survey revealed that more than 70 per cent of respondents had incurred debts from loans, having already sold possessions such as gold and other household items. Many single breadwinners had nothing to sell except their basic food – the food rations. In economic terms, when people from the middle income class and educated people turned into petty vendors, and when they got to the point where they sold their property and even the doors of their houses, it was apparent they were approaching the famine stage.[30]

A study of households headed by women revealed more disturbing scenes of life under sanctions. Such women had to endure additional responsibilities which were more than most of them could tolerate. Amina (aged 40 and the mother of three children) had lost her husband during the 1991 Gulf War. She complained of stress and permanent fatigue because of having to work so hard both inside and outside her home to provide for her three children. Even though she was living in a state housing area, under sanctions the collapse of her income as a laboratory assistant (from US$290 in 1989 to US$2 in 2001) meant it was not sufficient to cover even the most basic necessities. This meant, therefore, that she had to take a second job, working evening and night shifts in a pharmacy located in the neighbourhood.

Wafah (aged 42, from Area I) was a single breadwinner, living in a one-roomed house with her four children, the oldest of whom was a daughter aged 15. Wafah was employed as part time domestic at a hospital in the Baghdad area, and in addition to her work at the hospital, she travelled for more than two hours each way to work as a housekeeper. She described her situation:

> Every day when I get home, I am so exhausted that I don't even have the energy to eat. I just want to reach my bed and stretch out my suffering body and my troubled mind. However, I often experience sleepless nights. Being in bed is not the cure for what is troubling my mind. When everything falls silent, I am still awake thinking of my children, their future, and what their lives will be like if I die. This whirlpool of thoughts is taking the last drop of my energy. Before I close my eyes I know that my children will be looked after by God.

These women experienced the full impact of collapsing living standards and of Iraq's welfare state under sanctions. Most were under tremendous psychological pressure, and were living with their children below the poverty line and although most were far too proud even to complain, it was not difficult to recognize their depression and anxiety.

Health Responsibilities

The survey reveals that, regardless of their ages, education, and social backgrounds, respondents were expressing frustration about some of their basic needs,[31] and that lack of fulfilment of some essential basic needs had led to a deep sense of insecurity for many of the surveyed women, manifested in a permanent increase of tension both physical and inside the family. In general, the lack of basic essentials of life caused high levels of stress resulting from the inability of people to act upon their circumstances to remove or mitigate the source of such tensions.

Almost 95 percent of the sample complained of stress, depression, anxiety, insomnia, and health problems such as irregular menstruation, severe headaches, and high blood pressure. Young women aged between 20 and 29 years who were highly anxious, experienced the highest levels of tension caused by mounting social constraints and the unsatisfactory fulfilment of their basic needs. Most of these women, too, had to put up with the anxiety and fear of being 'wrongly' perceived by other people including their fellow women (colleagues) and their own families. Moreover, the decline of any adequate intervention by the state into their lives was reproduced through the deteriorating status of women as autonomous beings, and was reflected in women's perceptions of themselves as 'weak', 'helpless', 'tired', 'scared', 'ill', 'hopeless', 'worthless', etc.

Responsibility for the health and well-being of their children was another grim aspect of the impact of sanctions on Iraqi women. One of the most prominent and widespread effects of sanctions on Iraq was probably the collapse of Iraq's well-established public health and health intervention systems.[32]

Several official reports and professional studies reveal that during the 1970s and 1980s, Iraq's health system was heavily subsidized by the state and was oriented toward sophisticated curative care.[33] The people of Iraq, especially those who lived in urban areas, enjoyed beneficial health services, potable water, adequate nutritional foods, and a good standard of public health education. The government's policy during this period favoured population growth, which implied strategies to achieve a limiting of family planning and abortion. Driven by this aim, the state promoted programmes that were aimed at reducing mortality among infants and young children. These involved better vaccination coverage, promotion of breast-feeding, reduction of diarrhoeal morbidity, and improvements in domestic hygiene. UNICEF confirmed that Iraq's health policy promoted reproductive health through advances in antenatal and delivery services, particularly in relation to midwives, nurses and birth attendants.[34]

Specialists in public health emphasized that, because Iraq's health system, including medical services and medicine, was one of the most heavily subsidized sectors prior to sanctions, less attention had been given towards building the skills need to facilitate efficient reorganization or regulating decision-making in the system[35] Observations by the United Nations and other independent sources show that the sharp decline in the health condition of the Iraqi population had begun by August 1990. People began to suffer from an unprecedented decline in nutritional status, as well as from inadequate water supplies (in both quantity and quality), appalling sanitation, and falling immunization levels. The breakdown of health services during the sanctions era led to a huge increase in diseases that previously had been easily treated.[36] In fact, the deterioration of health conditions in Iraq happened concurrently with hyperinflation, stagnant salaries, a lack of medicines and medical equipment, deteriorating nutritional status, and other disturbing aspects of life under sanctions.

Images of sick and dying children with their mothers in Iraqi hospitals are well documented and well known to everyone. Information on child mortality, based on hospital records from the Iraqi Ministry of Health, proved that sanctions had claimed the lives of more than a million Iraqi children since 1993, although independent statistics and research on this issue allege serious methodological problems with the mortality data. Garfield argues, on the other hand, that not all the deaths from certain well-known illnesses were related to sanctions.[37] He also suggests that the mortality rates based on hospital records were not comprehensive because;

The deterioration in the condition of hospitals in Iraq due to the embargo meant that many people no longer went to hospitals, or went for only brief periods. Finding no treatments, they returned home to die in far greater numbers than before sanctions were imposed.[38]

Even so, the hospitals of Iraq displayed the effects of the sanctions at their most tragic. Due to the lack of adequate diagnostic and laboratory equipment, many hospital-based deaths were listed under 'unknown causes'.[39] The hospitals' databases were described as follows:

> Most hospital data systems are in disarray, with clinical notes written on odd scraps of paper or old patient charts. Most hospital statistical offices no longer generate routine reports and few of their computers still work. Though the Oil-for-Food Programme began to re-supply the system in 1998, little improvement has resulted, and many hospital-based deaths still go unrecorded or misdiagnosed.[40]

A joint survey by UNICEF and Iraq's Ministry of Health estimated that during the period from 1990 to 1997, around 500,000 children under five had died.[41] More cautious studies by foreign researchers also showed horrific rises in infant mortality, malnutrition and disease. Analysis from a health survey conducted by Garfield found that at least 227,000 children aged under five had died between 1991 and 1996 as a result of the Gulf war and sanctions.[42] This means that in the first eight months of 1990, there were 40 deaths per thousand among children under five years of age, while the corresponding number had increased to 60 deaths per thousand in the first quarter of 1998.[43]

Unprecedented and devastating scenes became common in Iraq under sanctions. Iraqi women sat openly in the streets, with their tiny malnourished children lying quietly in their laps, begging for the fees of a private physician and medicines for their desperately ill children. These sights of mothers with dying children were evidence of many tragic tales. Such people usually came from other city suburbs to wait for a chance to see one of the private doctors who were mostly based in Baghdad City.

As far as pregnant women and women giving birth for the first time are concerned, it is believed that malnutrition played a significant role in the high rates of low-weight births and high rates of embryo mortality.[44] The World Health Organization (WHO) reported that malnutrition among pregnant women was the major cause of pregnancy-related morbidities and low weight infants, and had increased dramatically since 1990.[45] The WHO also warned that many caesarean operations were performed with a minimum of anaesthetics because of the lack of medicines,[46] and called for international awareness of the health conditions of Iraqi women and children under sanctions.

> Severe economic hardship, semi-starvation diets, high levels of disease, scarcity of essential drugs and, above all, the psycho-social trauma and anguish of a black future, have led to numerous families being broken up, leading to

distortions of social norms. The impact of this unfortunate situation on the infant and child population in particular in Iraq needs special attention. It is not only the data on morbidity and mortality that tell the story but equally important are the crippling effects of many of these morbidities, which are often forgotten. This tragic aspect of the impact of the war and sanctions ... is rarely articulated but the world community should seriously consider the implications of an entire generation of children growing up with such traumatized mental handicaps if, of course, they survive at all.[47]

Long term food deficiency and the absence of good medical care left many women and their infants, especially from poor and limited income groups, at great risk from chronic diseases. A UNICEF survey of infant and maternal mortality revealed that lack of adequate antenatal care had resulted in the doubling of neonatal mortality rates.[48] The survey also calculated that during the 1990s, female-headed households, rural areas, and poor households had the highest rates of infant and child mortality. In addition it revealed the dramatic rise in mortality among females in the age group 5 to 49, and in the mortality rates among mothers during delivery.[49] In 1989, mortality of mothers during labour was rated at 1.5 percent (or 68 women) of total mortality of women in the age group 5 to 49. In 1999, the rate had increased to 30.7 percent (or 876 women) of total mortality among women in the same age group. Bleeding, ectopic pregnancies and prolonged labour were found to be among the main causes of the rise in maternal mortality.[50] The high rate of miscarriages was attributed partly to poverty and poor nutrition and partly to stress and exposure to chemical contaminants.[51]

Samira, a senior gynaecologist at the Obstetrical and Paediatric Department at the City Hospital (the biggest hospital in Baghdad), emphasized that 95 percent of pregnant women were anaemic because of malnutrition and noted that due to the malnutrition status of many Iraqi women, especially during the first six years after the imposition of sanctions, very few infants had been exclusively breast fed. According to a UN Population Fund survey of the high rates of maternal and infant mortality, the number of Iraqi women who died in pregnancy and childbirth almost tripled between 1999 and 2002.[52]

On the level of the surveyed women, many had suffered the death of a child or the birth of deformed child. Suhad (aged 36), a housewife and a mother of two children, had lost a baby before it was born. She said:

I'm lucky I'm still alive. I was about to die when I was pregnant with my third child. I used to have antenatal tests at the obstetric department of the hospital during my previous pregnancies, but during my third pregnancy, I tried to avoid going to the hospital because I heard horrible things about conditions there. However, my pregnancy went well until I realized that I had passed my time, and that I had had a high fever for three days. I went to the hospital, but the ultrasound machine was not working. The midwife looked at me briefly and decided that I should wait at home because there was no empty place for me at the hospital. She said I wasn't due yet. The next day at home I became unconscious. My husband took me to the hospital. My situation was very dangerous because the child had been dead inside me for over a week. My blood was poisoned.

Conclusion

In times of political and economic crisis women, regardless of their social and educational background, become subject to male institutionalized power. With little or no power at their disposal, Iraqi women became extremely vulnerable to all forms of patriarchal control, and their dependency on male guardians increased. Sanctions curtailed their rights and freedom by strengthening social attitudes that described women as 'weak' and 'dependent' and in need of male protection. The psychological being of women was significantly affected by the worsening aspects of the situation, which was demonstrated in an increase in all forms of violence against women, including domestic, public and state-induced violence. The impact of this situation was reflected on women's health in forms of depression, anxiety and other health problems.

The implications of these conditions were grave, especially for single women who were breadwinners. These women were not only deprived of material resources, but were also subjected to tremendous pressure by the lack of social (family and community) and medical support. In general, women's domestic responsibilities doubled, but it was especially difficult to quantify the frustration of single breadwinner women who were obliged to contend with the difficulties of life under circumstances marked by the almost total collapse of food, health, and social security.

Educated women, both students and professionals, constituted another group that was significantly affected by the economic and social disorder. These women in particular were exposed to higher risks of psychological pressure than housewives. The fact that they were obliged to be outside their homes on a daily basis obviously exposed them directly to different, and much more dangerous, types of pressure. As a consequence, many women left their jobs or their education, either out of fear or in an attempt to minimise the risks of harassment and violence in public places. In the same context, large numbers of young women resorted to Islamic dress (wearing *hijab* or headscarf), partly as an attempt to access an otherwise women-unfriendly public space. However, it is believed that increased veiling was also intended to demonstrate a more religious attitude among young women. Religious and veiling practices achieved an unprecedented popularity and encouragement from society and were in effect mandated by the state under sanctions.

The societal consequences of the sanctions were, and remain, multi-generational. Not only was the fabric of Iraqi society affected, but thousands of people, mainly young children, pregnant women, and the chronically ill and elderly, were also affected daily because of the sanctions. The collapse of public health and medical services led to high maternal and infant mortality, malnutrition, and the re-emergence of certain communicable diseases. The erratic supply of water and electricity significantly weakened health care systems and turned hospitals into extremely hazardous environments, not only for patients but also for health workers, the majority of whom were women. Because of the deterioration in health and sanitation systems in hospitals, many Iraqi women were giving birth at home, often with meagre medical facilities.

Thus, the UN's sanctions injured the very same people it claimed to help, but the suffering of the weakest – women and children – under these measures was unique.

7

CONCLUSION

International Sanctions: The New World Order

Sanctions in Iraq came within the context of 'countermeasures' in international law, whose objective is, by definition, to inflict punishment on the state that violates its international responsibilities, or to secure performance of a state with international responsibilities.[1] According to international law, Iraq's invasion and annexation of Kuwait in August 1990 constituted an international wrongful act; thus Iraq was held responsible for, and found guilty of, violating the primary rules of its international obligations. Moreover, not only was the invasion of Kuwait a breach of Iraq's international obligations, but more importantly its aggression against Kuwait was considered an offence against the whole international community.[2]

However, it must be noted that 'countermeasures' are on no account to be understood as measures that must necessarily involve the use of armed force.[3] They involve either economic sanctions or the use of armed force, or both. These measures are only to be authorized by the Security Council when it deems that the wrongful act of a state is a threat to international peace and security.[4]

When dealing with aggressors and others who violate fundamental principles of international law, sanctions as a prominent tool of international relations can be employed by the United Nations as an alternative to coercion through military force.[5] Significantly, the main subject of sanctions, as confirmed by the UN Law Commission, has always been the 'State', rather than other entities such as societies, groups, and individuals. Accordingly, the principal rights of a State suffering sanctions, such as its territorial integrity, sovereignty and independence, must be respected at all times, regardless of any claimed justification.[6]

Since 1990, the Security Council has imposed 14 cases of sanctions for various reasons and purposes.[7] Obviously, the end of the Cold War era in the 1990s signalled the end of a stalemated Security Council and created a climate within the Security Council in which comprehensive and partial sanctions became a viable policy option. The fall of the Soviet Union and the emergence of the United States as the only superpower marked the changing international geopolitical environment. Some argue that geopolitical sanctions had become more attractive because they allowed countries with quite different foreign polices an opportunity to forge shared responses to crises about which they might otherwise have disagreed.[8] The breakthrough in the impasse between the superpowers opened up the potential for the Security Council to deploy 'swift' punishment against those whom it deemed 'guilty'.

After the end of the Cold War, many diplomats, scholars, politicians, and citizens believed that economic sanctions were innovative, benign and non-violent. Others thought that economic sanctions offered an ethical foreign policy tool to combat threats to peace and security without causing unintended suffering. In general, either overridden by political motives or simply lacking sufficient knowledge about sanctions, the pro-sanctions constituencies assumed that the imposition of sanctions was a better alternative to the use of military force (war), an assumption based on the idea that economic coercion would have sufficient 'teeth' to impel citizens in the targeted country to exert political pressure to force either a change in the behaviour of the authorities or their removal together.[9]

International policymakers in particular often try to project economic sanctions as a more humane political instrument than military force, even though people's experience of sanctions frequently reveals that sanctions have little to do with humanitarian values. As has emerged from a variety of studies, this tendency has involved empirical generalization 'in favour' of sanctions, particularly evident from the case of South Africa.[10] Such generalizations have also provided opportunities for policymakers to debate expectations about which sanctions are awaiting outcomes – avoiding any debate about the acute civilian suffering from the economic sanctions in the target country – before acknowledging why they wait as long as they do to achieve any political gain. In other words, policymakers' debates are often driven by the notion of 'success', whereas policy analysts, paradoxically, appear not to be very confident about judging the success of sanctions. This has been clearly demonstrated by prominent analysts of sanctions policy who have expressed some doubt about the 'success' or 'effectiveness' of sanctions.[11]

Iraq: A Unique Target for Sanctions

A close look in the history of UN sanctions since 1945 reveals that specific vulnerability of the target was obviously the major factor influencing the choice of the comprehensive economic sanctions.[12] Scholars in the field emphasize that the efficiency of economic sanctions is determined by two crucial factors: the level of the target's economic strength, and the extent of the target's integration into the world economy.

This explains, for example, why South Africa was never subjected to comprehensive mandatory economic sanctions, in spite of the apartheid policy of destabilising its neighbouring states, occupying Namibia, and perpetuating the apartheid system within its own borders. South Africa had considerable built-in strengths, including a wealth of resources, a good infrastructure, and a potentially dominant position in the region.[13] Most importantly, it also had strong economic ties with western countries, particularly with the European Community, the United States, and Canada. Western countries imported extensively from South Africa, especially uranium, gold, iron, coal, steel, and agricultural products, as well as investing hugely in South Africa. These interests were behind the 'soft' and 'hesitant' will of the western states to impose mandatory comprehensive sanctions on South Africa. In 1977 the UN imposed the embargo on arms exports to South Africa, and in 1984 placed a voluntary ban on imports from South Africa; however, due to vetoes by the United States, France, and Britain, sanctions became more or less 'voluntary' measures taken by some states, businesses and institutions.[14]

In the same context, policymakers favoured the use of sanctions because of their low domestic cost and low risk of lost credibility in case of failure, as compared with the 'overall' high destructive cost of sanctions on the target state. These are some of the factors that have made sanctions an increasingly attractive alternative to the use of armed force.

The Iraq case of sanctions is unique. Exposed to the hardest set of sanctions ever employed by the UN in its whole history, Iraq was subjected to comprehensive multilateral sanctions: an arms embargo; economic sanctions including a complete ban on all imports and exports except for humanitarian purposes; commercial and financial sanctions; diplomatic sanctions; sport sanctions; and culture sanctions.

Iraq was also an 'ideal' target for this type of sanctions.[15] In an attempt to examine the economic statecraft of sanctions, Baldwin defines economic sanctions as 'a governmental technique relying primarily on resources that have a reasonable appearance of a market in terms of money'.[16] This may explain why Iraq was considered right for comprehensive economic sanctions. The fact that Iraq was dependent on foreign trade of a single product (oil) as a source of exchange earning, and that 75 percent of Iraq's foodstuffs were imported from abroad, meant disaster if these markets were lost. Additionally, Iraq's economy prior to the 1990 Gulf crisis had also been suffering from devastation and heavy debts resulting from the eight years war with Iran. Thus the state of Iraq's economy indeed corresponded to the main goal of imposing economic sanctions (i.e., to 'inflict serious deprivation on the target with severe punitive and coercive intent',[17] since such a goal could only be reached 'effectively' if the target's economy was weak. Iraq met the criteria. In 1989, revenues from the sale of oil had accounted for 61 percent of its Gross Domestic Product (GDP) and over 95 percent of its foreign currency earnings.[18] By 1991, real GDP had fallen by 75 percent and was estimated to equal that of the 1940s.[19]

In an open economy such as Iraq's, foreign trade plays a vital role in shaping economic and social outcomes, including, but not limited to, economic growths, levels of public and private consumption, economic diversification, technology and research and development, social services, health care and welfare, etc. However, against the scale of devastation that befell Iraq's economy due to sanctions, the oil embargo caused no significant consequences on the international oil market. Apart from a short period of oil price increases, the oil market was quickly restored to previous levels in terms of both prices and supplies.

Moreover, there were no substantial costs to the 'sanctions-imposing' states in terms of losing market share or foreign investments.[20] Notably, and with the exception of problems that emerged due to Iraq's delay in repaying the huge foreign debt owed to many countries, no essential western interests were adversely affected by the sanctions against Iraq. In any event, Iraq's subsequent government(s) will remain obliged to repay Iraq's debts to other countries, enterprises and individuals, naturally at exorbitant interest rates and of course to their advantage.

The Sanctions on Iraq: The Political Failure

The painful case of sanctions against Iraq ended without any substantial political gain. The UN maintained the comprehensive sanctions on Iraq for almost 13 years (August 1990 – May 2003), claiming that Iraq possessed weapons of mass destruction (WMD). However, whatever the proclaimed objectives behind the sanctions might have been, it is believed that the overthrow of Saddam's regime was one of the main strategic aims.[21] Saddam managed to stay in power until he was removed by another attack on Iraq in March 2003, but sanctions did not contribute to his removal. Indeed, as Donald Rumsfeld, then US Defence Minister, proclaimed, 'sanctions have failed to topple the regime in Iraq', and 'Economic sanctions against Iraq was a useless policy'.[22] The UN finally decided to lift the sanctions in May 2003.

In March 2003, George W. Bush and his closest ally, Tony Blair, had decided to end Saddam's regime and the 'threat' to the international community by invading and occupying Iraq. The Anglo-American coalition claimed that they were going to 'save' world peace and security which were threatened by Iraq's alleged WMD; a decision that had led Iraq to the sink into another everlasting conflict, with hundreds of thousands people losing their lives and further destruction of the country's civilian infrastructure.

Iraq's Weapons of Mass Destruction: The Myth

By the last two or three years of sanctions, and as the war was beginning to loom, the American and British intelligence communities were charged with telling policymakers what they had discovered about Iraq's nuclear, biological, and chemical weapons programmes. The answer was that Iraq was still pursuing its programme for WMD, and that it had biological weapons and mobile facilities for producing biological warfare devices.[23] An additional claim was that Iraq had renewed its production of chemical weapons, and was also developing unmanned aerial vehicles that were probably intended to deliver biological weapons agents. UK Intelligence went even further by stating that Iraq would be ready to put its WMD in operation within 45 minutes.[24]

Against this background, the war and the subsequent invasion of Iraq were carried out, even without legal sanction from the UN. However, after two years of occupying Iraq the allies were unable to establish a single factual proof that Iraq had retained production of WMD, and two years later, in January 2005, the UN elected to terminate the programme of inspection for Iraq's alleged WMD, against a background that indicated an absence of any evidence that Iraq even had conventional weapons in its possession. Its official termination of the inspection/search for these alleged WMD fuelled another scandal. An investigation carried out by the US Commission on the Intelligence Capability of the United States regarding WMD revealed that all the assessments by US intelligence about Iraq's WMD 'were wrong'. The Commission's report asserted that there was no evidence that Iraq had tried to reconstitute its ability to produce nuclear weapons after 1991, and that no evidence at all had been found of stockpiles of biological weapons agents, mobile biological weapons production facilities, or substantial chemical warfare capability.[25]

It would appear that the claim about Iraq's WMD had been made because of 'mistaken' intelligence, rather than from any belief that Iraq still had major WMD potential, but certainly the 'manoeuvre' that linked the alleged WMD with the invasion of Iraq was part of a deliberate policy for a new global agenda which had begun after 11 September 2001. It demonstrated an amalgamation of ideological concerns. On one hand, the neo-conservative American administration announced a globally-reaching war on all 'terrorists' and forewarned state sponsors of 'terrorism', while on the other it deployed a grand vision for political and economic liberalization in the Middle East. The attack on Iraq explicitly linked these ends, arguing that the creation of a democratic state in post-Saddam Iraq would contain terrorism and stimulate the spread of democracy through the whole Middle East region.

Thus, when the allies failed to establish evidence about Iraq's possession of WMD, they began to justify their action by deploying the rhetoric of promoting democracy and declaring that it was their ethical and moral duty to protect the rights and interests of the Iraqi people. Ironically, the US administration – having seemingly forgotten the years of mass deprivation of the Iraqi people resulting from the US-induced sanctions, and its long history of providing support to authoritarian regime(s) in Iraq and in the Middle East region generally – 'promised' that the war on Iraq would improve the situation of women in Iraq, and would 'bring' democracy, 'improve' human rights, and so on. The neo-conservative US administration wanted to impose democratic reform, principally as a way of combating 'terrorism', a catchword that took no account of history, context, society, or anything else.

There is currently a growing body of literature that addresses the obvious shift in international politics from the openly-declared pursuit of national interests towards an increased emphasis on ethical and moral democracy, human rights, gender equality, and so on.[26] Such work argues that while an ethical foreign policy may be ideally suited to buttressing the moral authority of governments, particularly if such authority is questioned domestically, it may have quite different (unethical) outcomes in the international sphere.[27] Moreover, regardless of its international effects, the ethical rhetoric of foreign policy seems easier in the sense that policy-makers are less accountable for matching ambitious policy aims with final policy outcomes on the international level.[28] The case of Iraq for the last 15 years is an obvious example of how international politics maintains its unaccountability for the relentless suffering of Iraqi people.

Sanctions on Iraq: The Humanitarian Failure

Indeed, if sanctions had been imposed with the aim of removing Saddam from power, they had failed miserably, but if they were aimed at destroying the economy and the people of Iraq, they have very definitely succeeded. The cruel irony is that the dictator and his henchmen grew obscenely rich as a direct result of sanctions, which were meant to punish them, while helpless civilians – especially the most vulnerable groups among them – were made to suffer hunger, disease, or even death as a result of those very same sanctions that were said to be helping them.

It is true that Saddam's regime had ruthlessly oppressed his political opponents and had plunged the nation into the furnace of wars with neighbouring countries, but sanctions stripped the Iraqi people of the economic rights essential to preserve their dignity and respect as human beings. The people of Iraq died in large numbers, and the extent of hardship, suffering and death may have been greater, especially for civilians, than the deaths that were a direct result of armed hostilities.

It is now clear that economic sanctions in Iraq hurt large numbers of innocent civilians, and also disrupted the social fabric of the Iraqi society. Thus, comprehensive economic sanctions in Iraq were neither benign, non-violent, or ethical. In light of the facts introduced about the humanitarian impacts of sanctions and the failure of sanctions to achieve their political aim, one wonders whether advocates of sanctions still consider that heightened civilian pain is justified, and whether the political failure of sanctions, particularly in the case of Iraq, touches upon the persuasiveness of the policymakers.

However, the sanctions 'episode' reflects upon the convergences of two major policy trends in the immediate aftermath of the end of the Cold War. The first is the dramatic increase in the way international sanctions are resorted to as a means of multilateral coercive action against states or political authorities which violate basic norms of international relations. The second is the increased international critiques of sanctions, especially with regard to the humanitarian consequences of economic sanctions and the consequent willingness of the international community to respond to humanitarian emergencies. However, while concerns about humanitarian consequences have been sparse in the academic literature, they have always been part of the policy debate within international organisations.[29] Generally speaking, policy analysts have regarded as naïve the underlying assumption that sanctions are a means of achieving political gain.[30] However, the separation of the equation – the humanitarian costs of the sanctions and the political goals of sanctions – into two fundamentally different matters began only during the later years of sanctions in Iraq.

In stark contrast to the rationale of the sanctions policy, the case of Iraq later opened up an unprecedented critique of economic sanctions, and particularly their impact on civilian populations. The contradictions of the sanctions policy put the UN in an unpleasant position, especially as the organization is entrusted to preserve the primacy of human rights, whatever the political objectives might be. In a self-critical mood, the UN Inter-Agency Standing Committee stated:

> Humanitarian and political objectives do not always coincide and even may be contradictory. Economic sanctions, for example, often have negative consequences for vulnerable groups and often directly affect the poorest strata of the population.[31]

Several UN agencies conducted studies with a particular focus on specific segments of the population, particularly children, and also examined the impact of sanctions in particular sectors such as health. Also, the former UN Secretary-General, Boutros Boutros-Ghali, noted that sanctions were 'blunt instruments' that inflicted suffering on vulnerable groups.[32]

However, in spite of criticisms, the UN and the policymakers were not willing to discuss the lifting of sanctions in Iraq while Saddam's regime remained in power, arguing that Iraq's possession of weapons of mass destruction made the country dangerous to world peace. Instead, they resorted to a 'middle way', which was to allow Iraq to export some oil while keeping sanctions in place. Along with the UN, Western politicians also pressed for the Oil For Food agreement, in order to avoid having to take responsibility for the humanitarian catastrophe in Iraq. The UN managed to maintain its comprehensive regime of sanctions against the country for such a long period of time only because it had manufactured a 'similarly' unique set of policies to sustain it.

Through the Oil-For Food programme (May 1996 to May 2003), the UN was able to control the flow of goods necessary to sustain life in Iraq through the proceeds of the sale of Iraq's oil, thereby keeping sanctions intact. For the whole period Iraq witnessed unprecedented hyperinflationary rates, high unemployment rates, excessive pressure on wages, a slump in labour productivity, and social tension and uncertainty.

The OFF programme was the largest humanitarian operation in the history of the United Nations. Even so, it proved to be insufficient to alleviate the wider-scale deterioration of life under sanctions, in spite of a relative improvement in humanitarian conditions in 1997 compared with the first six years of sanctions. By mid-1997 when the first proceeds of OFF were received, the monthly food ration had shown a slight improvement – from 1,800 kilocalories in the pre-OFF period to 2,400 kilocalories per person – although doctors throughout Iraq continued to report shortages of essential medicines and equipment, paediatric cancers, and malnutrition.[33]

It is also important to note that in September 1990, a month after the imposition of sanctions, the Iraqi government instituted a system of food rationing which was seen to be critical for sustaining the population and thereby preventing wide-scale famine.[34] The public rationing system was highly efficient in reaching the whole population on a monthly basis. This may appear paradoxical, especially given the regime's notorious record of brutality and oppression within the country. Some argue that the government's active role in preventing the onset of mass starvation served its narrow and cynical aim of prolonging its rule by averting political strife.[35] However, even if this line of argument is correct, there is no doubt that the sanctions regime did poorly in its attempts to alter the excessive abuses of political rights in Iraq. It also succeeded in destroying the well-being of Iraqi citizens by damaging education, public health care, infrastructural developments, and many other reforms that had been consistent and substantial features of the public policy carried out by the state in Iraq since 1970.[36] The distribution of food to more than 18 million people (in the Central and South governorates only) on a monthly basis for more than 12 years was one of the most enormous logistical operations in world history. It is worth mentioning that, although more than three years have passed since the sanctions were lifted and Saddam's regime was overthrown, the rationing system is still being used (Autumn 2006).

However, the impoverishment of the Iraqi people under sanctions is multi-dimensional. The lack of food and medicine, or the paucity of income to secure these basic needs, is only one aspect of human poverty. Deterioration in public health care systems, shortage of work opportunities, inability to afford education, feelings of personal insecurity, and so on, are all indicators of human poverty that the Iraqi society witnessed to an unprecedented degree under sanctions.

Sanctions stripped the broad majority of the Iraqi people of the economic rights essential for preserving the dignity and respect of human beings, and Iraqis died in large numbers because of hunger and disease. This was seen in the dramatic increase in communicable diseases, in maternal, child and infant mortality and morbidity, and in the immense suffering of the chronically ill and of a large number of physically and mentally disabled people. Due to the collapse of public health care, and to increased environmental pollution, malnutrition is widespread and other new kinds of disease have emerged, including a array of physical abnormalities among the new born

The OFF Programme lasted for seven years (May 1996 to May 2003) with more than US$100 billion in transactions (including over US$64 billion in oil sales and approximately US$37 billion for food and services).[37] However, the Volcker Report (the Commission of Enquiry into allegations of OFF scandals) shows that the amount that was in fact used for the reconstruction of public services and civilian infrastructures was rather less than half of the real proceeds received from the sale of Iraq's oil. It concluded that 'things had gone wrong, and that the reputation and credibility of the UN had been damaged', and called for a stronger executive leadership. The findings of the Volcker Commission revealed that the OFF Programme was one of the most corrupt operations in the history of the UN. Evidence suggests that UN officials were aware of the abuse, and there are now arguments that proper scrutiny would have limited the scale of the fraud. It will be clear to many people that Saddam's regime was involved in oil smuggling and corruption (oil commissions), but those who managed his oil trafficking and purchases, and those who inspected and monitored Iraq's oil exports, constitute another group that is badly in need of investigation. In fact, the scandal of oil smuggling and payoffs was not a secret, but was encouraged and facilitated by high-ranking UN officials, particular countries and politically-backed individuals. These actors were all united through clumsy get-rich-quick ambitions at the expense of the Iraqi people.

Iraqi Women: The Gender Impact of Sanctions

This book has, through its various chapters, demonstrated insights in the cases where international sanctions were being felt, within a society and by women as a specific group. The recasting of Iraqi women's experience during the 1970s and 1980s revealed that construction of a 'gender regime' in Iraqi society, as any other Middle Eastern societies, depended, by and large, on the social role of the state/nation-state.

By the term 'gender regime' is meant the construct of labour market structures, social policies, historical division of production and reproduction, cultural norms and historical discursive practices concerning the roles of women and men.[38] Building on this base, the main concern of this book was to illustrate ways in which the 'gender regime' was moved and affected by the UN sanctions, by reflecting on women's experiences in their daily life under sanctions. The main research questions asked: What did the withdrawal of the state from its interventionist role in the economy and society mean to Iraqi women? What was the fate of women when the state was unable to implement the socio-economic programmes of which they were the prime beneficiaries?

This book was structured to provide a background into the case of sanctions in Iraq, and to examine the impact of sanctions on Iraq's macro-economy. This was done against the backdrop of the Iraqi economy in the 1970s and 1980s, as a contrast to the situation of the economy under sanctions.

This was followed by a historical review of gender dynamics in Iraqi society over a specific period of time. Iraq's experience in the 1970s and 1980s revealed that through the nation-state, various groups of men and women were able to articulate their interests and rights, and their success or failure with regard to claims over material resources. The realization of the nation-state in Iraq led to adoption of the most important labour and family laws, regulating women's productive and reproductive rights. During this period, Iraq witnessed a high level of upward social mobility that resulted in an important shift of material and living conditions for the majority of Iraq's population. For Iraqi women this could be perceived in the increased participation of women in male public life. The state was a key player in organising a labour market in which new graduates, females as well as males, were centrally distributed throughout the country's extensive public/state sector. The state-building process resulted in the formation of a large middle class with new priorities in their economic and social relationships. Through this kind of institutional framework, Iraqi citizens, both men and women, were offered a range of alternatives to primordial groups for meeting their social, economic and political needs. In return, political allegiance with the state implied the freeing of the individual from the familial and tribal matrix and her/his reintegration into the nation-state. In this way, the state in Iraq was able to assume more authority over duties traditionally associated with patriarchal and tribal kinsmen.

The rights of Iraqi women were envisaged when the 'secular' Ba'th ideology and the country's oil wealth enabled the emergence of a 'strong' centralized nation-state, with institutions capable of penetrating most aspects of society. Changes in the status of Iraqi women brought about by family law or by socio-economic policy were always dependent principally on the potential economic power of the state and the social agenda of the political elites. However, the state's support for women's rights was not unwavering. Gender identities and relations were constantly re-negotiated and transformed, in response to the consolidating of power and alliances. This was the particular feature of the regime after Saddam arrived at the top of the political power structure in Iraq in mid-1979, especially because the period of his rule was associated with wars and political strife.

Iraqi women's rights, as demonstrated by laws and legislation, and public policies during the 1980s were subject to contradictory change according to the exigencies implied by political and economic circumstances. In particular, the economic crisis that resulted, by the mid-1980s, from the effects of the war with Iran and the escalation in costs that resulted from the fall in oil prices, directly reflected on the state's attitude toward women's productive and reproductive rights. However, in all cases the nation-state in Iraq retained its position of strategic importance to Iraqi women, through which they could gain or lose crucial legal, social and political protection from discriminatory practices in various aspects of life.

Thus, the exploration of the gender impact of international sanctions on Iraqi women was linked to the situation of the state being unable to control the external and internal factors that interfered with and influenced changes in all aspects of life in Iraq. Analysis of the situation and conditions of women under economic sanctions was therefore concerned with more than simply describing women's daily lives in this particular situation. Rather, it expanded to observing how the impact of sanctions extended to the family, kinship and the polity, and from there, to the way they affected the roles and status of women in the society and the family.

The lives of Iraqi women underwent a rapid change as a result of the massive collapse of the Iraqi economy and the social discontent with the political regime in Baghdad that began in the aftermath of the invasion of Kuwait in August 1990. This was seen not only in the lack of access to food, medicine and public heath care and services, but also in the sharp deterioration of women's participation in public life. Given that the participation of Iraqi women in the labour force had historically been envisaged through state-sponsored education, state-led economic development, and public sector employment, the impact of sanctions on Iraqi women was specifically seen as a result of public sector downscaling, devalued wages, and diminishing opportunities for other earnings. Women's experiences revealed that the collapse of the public sector due to the economic crisis reflected directly on their lives, precisely because women were 'typically' concentrated in this sector. The significance of the public sector's role in the lives of Iraqi women was not simply because it provided a 'good' income, but most importantly because women's participation in economic activities and formal earnings generated from jobs in the public sector was also socially and culturally accepted. Through the realization of Iraqi women's right to participate in formal labour, and their consequent economic independence, the public sector contributed indirectly to the breakdown of the traditional resistance to women's involvement in public life.

While the majority of Iraqi women were affected by sanctions, different groups of women were differently affected.[39] The collapse of Iraq's economy under sanctions had led to high rates of unemployment and shrinking wages for both men and women. However, while sanctions limited the potential economic opportunities of all Iraqi women, they also exerted further pressure on highly educated women from middle-class backgrounds. Prior to sanctions such women perceived education and a professional career as the main path to independence, freedom and equality. Because of the economic collapse, their employment options were reduced to taking low paid jobs in the public sector or to becoming full-time housewives. While a large number of middle-class educated women, were engaged in informal income earning because of their desperate need for income, the overwhelming majority of these women perceived formal employment under sanctions as socially and economically degrading. As such, women's professional careers and earnings were widely perceived as secondary, less important (than those of men), and temporary. This explains why many women who were working and generating income, whether through formal or informal jobs, were subjected to an intensified form of male control, both in the home and at work.

As educated middle-class women were pushed 'back home', women from lower-middle and poor class backgrounds were encountering inadequate work conditions and low wages at the bottom level of informal economic activities, such as petty trade, retail sales, housekeeping, and so on. Although informal economic activities have always existed in Iraq, they have been concentrated largely in agricultural areas and carried out mainly by the poorest segments of the Iraqi society. Under the economic crisis of sanctions, informal economic activities began to re-emerge strongly, particularly as an alternative to the ruined economic infrastructure, and as a potential means for earnings. The concentration of women workers in this informal economic activities sector made them essentially vulnerable to discrimination and abuse. On the intra-household level, the situation indicated a further increase in women's dependence on the male provider and a further exposure of women to familial and patriarchal control.

Paradoxically, while kinship and family increasingly became the focus of everyday life, the economic crisis placed the Iraqi family, both nuclear and extended, under tremendous stress. Middle and poor income families were unable to offer the same forms of support previously provided for their members. The economic crisis born out of sanctions penetrated deeply in the social fabric of Iraqi society, affecting the internal relational system implicit in the connective familial and patriarchal relationships between members of the same family. The statements of respondents given throughout the earlier chapters clearly show that, regardless of their class, income, and familial status, Iraqi women were caught up in an 'unusual' economic and social insecurity. Deprived of the economic security previously provided by the state, they were also unable to receive the 'socio-economic' support offered by family and kin that the family/extended family, under 'normal' economic circumstances, would have been able to give. The result of this situation was seen in the increase in women's susceptibility to poverty, as well as to more intensified forms of patriarchal abuse and domination.

The most disadvantaged group in these circumstances was the single women breadwinners. As a result of the economic crisis, the situation of widowed and divorced women deteriorated further, and the social stigma against young women in these categories was particularly reinforced. They were particularly affected by the state's withdrawal from the social sphere and by the increased 'materialization' of social and emotional relationships between members of the immediate family. One aspect of the problem could be seen in the further strengthening of the traditional importance attached to marriage as the 'only' option for women's recognition and respectability in society. This situation also strengthened the social stigma that portrays divorced women as a potential risk to themselves and to their families, and perpetuates the placing of women into ill-conceived marriages. Indeed, the loss of security, whether through adequate income earnings or through the security provided by the extended family and kinship, increased women's subjugation to new forms of 'nuclear' and 'impersonal' patriarchal domination.

Of course, in an increasingly insecure environment, marriage had become the option through which many girls expected to find more security than was to be had through education and work. The turning point in social attitudes towards female education took place when education became an additional burden to families, especially those with limited income. Prior to sanctions, Iraq had a promising education sector that was also one of the state's priorities. The compound effect of sanctions on this viable sector was seen in the destruction of educational establishments, shortage of material and human resources, increased rates of failure and dropout, and the emergence of private education. For female education this situation was translated into an increased financial burden on families and the declined value of female education, especially since female graduates were not able to find jobs, or were confined to jobs at the lowest level of the salary scale.

Under the immense pressure of the economic crisis, Iraqi people began to adopt atypical strategies which were unfavourable to women and girls. Large numbers of families with limited incomes were forced to put their children into premature employment, often in hazardous conditions. Small girls were leaving school, either to take up responsibilities at home, or were going outside the home to seek informal earnings, often in demeaning jobs such as cleaning houses and gardens, or begging around the streets.

In this situation, too, early marriages and polygamous marriages were often perceived to be the 'best' alternative for girls and their families. However, while the economic crisis was intensifying the chronic dilemma of declining marriage rates in Iraq, it was also increasing the inclination towards the materialistic gains of marriage, because of other traditional values. Polygamous marriage became an alternative solution for lost social and economic security. The move towards compromising on the stigma of polygamy as 'uncivilized' and 'old fashioned' was motivated in particular by the overwhelming and disparate need for material security, rather than the fact of increased numbers of unmarried women.

In addition to economic impoverishment, Iraqi women encountered tremendous domestic responsibilities as well as health responsibilities. While collapse of the economic infrastructure and public services eroded all aspects of life, there was no clinical or professional help available for the unfortunate population. In addition to their usual household responsibilities, women had to manage household supplies, and needed to be constantly aware of the frequent fluctuations in market prices when planning and purchasing food and basic necessities, such as water and fuel, both rationed due to shortages. The most tragic situation was illustrated in households headed by women who were responsible for children. Economic hardship perpetuated their psychological trauma. A large number of Iraqi women whose husbands or fathers had been killed by wars or executed or 'disappeared' by the regime, had to manage the rising cost of living and declining incomes on their own. Divorced women with children, particularly girls, also had to contend with regressive societal attitudes that imposed extra pressure and restrictions on them. This very unfortunate group of women had to deal with economic hardship while their reputations were under constant scrutiny by society and family alike.

Women – because of to their essential roles as mothers – were especially affected by the declining of state subsidies and public expenditure on health care and services, and the deterioration in public health education. During the sanctions era Iraq witnessed an unprecedented collapse of public health and medical services that led to high maternal and infant mortality, malnutrition, and high rates of infants' deformity. Most pregnant women also suffered from anaemia and malnutrition due to the deteriorating quality of food, water and sanitation.

The other face of the crisis was seen through the immense psychological pressure encountered because of growing gender-based violence that included domestic violence, street/public violence, and a centralized form of violence (by the state) against women. Although there were several reasons for the increasing violence against women, the deteriorated welfare of the Iraqi society under sanctions is believed to have been the main reason behind the surge of violence against women. Indeed, the strengthening of male dominance over the 'weakest' (women and girls) while the male role as provider weakened under sanctions, made a 'perfect' recipe for exacerbating the phenomenon of gender-based violence against women, especially young women. Moreover, because of being obliged to be outside homes on daily basis, students and working women also encountered the increased risk of public violence. This explains why a large number of young Iraqi women left their jobs and schooling in attempt to distance themselves from the increased risks of aggression and harassment in public places.

Paradoxically however, the dramatic deterioration in the status of Iraqi women that occurred under sanctions did not coincide with any potential change in their legal status (rights and obligations). It seems rather surprising and unexpected that women's legal rights, as stated in Iraqi law, stayed more or less unchanged during the whole period of sanctions. Apart from a few amendments, the important body of laws and legislation concerning women's rights in labour, education, and most importantly, family law remained untouched.[40] In fact, the strictest decrees ever issued by a Ba'th government against Iraqi women, including the decree allowing them to be killed for 'honour crimes', were actually adopted during the late 1980s (i.e., in the period between the end of the Iraq-Iran War and the beginning of the Gulf Crisis in 1990).[41]

However, if the laws concerning women did not change, how could the situation of women have deteriorated to the degree found in this study? It is true that the implicit understanding of gender that might be invoked within a community depends, in part, on laws and legislation concerning women and men, but the actual realization of laws regarding the relative replacement of men and women in the economy and society depends on the capacity/incapacity of the state to enforce these laws.[42] In political and economic terms, the fact that only a 'strong' state is capable of enforcing its laws and legislation explains why the situation of Iraqi women deteriorated steadily under sanctions, despite the fact that women were 'legally protected'.[43]

The bringing about of change in the status of women, particularly if improving that status is intended, implies more than just laws and legislation, nor is it simply a legal issue. It is rather more of an intertwined economic, social and legal issue, where the realization of economic, social and cultural rights involves a positive responsibility on the state involving financial and human resource allocation, follow-up programmes and control. However, this is not in any way to underplay the importance of state laws and legal reforms concerning women and women's legal entitlement to rights – rather it emphasises the reciprocal relationship between state laws and legislation, and the state's economic and political power to enforce these laws.

The imposition of sanctions on the Iraqi economy had serious consequences for the positive obligations of the state as implied by its laws and regulations. The state was able to deliver on its legal responsibilities as implicit in its laws, particularly those stated in the interim constitution of 1970 and in other important provisions concerning the social and economic dimensions of the principle of equality between citizens (Articles 1, 2 & 19 of Iraq's Interim Constitution, 1970). Moreover, under sanctions, while the Ba'th regime was living through the most intense crisis of its rule, with uncertainty looming as to its hold on power, the government turned a blind eye to legal offences that did not directly threaten the political system. Most importantly, the regime's public support was narrowing at this time, especially among the urban middle-classes who were severely hit by sanctions-induced economic deprivation. Saddam responded by appealing to tribalist support. In contrast to the earlier pre-crisis period, Saddam made sure, by word and deed, that tribes and kinship were in the forefront of Iraq's political and ideological concerns.[44] In response to the anti-regime disturbances of April 1991, Saddam called attention to the tribes as 'the swords of the state', and in the process undermined the state's judicial authority, a price he was willing to pay in return for the tribes' allegiance to the regime.[45]

In this environment, many of the progressive accomplishments that had been behind the expansion of Iraqi women's participation in the formal labour force and in education were reversed. The examples given in this book provide some insight into the kind of power relationships that were being constructed in the Iraqi society under sanctions. Patriarchal kinship systems and conservative religious attitudes towards women were encouraged. Thus, sanctions strengthened the social attitudes that prescribed women as 'weak' and 'dependent' human beings in need of male/kinship protection. Moreover, corruption had made it possible to get away with various offences, particularly against women. Such matters were largely seen as internal familial affairs. In this way, while sanctions turned life in Iraq towards widespread impoverishment and the systematic curtailment of economic and social rights, they also managed to transmit the overall political and ethical crisis of Saddam's regime directly to women's lives.

Women in Post-Invasion Iraq

Since March 2003, the humanitarian and the political situation in Iraq changed dramatically for the worse. The US and the UK-led war and invasion of Iraq put an end to Saddam's regime, but at the same time opened for a new era of devastation, violence, hardship and uncertainty for the Iraqi people. Ironically however, after the myth of Iraq's weapons of mass of destruction had been demolished, one of the proclaimed aim of the war and the invasion of Iraq was marketed under the slogan of 'democracy' and 'liberating' Iraqi women and making them more 'free'.

However, since March 2003, Iraqi women's daily lives seem different from anything they ever experienced previously. Their lives were further reduced to the sheer struggle for survival.

In the immediate aftermath of the war and the occupation of Iraq, gangs of armed men broke into state institutions, private residences, police stations, the courts, hospitals, museums, and so on, looting everything. Sometime later the Americans disbanded the police and the armed forces, leaving the whole country open to criminals and organized gangs who specialized in killing, kidnapping, and theft. In most Iraqi cities, numbers of women and/or girls were seized in public while walking along the street, even in daytime. Gangs of savage criminals kidnapped hundreds of girls/women to sell them, or killed them after they had been raped. A report by Human Rights Watch (HRW) in 2003 states:

> Between the end of May and end of June, in Baghdad only, there were more than 400 women have been raped, kidnapped, and sometimes sold ... Many women/girls, especially in Baghdad City stayed at home out of schools and even from work because of fear and lack of security.[46]

The political situation and the widespread violence in Iraq since the invasion also reduced women's potential to protect themselves. Even staying within the domestic domain had ceased to be the last resort for avoiding risks and violence outside the home. Most notably, immediately after the invasion, the allied army (particularly Americans) began bursting into people's houses, breaking down doors and destroying furniture, and summarily arresting all military-aged men – actions that made them unwitting recruits for the insurgency. Arbitrary arrests, beatings and sometimes killings were carried out, often based on the flimsiest intelligence, while Iraqi people had no recourse to justice. The brutal behaviour of American soldiers in the face of the sense of helplessness of Iraqi civilians was witnessed worldwide. The sight of American soldiers breaking into the homes of Iraqis in the dead of night, searching for resistance, terrorizing children and women, was and remains extremely shocking.

The exposure of the crimes perpetuated by American soldiers in Abu Ghraib prison against Iraqi detainees of both sexes revealed that Iraqi women were systematically arrested, detained, abused and tortured. In most instances, women were detained and tortured (in many cases, with their infants) not because of anything they had done, but because they were being used as 'bargaining chips' to inform and collaborate with the occupation against insurgence from their close relatives (spouses, sons and brothers). Although the Abu Ghraib scandal raised a general awareness of offences committed by the coalition forces, particularly sexual offences perpetrated by American soldiers against Iraqi women, nevertheless the numbers of Iraqi women detained in both US-run and Iraqi prisons are constantly increasing.[47]

There have been a number of reports published by agencies such as Human Rights Watch (July 2003) and Amnesty International (February 2005) that speak of the increasing sexual violence against women since the war in 2003, including the group rape of Iraqi women prisoners by American soldiers. However, most of the reporting on the situation of Iraqi women after 2003 notably emphasizes the culturally-specific consequences of the fact that sexual dishonour of a woman is often punished by death. The interpretation of violence against women in these terms is quite misleading because this approach attempts to direct our attention from the facts that have led to increasing violence and gender violence against women. It seems to want to make us aware that 'after all' a much worse fate than mere rape awaits these unfortunate women. Addressing the surge in violence against women in Iraq since the 2003 war and occupation in this manner is disingenuous. Rather, it is war, mass displacement of the population, and political hostility that increases Iraqi women's vulnerability to aggression, making them at the same time an easy target for sexual violence and honour crimes.

It should also be noted that crimes against women and honour killings have always existed in the Iraqi society. However, honour killings became worse under sanctions when Saddam made his first attempts to strengthen alliances with tribal and extreme religious groups. He revived mores and practices sanctioned by tribal law that allowed women who betrayed their family honour to be killed by their paternal relatives. This decree was followed by many similarly hasty government decrees, all of which were intended to foster tribal and extreme religious alliances.

Far more extensive, however, is the number of innocent Iraqi people who were killed in bombs explosion and because of accidents and errors of shooting by American soldiers. Such deaths run into hundreds of thousands. There is no question that the number of Iraqi non-combatants killed hugely exceeds the number of allied troops killed in hostile actions.[48] Estimates of the number of Iraqi civilian deaths significantly exceed actual Iraqi military casualties. In general, Iraqi civilians have suffered the bulk of fatalities in this conflict. Iraqi women and children under 15 make up some 53 percent of these deaths.[49] Most are caused by random shooting, terrorist suicide bombs, and criminal mafia-type gangs that specialize in kidnap and killing.

HRW Report noted that 'Although, by the end of 2003, women formed more of a public presence, their movements in public remained limited due to fear of attacks, explosions, kidnaps and sexual violence'. The political and religious climate in Iraq since the invasion particularly emphasizes women as sexual objects and transmitters of the culture. Expert assessment of the impact of armed conflict on women and women's roles in peace-building, based on firsthand data and testimonies of women who were victims and survivors of wars in 14 areas around the world, reveals the prevalence of violence against women, before, during, and after armed conflict.[50] Conditions during armed conflicts and in the post-conflict 'reconstruction' periods often leave lasting psychological consequences, including depression and stigma, which also open the way for further cycles of gender-based exploitation.[51] However, it seems that these tendencies are particularly enforced in societies where cultures of violence and discrimination against women/girls have existed prior to the conflict.

As previously mentioned, regressive tribal and extreme religious attitudes towards women were increasingly intensified as Saddam's regime had to face up to the pressure of sanctions. In an attempt to consolidate his power Saddam looked to the religious establishment for support, thereby sharpening the divide between Sunni Muslims (35 percent of the population) and Shi'i Muslims (60 percent).[52] He also launched a 'faith campaign' in the early 1990s that attempted to co-opt the support of conservative religious (Sunni) leaders while eradicating Shi'i leadership, forcing back women's protection in the process. Under occupation, different religious extremist groupings became notorious, either in opposition to the occupation, or as masked men carrying out arbitrary acts of death and destruction and terrorizing the entire population. However, in this destructive and horrific setting the least alarming aspect is that Islamic extremists are now pressuring women to put on the veil as the price of their tranquillity. By far the worse aspect is the phenomenon of ethnic cleansing and revenge-motivated attacks that make women sensitive targets for rape and killing. Constant fear is spreading throughout the different segments of Iraqi society, especially after many incidents of kidnap, gang rape and killing of women in one community by terrorists and gangs from another community/sect. However, it is widely believed that behind these crimes lies a more vicious interest in waging civil war in Iraq.

While conditions are far more difficult than they were under the Ba'th regime, a few Iraqi women 'elites', especially repatriates from the West, are obviously seizing opportunities, particularly through their contacts with the new political leaders. A 'civil society', largely in the form of women's organizations, is perceptibly emerging, especially in Baghdad; most of these organizations are backed financially and politically by the numerous political parties that have rapidly arisen in the aftermath of the events of 2003. Meanwhile the majority of Iraqi women are simply trying to survive from day to day in deteriorating circumstances. It is noticeable that many reports dwell constantly on quite trivial issues, such as the fact that increasing numbers of Iraqi women are veiling (covering their hair with scarves), and no longer wear make-up or drive cars. There is less consistency in reporting the calamitous shortages of food, water, and electricity, the lack of medicine, the overall deterioration of health and sanitation, the looting, and the corruption at high levels, etc. All these are forms of restriction of women's freedom and rights, and should be addressed in relation to occupation and war and the consequent political and public upheavals. The diminished aspects of life in Iraq under occupation have a much greater impact on the most vulnerable groups of the population, including women, poor households, children, the elderly and sick, and single breadwinners.

The situation since 2003 is further increasing Iraqi women's vulnerability, particularly due to detention, disappearance and – in the on-going armed struggle – the mass killings of men and boys, either by the coalition forces or by anti-coalition violence, or by vicious terrorists. It is now estimated that one in ten Iraqi women is a widow, especially young women. Sectarian killings and the displacement of hundreds of thousands of families from their homes into refugee camps in their own country have made an already dreadful situation worse, and has increased the numbers of households headed by women only.[53]

Iraqi women suffer, now more than ever, from the destroyed infrastructure of the country, especially because it had become the target for actions by various groups of insurgents as way of bringing themselves to public attention. This was seen through cuts in water, electricity, gas and fuel supplies, food rations, and so on. All essentials and the basic civilian infrastructure, which were already disintegrating because of decades of wars and sanctions, are now further damaged and vandalized. The situation of widespread disorder and impoverishment has encouraged various corrupt mafia types in all levels of the government administration; through their long arms they dominate 're-construction' contracts and food distribution channels. These networks manage to earn fortunes by manipulating prices of the basic essentials of life, and through indulging in fraud and thievery.

Is it Democracy or a Backward Move?

It is argued that during and after the stress of armed conflict/war in societies where political culture prevents women's participation in decision-making structures, women are unlikely to become involved in decisions about the conflict and about the reconstruction process that follows.[54] This is very much expected to be the case in Iraq. When political and business interests collide, it is typically women and other vulnerable groups who pay the price. In these circumstances, women suffer from lack of protection, in addition to shortages of basic primary and reproductive health care and the absence of psychological support for victims of gender-based and sexual violence and physical trauma.

The situation in Iraq since the occupation reveals the difficult conditions of women, whose lives became considerably constrained after the US forces had embedded conservative religious and tribal leaders in positions of power. In February 2004, the US-led Coalition Provisional Authority (CPA) introduced Resolution 137, which would have abrogated Iraq's Code of Personal Status of 1959 (amended 1978), and given the religious courts jurisdiction over such matters as inheritance, marriage, and divorce. Resolution 137 opened the door to religious laws permitting polygamy, child marriage, and the loss of custody by divorced mothers of male children at age 2 and female children at age 7. The proposal was backed by the majority of CPA members, including the few pro-secular figures; all were enthusiastic about replacing all the provisions (marriage, divorce, custody, inheritance) of the civil laws on 'family status' with Islamic laws. Fortunately,

Resolution 137 was overturned, but only after strong opposition by some Iraqi women's groups backed by American supporters.

Although the pro-secular Code of Personal Status was able to pre-empt the backlash against women's reforms on this occasion, there is no doubt that debate on such proposals will resurface. The question as to whether elected Iraqi governments would enable women to preserve and improve their rights is extremely unclear at the present time. However, it is strongly believed that an 'emancipatory' struggle operating entirely within a secular framework after the Anglo-American occupation would be extremely unlikely to succeed in Iraq. Even though there are strong attempts by Iraqi women activists, and their equivalent among male politicians, to protect the secular provisions of the 1978 Code of Personal Status, these attempts would certainly face a strong opposition in the 'new' political structure of Iraq. Therefore, it seems more likely that the present political (sectarian) situation in Iraq implies that equality between the sexes must be negotiated within Islam. Indeed, this could be done through countless possibilities for interpretation of the sacred texts of the Qur'an and the Sunna in ways that would enhance women's rights and equality between the sexes.[55] However, under the present sectarian divisions and the threat of political and religious fundamentalism, the abandonment of the struggle for equality between the sexes within Islam would more than ever leave the path clear for various religious extremists to curtail women's rights.

The 'quota' achieved by the 'Transitional Law' – i.e., that every third seat in the Iraqi Assembly was set aside for a woman – aims for the time being to ensure 'preferential treatment' for Iraqi women in political participations until equality between men and women will have been achieved. However, the matter is not simply concerned with the number of women in the Iraqi Assembly but rather has to do with whether these women are genuinely concerned about improving women's rights, and aware of how they should lead the battle to achieve this goal. In this context, if we are to envisage a 'democratic' Iraq, women should be careful not to be treated as objects defined according to the political needs and exigencies of the male elites.

Prominent scholars concerned with Muslim societies emphasize that if support and solidarity for women's rights comes from international society and/or is given by international feminist movements, it will not be influential without a struggle that originates from within those societies.[56] It is argued that international norms, such as a Women's Convention (CEDAW), may operate as a 'political lever and a point of reference' when attempting to articulate specific demands in Muslim societies, but it will not provide sufficient grounds to bring about equality of the sexes.[57] If this is to be successful, the norms and values of international human rights must be interwoven with the struggle to articulate women's human rights from within the Muslim community.[58] Indeed, there is a fertile human rights discourse within the Islamic tradition, but it can only be developed into legal rules through a progressive interpretation of Islamic religious texts (Qur'an and Hadith). A moderate and real interpretation of Islam would incorporate international women's human rights values, and enable Islam to work across socio-cultural and religious diversities.[59]

However, the escalating antagonistic foreign policy of the neo-conservative American administration towards the Middle East is adding the complexity of the heightened confrontations between Islamic extremists and the more moderate Islamic schools of thought. This situation increases uncertainty that the battle will produce a progressive interpretation of Islam. Such a result now seems more difficult than it has ever been. Muslim societies around the globe increasingly see that women's human rights are predominately based on 'Western', 'liberal', 'secular', and individual values and norms and hence disregard the historical, cultural and ethnic specificities of these societies.[60] Iraq, under the effect of occupation and terrorism, is now witnessing an unprecedented tendency towards identifying 'secular' women's rights as synonymous with 'un-Islamic', i.e., culturally and religiously alien to the Iraqi society. However, there is an increasing hope that when Iraq regains its integrity and independence, and re-establishes its economic strength, this will enable a more acceptable environment for a progressive interpretation and enshrining of women's human rights and family laws in the country's new constitution, as well as their enforcement on the ground.

NOTES

Chapter 1

1 See Alnasrawi (1994: 83); and Gazdar (1997: 8).

2 The UN's reaction to Iraq's invasion of Kuwait involved the use of military force in addition to comprehensive sanctions. The UN SCR 678 of 2 November 1990 called for the use of 'all necessary means' in order to end the crisis (SCR 678: Paragraph 2). Accordingly, this resolution opened the door for the war against Iraq.

3 According to a US Air Force planner, 'What we were doing with the attacks on infrastructure was to accelerate the effect of the sanctions': quoted in Gellman (1991). See also Nagy (2001).

4 For an account of this war, see Bulloch and Morris (1991); Hiro (1992); and Sluglett and Farouq Sluglett (1992: 435).

5 The bombing campaign dropped more than 88,000 tons of explosives over a six-week period, more than were dropped by the US in the Vietnam War. This comparison was made by Parker Payson, drawing on Pentagon and Department of Defence figures, in 'Figure it Out', in *The Washington Report on Middle East Affairs in May/June 1991,* page 37. Online: HtmlResAnchor http://www.wmea.com/backissues/0591/9105037.htm (last accessed 13 September /2005).

6 See Ahtisaari (1991: 5).

7 See Arab Monetary Fund (1992: 18).

8 See Alnasrawi (1994:122); and AMF (1992: 18).

9 See MEED (1991: D6).

10 See Boutros Ghali (1996: 2).

11 Including: acknowledgment of Kuwait's boundaries for which the SC established the Iraq-Kuwait Boundary Demarcation Commission (IKBDC); compensation for damage caused by the invasion and the establishment of the UN Compensation Commission (UNCC); and the dismantling of Iraq's weapons of mass destruction (WMD) and the establishment of UN Special Commission (UNSCOM), later named the United Nations Monitoring and Verification Commission (UNMOVIC).

12 Contrary to common perceptions, the OFF programme was not 'humanitarian aid'. No foreign government or NGO donated food, medicine or other necessities to Iraq under the programme. Humanitarian aid was paid for by Iraq's own revenues – prior to the invasion, payments were made from its oil revenues, and later from the sale of a limited amount of oil. See Niblock (2001b).

13 SCR 706, 15 August 1991 and SCR 712, 19 September 1991. See also Niblock (2001a)

14 See United Nations (1996c: 101).

15 Among others, the Iraqi funds from the sale of Iraqi oil prior to 6 August 1990, for which Iraq had not received payment (SCR 778, 2 October 1992). These assets had not been formally frozen, but Iraq had been denied access to them on the basis of SCR 661 of 6 August 1990.

16 Some sentences were added: 'Commitment of all member states to the sovereignty and territorial integrity of Iraq' and 'Nothing in this resolution should be considered as infringing the sovereignty or territorial integrity of Iraq', and 'Kurdish areas are sovereign territory of Iraq'. SCR 986 allowed the export of US$2 billion-worth of oil every six months on condition that all transactions would be channelled through the UN Escrow Account (the same mechanisms envisaged by SCR 706 and SCR 712).

17 See details in United Nations (1996b).

18 According to the Secretary General this was: 'to prevent further deterioration in the humanitarian conditions, health, and nutritional status of the Iraqi population'. See Anan (1998b).

19 Secretary-General's Reports to the SC on the implementation of the OFF programme in Iraq. See also reports of UN Office for Iraq Programme (UNOIP) to the Secretary-General. See Internet sources: HtmlResAnchor http://www.un.org/depts/oip/background/inbrief.html; and HtmlResAnchor http://www.un.org/depts/oip/ (last accessed 12 September 2005).

20 The Security Council continued the Oil-for-Food Programme in 180 periods called "phases". Phase 1 ran from 10 December 1996 to 7 June 1997. The first oil was exported on 15 December 1996. The first shipments of food arrived in Iraq in March 1997, and the first medical supplies in May 1997. The final oil exporting period (Phase XII) authorised by Security Council Resolution 1447 (2002) was in effect from 5 December 2002 until 3 June 2003. See: HtmlResAnchor http://www.un.org/depts/oip/background/inbrief.html (last accessed 12 September 2005).

21 Despite the fact that Iraq was allowed to increase its oil exports, the oil industry and its refineries were unable to raise production due to the shortage of spare parts. By mid-1998, in response to the escalating problem, the SC had authorised the import of up to US$300 million-worth of oil industry spare parts and equipment (on the basis of UN SCR 1175 of 19 January 1998). On 4 November 1998 the Secretary General reported to the SC that US$300 million was not sufficient for comprehensive repairs (see Anan, 1998b, and 1998a). However, the Security Council continued to refuse Iraq's demand for US$600 million for spare parts imports until March 2000.

22 For detailed information on this issue see United Nations Press Release, online at HtmlResAnchor http://www.un.org/news; HtmlResAnchor http://www.un.org/Depts/oip/; HtmlResAnchor http://www/casi.org.uk/info/sciraq.html#1990; and UN Office of Iraq, OFF Programme HtmlResAnchor http://www.un.org/Depts/oip/sector-displaced.html (last accessed 12 September 2005).

23 Stated in the Independent Inquiry Committee (Volcker) Report published online on 7 September 2005 at: HtmlResAnchor http://www.iic-offp.org/Mgmt_Report.htm.

24 For more details see Von Sponeck (2006).

25 Paul A. Volcker, former chairman of the US Federal Reserve Bank, was appointed by the UN in 2004 to head the Commission of Enquiry established to probe allegations that UN officials had received payoffs from Iraq. The scandal emerged after a report by Charles Duelfer, a senior CIA advisor, alleging that the director of Iraq's OFF programme, Sevan Benon, was involved in this discreditable behaviour.

26 On this particular issue, Denis Halliday commented when reviewed the draft copy of this study. He said: 'The US and the UK enabled Saddam Hussain to sell oil to Jordan and Turkey throughout sanctions yielding some US$10 billion directly to Baghdad. In later years, bribes, kickbacks and surcharges added to that accumulation of wealth, and created those well connected to whom a case study refers, who profited from the pain of others'.

27 See Economic Intelligence Unit (2001: 25).

28 See Economic Intelligence Unit (2000: 27).

29 See Dreze and Gazdar (1991a: 18).

30 See Economic Intelligence Unit (1997: 22).

31 See Economic Intelligence Unit (September 2003: 29).

32 Ibid.

33 See Annan (1998a) and (1998b).

34 See Economic Intelligence Unit (December 2003: 11).

35 Imports of foodstuffs, medicine medical equipment, and water and sanitation equipment and supplies rose from US$4.2 billion in 1978 to US$21.6 billion in 1982. See Alnasrawi (1994: 118); and Economic Intelligence Unit, *Iraq Country Profile* (1995–6); and EIU, *Iraq Country Report* (1997).

36 See Economic Intelligence Unit (1995–6: 6–7); and (2001: 27).

37 See Van der Stoel (1991: 45).

38 See Economic Intelligence Unit (1999–2000: 21).

39 See UNHP (1999a).

40 See Anan (1998a).

41 Ibid.

42 See Anan (2001).

43 See UNHP (1999b).

44 See Von Sponeck (1999).

45 See Reuters (29 March 2000).

46 See Von Sponeck (2001). For more information about Iraq economy during the 1970s and 1980s see Al-Ameen (1981: 263–275).

47 See MEED (9 December 1977); and MEED (29 August 1980).

48 See Hoskins (1997: 112).

49 See for example, Simons (1998); and (2002), and Graham-Brown (1999).

50 See Boone et al. (1997: 21).

51 Among the early reports about the humanitarian situation in the after math of the Gulf War 1991 and sanctions see Khan, Aga Sadruddin (1991); and Cainkar (1993).

52 See Hoskins (1997: 109); and UNHP (24 March 1996b).

53 Many scholars who work within or outside the discipline of International Relations (IR) argue that IR has shown strong resistance to incorporating an analysis of gender in general and of women in particular. See for example, Pettman (1996); Tickner (1992 and 2001); Jabri and O'Gorman, eds. (1999); Whitworth (1994); Grant (1992); Grant and Newland, eds. (1991); Connell (1987); Enloe (1990a); Peterson (1992a: 1–29); Peterson and Runyan (1993), and Halliday (1991 and 1994). In this context, Halliday (1994) argues that because 'conventional' IR theory, in its assumption and explanations, is considered almost entirely on activity of states, it makes the world international politics a masculine, and therefore not pertain to women (Halliday, 1994: 149). Fred Halliday asserts that the resistance of the field IR to gender analysis of international politics, not because it is 'gender neutral', but rather because it is thoroughly masculized by a hierarchal relationship of power (ibid).

54 There are some groundbreaking works emphasizing that international relations (politics) is also based on different access of power and resources thus, are no different from other social relations. See for example, Jabri and O' Gorman, eds. (1999); Enloe (1988 and 1990a and 1990b); Cockburn (1999); and Goldstein (2001). These works raised questions that are central to gender relations such as, for example, how women relate to other both within and outside societies, especially referring to issues of pre-war conflict, militarism, war, security, migration, peacemaking and reconstruction.

55 The terms 'gender' and 'gender differences' become way of denoting 'cultural' constructions of the appropriate roles of women and men, and a way of referring to subjective identity of women and men. See Scott (1996); and Flax (1990). In this way, the term 'gender' is used to explain why and how system of power (social relations) operates the way it does. See Radtke and Stan (1994).

56 See Pettman (1996); and Cockburn (1999).

57 This research brings to light a problematic of gender relations as associated with conditions of life and conditions of dominance and inequality. Therefore, the multiple methods of research is seen most appropriate. Multiple methods include, a combination of quantitative data (survey) and qualitative data collections (open-ended interview and case-study). For more detail see Reinharz (1992); and Harding, ed. (1987).

58 This is because many Iraqi families now build extensions to their houses to shelter family members with their own households. In many cases, an extension, especially one with a separate entrance but sharing the same house number, is rented out to a young nuclear family.

59 Frequently, female heads of household were not young women living independently, but were widows (10 women, in the survey), or women whose husbands had been in captivity since the Iraq-Iran war (2 women, in the survey). There was one case where the oldest sister was the head of the household.

Chapter 2

1 See Al-Juma'i' and Mohammed-'Ali (1989: 195–222); Farouk-Sluglett (1993: 51–73); Joseph (1982: 69–90), and (1991: 176–200); Rassam (1992: 82–95), and (1982: 88–99); Al-Sharqi (1982: 74–87); Cobbett (1989: 120–137); Omar (1994: 60–71); Efrati (1999: 27–44); Al-Khayat (1990); and Moghadam (1993: esp. Ch.2).

2 See Davis (1991: 7); Hajjar (1985: 8–10); and Keddie (1988).

3 The officers' corps was composed predominately of Arab Sunnis, from a middle-class background; some few were Shi'a. The leader General Abdel Karim Qassim was from mixed background; Sunni father and Shi'a mother (see Batatu, 1978).

4 See Batatu (1978: 764–807); and Tripp (2000).

5 See Farsoun, ed. (1985: 5); Batatu (1978); and Zubaida (2002: 205–215).

6 For example, according to Article 4 of the Ba'th Party Constitution of 1949: 'the party strives to formulate a constitution, for the state guarantees absolute equality for Arab citizens before law ... [to] safeguard the freedoms of speech, publication, assembly, protest and the press ... and [to] allow the setting up of clubs, societies and parties'. However, in spite of these 'democratic' provisions, particularly concerning parliamentary democracy, pluralism, and the four freedoms, the Ba'th regime(s) in both Iraq and Syria have, in practice, always ruled by iron and blood. An extremely violent and tyrannical history against political opponents has been comprehensively revealed. See Arab Ba'th Socialist Party (ABSP- Constitution 1947).

7 See Al-Hassan (1988).

8 According to the ASBP Constitution, 'Arab women enjoy the full rights of Arab citizens. The liberation of women is an integral part of the liberation of the Arab nation' (see ABSP, 1976; 1974b). Such slogans were often repeated by the Ba'thist elites.

9 See ABSP Doctrine (1974a: 153).

10 In 1971 Iraq ratified two of the most important human rights conventions, namely the International Covenant on Civil and Political Rights (ICCPR) and the International Covenant on Economic, Social and Cultural Rights (ICESCR). The latter is viewed as being essential to the equality of men and women.

11 See Abdallah (1987).

12 The Interim Constitution of 1970 embodied a new spirit that was different from Iraq's previous constitutions. Although the principle of equality between citizens had been stated in the 1958, 1964, and 1968 constitutions, these had stopped short of specifying areas in which discrimination against women accrued, nor did they identify the state's responsibilities in this regard. The ambiguity of these constitutions was rectified in the Interim Constitution of 1970, which stated clearly that work was one of the areas where discrimination against women might accrue. The state was therefore responsible not only for alleviating discrimination by ensuring that women's rights were put on an equal footing with those of men, but also for providing female workers with good working conditions, raising their living standards, and improving their professional skills.

13 Labour Law No. 151 of 1970, the Agrarian Reforms Law No. 117 of 1970, Reforms of Legal System Law No. 35 of 1977, Social Security and Labour Pension (Welfare) Law No. 39 of 1971, Civil Services Law (amendment) No. 94 of 1977, and the 'Political Report of the Eighth Regional Congress of the Ba'th Party' (ABSP-Doctrine of 1974) which was regarded 'important law' Party recommendations.

14 Labour Law No. 151 of 1970 (published in the Iraqi Gazette issue No. 2200 of 1972). Article 79, Paragraph (A) stated that the employment of women on night shifts in industrial plants and factories was banned, except in a handful of specified cases and on condition that in these cases, acceptable health and other facilities were provided. It also prohibited the employment of women in jobs of a heavy or harmful nature. These rights were also mentioned in the reformed Legal System Law No. 35 of 1977, in which Article 83 stipulated that special facilities, such as comfortable seats modified according to type of work, should be provided, and were stipulated in 'Special Regulations Concerning Working Women', No. 36 of 1972. According to Articles 81, 82 and 84 of Labour Law No. 151 of 1970 (published in the Iraqi Gazette issue No. 1906 of 1971), a pregnant working woman was granted 'special' rights, such as special health care, a maximum prohibition on jobs and duties with the potential for causing damaging effects, a working day limited strictly to seven hours, and so on. These laws were also stated in the Pension and Social Security Welfare Law No. 39 of 1979, Article 45, Paragraph (b). Article 84 of the Labour Law 1970 among other it obliged employers of 20 or more women to establish a nursery or kindergarten at the worksite, and entitled working mothers to bay-feeding breaks during working hours.

15 Both parents (mothers and fathers) were entitled to receive children's allowances on an equal footing, regardless of whether they were living together, or were divorced or separated. (see Financial Rights and Benefits: Equality between Men and Women, Law No. 191 of 1975).

16 Labour Law No. 151 of 1970, Article 80, granted pregnant women a month of antenatal leave, and six weeks of postnatal leave on full pay. In special cases such leave could be extended, provided that the extension did not exceed nine months (including the original

maternity-leave period) in total. A woman received 75 per cent of her original salary for the period of such an extension. This right was also stated in Pensions and Social Security Welfare Law No. 39 of 1971, Article 48.

17 The nationalization of Iraq's Petroleum Company in 1972 and the oil price increases in 1973–74 led to sharp increases in Iraq oil revenues, from about ID 280 million in 1970 to ID 2.4 billion in 1974. By the end of 1970s, Iraq's oil revenues had reached about ID 9 billion (US$30.5 billion), having in mind that exchange rate in the 1970s was US$1 to ID 0.311.

18 Civil Service Law amendment No. 94 of 1977 (amending CSL No. 34 of 1960), published in the *Iraqi Gazette*, issue No. 2602 of 1977.

19 Revolutionary Command Council (RCC) Decree No. 1534 of 13 November 1979, published in the *Iraqi Gazette* issue No. 2742 in 26 November 1979.

20 The Code of Personal Status (amendment no 2) Law No 21 of 1978, published in *Al-Waqa'e al-irakiyya* [Iraqi Gazette] No. 2639, 20 February 1978.

21 The PSC, paragraph 9 {1} , Chapter 2 paragraphs 23–32, and Chapter 3 paragraphs 19–22.

22 See ABSP Doctrine (1974a: 185).

23 The PSC, paragraphs 3 (4), 3 (5), and 7.

24 The Code imposes a penalty of imprisonment for a period of no less than three years and no more than five years on men who fail to register their marriages at court. The legislation makes a distinction between two categories of relatives when applying penalties for those who are found guilty of forcing a marriage. Parents are to be penalized by imprisonment for a period of maximum 3 years or/and by the payment of an unspecified fine. Relatives other than parents, including brothers, uncles, cousins and other kinsmen are to be penalized by imprisonment for a period of no less than three years and no more than ten. See CPS, paragraphs 8 (2), 9 (2) & 9 (3).

25 The PSC, paragraphs 34, 35, 36 & paragraphs 1–39; CPS- amendments of 1980, Law No. 156, paragraph 1.

26 As such, the 1978 PSC was significantly different from the original code of 1959, where a husband's infidelity was not considered as adultery and thus was not a valid cause for divorce unless it was committed within the confines of the conjugal home. On the other hand, according to the 1959 code a woman's affair with another man was considered to be adultery, no matter where it took place. It should be noted that the 1978 Personal Status Code referred to marital infidelity in terms of adultery (*khiyana zawajiyya*), rather than the old term *zina* (fornication), which is strongly connected to the concepts of women's 'purity' and their role as guardians of male honour. Substituting the religious term of adultery for more natural and 'secular' conceptions was obviously an attempt to draw attention away from the issue of patriarchal honour and women's purity and towards the responsibility of both husband and wife to live up to their marital commitments (Law No. 125 of 1981, 7th amendment of PSC, *Al-Waqa'e al-irakiyya* [The Iraqi Gazette] No. 2863, 21 December 1981).

27 The 1958 government abolished the tribal code of honour killing and declared all Iraqi citizens to be subject to the same national legal codes, thereby rendering tribal customary laws void.

28 According to *shari'a*, a woman's right to her parents' inheritance is equal to half the share of what a man may inherit.

29 Under Ba'th rule the RCC was the 'only' real governing body in Iraq, although its membership changed repeatedly due to the systematic executions of some of its members. Saddam Hussain was believed to be behind all these killings. However, the most notable

massacre in the RCC occurred on 22 July 1979, when Saddam participated 'physically' in the execution of one third of the RCC's members. In 1982, the RCC was made up of 24 members, two thirds of whom were his relatives.

30 See Joseph (1991: 178–9).

31 United Nations' analysis of main aggregates suggests that Iraq's average growth rates for different economic sectors for the period 1970–80 were 19.5 percent (with the exception of the agricultural sector, which registered a growth rate of only 1.4 percent) (see United Nations, 1991: 126–197).

32 See Republic of Iraq (1983a: 20).

33 See Jiyad (2002: 141–169). An examination of the problem of disparity between oil revenues and announced allocations for the three-year period from 1981 to 1983 gives an idea of the financial support that was offered to Iraq during its war with Iran. During this period, total allocations were ID 19.8 billion, yet one half of the oil revenue in the same period was only ID 4.7 billion; i.e., less than one fourth of total allocations (for more details see Townsend, 1984: 62; and EIU, 1984: 11).

34 Until this time, there are no accurate official statistics concerning the scale of human casualties of the Iraq-Iran War, although it is estimated that over one million people from both countries were killed. According to some conservative estimates, the number of Iraqi soldiers killed was 105,000, with a further 700,000 solders injured (see Hiro, 1991: 250; Alnasrawi, 1994: esp. Ch. 5).

35 Saddam said: 'Every Iraqi family should have at least five children. A family with less than four children should be severely rebuked … Iraq's geographic location requires a 'larger' population capable of defending the country' (*Al-Jumhuriyya* newspaper, 4 May 1986). Manal al-Alusi, Secretary-General of the General Federation of Iraqi Women (the female arm of the Ba'th party), said in June 1986 that the Federation was setting up a three-year working plan to implement the President's directive on women's roles in various fields, including procreation (*Al-Jumhuriyya*, 7 June 1986). The participation of government ministries in the national campaign for increasing the birth rate was also reported officially.

36 The 1985 amendment of CSL No. 48 of 1975 (Article 51, no.5).

37 A condition of the legislation was that these allowances would be void if the workers left the service for employment in non-military institutions.

38 RCC Decree No. 730 of 25 June 1985, the *Iraqi Gazette*, No. 3054, 15 June 1985. The shortage of labour was reflected in RCC Decree No. 208, Paragraph 5, issued in 1982, urging the state sectors to employ individuals with physical deformities, both male and female, who were able and willing to work.

39 Amendment to Article 44, Paragraph 4, Civil Service Law of 1977, published in the *Iraqi Gazette*, No. 2807, 15 December 1980.

40 RCC Decree No. 1283, published in the *Iraqi Gazette*, No. 2793, 8 September 1980.

41 Actual service did not include maternity leaves. RCC Decree No. 959 of 18 July 1981.

42 RCC Decree No. 1283 of 23 November 1983, published in the *Iraqi Gazette*, No. 2970, 15 December 1983.

43 RCC Decree No. 521 of 17 May 1983, published in the *Iraqi Gazette*, No. 2939, 16 May 1983.

44 RCC Decree No. 179 of 1980, published in the *Iraqi Gazette*, No. 2807, 15 December 1980.

45 Decree No. 92/81 issued by the RCC's Control Committee (*Majlis al-indhebhebat*), published in *Al-Adalah al-Iraqiyya* [Iraq Gazette]) Vol. 1, No. 7, 1981, p. 85.

46 RCC Decree No. 581, 2 May 1982, published in the *Iraqi Gazette*, No. 2884, 17 May 1982.

47 In fact, the word *tjeeb* has a second meaning when spoken with an Iraqi accent. In classical Arabic, it (*tujeeb*) is the feminine form of the verb 'answering', but when said in an Iraqi accent, it (*tjeeb*) often applies to terms to do with 'giving birth to' or 'the delivery of' a child or a thing'.

48 See GFIW (1989). According to the 1990 World Average Fertility figures, the average of total fertility in Iraq increased from 6.5 births per woman in 1977 to 7.4 births in 1987, which is far higher than the world average of 5.5 births, 5.6 births for western Asia, and 2.8 births for the developed countries.

49 The ministries of health and education co-worked a two-year plan aimed at increasing women's fertility, improving mother and child care, preventing sterility, increasing penalties for illegal abortions and restricting the sale of contraceptives, increasing the number of paediatric hospitals, clinics and other medical institutions providing services to mothers and children, training more midwives, improving public education, and promoting the campaign through the media (*Al-Jumhuriyya*, 31 January 1988). The media also directed its attention towards raising women's awareness of the national and the pan-Arab importance of increasing reproduction, stressing the significance of marriage and the need for reducing its costs, including those of the dower.

50 See GFIW (1990: 10); and Al-Khalidi (1991: 22–29).

51 RCC Decree No. 44 of 1986.

52 RCC Decree No. 43 of 11 January 1986, published in the *Iraqi Gazette*, No. 3081, 11 June 1986.

53 RCC Decree No. 703 of 5 September 1987, published in the *Iraqi Gazette*, No. 3168, 21 September 1987.

54 RCC Decree No. 727 of 11 September 1987, in the *Iraqi Gazette*, No. 3169, 28 September 1987.

55 RCC Decree No. 882 of 29 November 1987, in the *Iraqi Gazette*, No. 3179 in 7 December 1987.

56 Issue of the new Labour Law No. 71 of 1987 was ordered by RCC Decree No. 536 of 27 July 1987, published in the *Iraqi Gazette*, No. 3143 of 30 August 1987.

57 These provisions granted women employees in the private sector the right to an extended period of maternity leave to a maximum of nine months, including the original period of 72 days. The first 72 days were to be fully paid by the private employers while the rest (the extension) could be paid by the Social Security and Welfare, provided that the mother had had full membership (paid contingent) in the Social Security System for a minimum of one year of actual service in the same job.

58 Iraq's economically active population increased in size from 1,631,000 in 1960 to 3,134,000 in 1977, an increase of 195 per cent, or an annual average growth of 4.3 percent (see Mehdi and Robenson, 1983: 18–26). Iraq's labour force increased from 3,929,550 in 1972 – to 6,628,560 in 1978, and to 7,387,000 in 1979. For more details see, 'Situation and Development of Iraq's Labour Force: A Detailed Study' Ministry of Planning (Republic of Iraq, Ministry of Planning, 1971a: 103); (Republic of Iraq, Ministry of Planning, 1977b: 6).

59 Rates of female labour force in the public sector increased from 14.83 percent to total labour in the sector in 1967 to 22.45 percent in 1979 (Republic of Iraq, Ministry of Planning Iraq, 1980: 32).

60 See GFIW (1994b: 29).

61 Ibid.

62 See Alnasrawi (1994: 92).

63 Ibid.

64 See Farahni (1986: 2).

65 Ibid: 12–13. During 1982, and in order to minimize the hard currency crisis, the government halved the hard currency transactions permitted to foreign workers.

66 Cited in Al-Alusi (1985: 22–23).

67 Apart from the agricultural sector where female labour was highly concentrated, the biggest increase in female labour during the period 1977 to 1984 occurred in the banking and finance sector (37.9 percent of the total labour in the sector) and the service sector (26.1 percent).

68 Republic of Iraq, Ministry of Planning (1984: 14); GFIW (1983b: 10); GFIW (1987: 67).

69 See Chaudhry (1997) and (1991); Springborg (1999); and Alnasrawi (1994).

70 In 1987, the unemployed and those who had never been in work numbered 176,393 individuals, of whom 81 percent were male and 19 percent (33,104) were female. This rate was higher than in 1977, when total unemployment in the country was 101,714 individuals, of whom 11,575 were female (i.e. 11 percent of the total unemployed). According to the statistics, 67 percent of unemployed females were educated to above high school level, compared with the majority of the unemployed males (stated in GFIW, 1987: 14). This meant that suitable opportunities for female employment had declined less, especially for those who were highly educated. For these groups of women it was particularly difficult to take lower level jobs outside their professional field (ibid: 22).

71 See GFIW (1994a: 61).

72 Ibid.

73 This is evident in the increased share of the agricultural sector in Iraq's GDP from ID 860.9 million in 1987 to ID 1073.2 million in 1990 while the manufacturing industry's contribution to GDP declined from ID 942.5 million in 1987 to ID 719.8 million in 1990. See Iraq's *Annual Abstract of Statistics*, 1987a & 1991.

74 'Umma is the Arabic word for 'community'. The concept of 'umma connotes a united people or the nation through Islamic tradition or Arab identity. However, the Islamic 'umma or united Muslim community is more important than national identity. It was only in the aftermath of the First World War that the 'Arab nation' emerged as a significant concept, and Arab nationalism gradually took the form of a political movement with the idea of a secular Arab nation/'umma/community. 'The 'umma of Islam' has a broader catchment area than pan-Arabism because it does not differentiate between Arab and non-Arab. The Muslim 'umma is a unity in which ethnicity plays no part (see for more details, Dawisha, 2003).

75 See Yuval-Davis and Anthias (1989).

76 Apart from unpaid household work, unpaid family labour in agricultural and small manufacturing enterprises is unlikely to be included in the figures presented in statistical tables. Iraqi women may well be making larger economic contributions than they appear to be, but because they are not salaried, they may not control the yields of their labours. For this and other reasons, women's labour participation remains low, partly because it reflects unpaid family labour in the household and agriculture, but also because many women are still economically dependent upon men.

Chapter 3

1 It must be noted that the MENA is not a uniform entity and the countries that make up the region differ in their historical evolution, social composition, economic structures, and

state forms. They also differ as regards the construct of patriarchal/gender systems. As a primarily cultural construct, the patriarchal system is constituted according to social structure, historical processes, and political and economic conditions. Thus, patriarchal systems are differently manifested in different countries in the region. For example, patriarchal kinship-ordered relationships are more influential in the tribal and homogenous society of Saudi Arabia (and other Gulf states) than it the case in the heterogeneous and secular societies of Turkey and Tunisia (at least at an official level) (cf., Kandiyoti, 1988: 274–290), and (1991d); and Moghadam (1993).

2   See UNICEF (1997) and (1998).

3   See UNDP (2002: 82).

4   A UNICEF Report noted that teachers were the group most affected by the embargo. The inadequate salaries discouraged large numbers of teachers, especially women, and many qualified teachers and professors went out of teaching, either to move into another occupation for much better pay, or else left the country altogether in search of a better life (see UNICEF 1997: 81).

5   The nominal income salary of a civil servant constitutes the 'net' payment. Above the net salary every civil servant has the right to other financial allowances, including housing allowance, children's allowance, transport allowance, and in many cases special health insurance.

6   See Chaudhry (1997); Alnasrawi (1994); and Jiyad (1998).

7   For further reading on the experience of women in other part of the Middle East see Moghadam (1998); World Bank (1995), and Anker (1998).

8   See Johnson & Rogaly (1997); and Khandker (1998).

9   Several studies have contributed to the definition of the informal sector in Third World economies. See for example, Abdel-Fadil (1989: 18–21); Hopkins, (ed.) (1991); Lobban & Richard (eds.) (1998); ILO (1991), and (1999: 180–4); Singerman (1995: 177); and Bibars (2001).

10 See Mustafa-Yasin (1990).

11 The ILO maintains that the informal sector has been growing rapidly and continuously in almost every corner of the globe, but it has increased considerably in recent years due to the inability of workers to find jobs in the formal economy. The informal economy covers all types of economic activities outside the formal economy; these are generally unrecognized and lie beyond the control of the state. Workers in the informal economy have uncertain wage rates and uncertain working hours, do not enjoy legal protection and are not insured by health and pension security (see ILO, 1991).

12 See UNDP (2002: 94).

13 See ILO (1999: 182).

14 Ibid.

Chapter 4

1   See ABSP (1974b: Article 45).

2   See Reynolds (1985: 25).

3   See UNESCO (2003a: 29).

4   See Van Eeghen (2000).

5   See Solomon (1999).

6   For example, education expenditure in the United Kingdom for the financial year 2003/4 was planned to reach 5.29 percent of GDP, the highest level since 1982/3 (in United Kingdom, 2002, 'Social Indicators', Research Paper 02/01, 9 Jan 2002, p. 32. Online: HtmlResAnchor http://www.parliament.uk/commons/lib/research/rp2002/rp02-001.pdf.

In Malaysia, educational expenditure averaged some 17 percent of total expenditure, and 5 percent of the ever-growing GDP over the period 1970–2000 (see Doling and Omar, 2000: 33–47). In Singapore, according to the World Bank's *World development Indicators, 1998*, public education expenditure in 1980 was 2.8 percent of GDP and in 1995 was 3 percent of GDP. In Chile it was 4.6 percent and 2.9 percent respectively for the same years, in Indonesia it was 1.7 percent and 1.3 percent respectively, and in South Korea it remained the same at 3.7 percent for both years.

7   See UNESCO (2003a: 15).

8   Ibid.

9   See UNESCO (2003a).

10 See UNESCO (2003).

11 Starting in 1988, the government ordered the construction of seven universities, including Kirkuk University (Northern Province), which was opened in January 2003 – three months before the allied (US and UK) war of 2003.

12 Iraq's formal education is divided into the following categories: (a) illiterate and read only (pre-primary level); (b) primary school (six years); (c) secondary education (three years intermediate and three years preparatory/high school); (d) vocational school (three years); (e) Bachelor's degree (four years); (f) Higher diploma (three years), Master's degree (two and half years), PhD/high professional degree (three to five years), and others. Students who completed the preparatory route and obtained minimum entry qualifications could proceed directly to university or to the technical colleges for a minimum of four years. Students could choose to select programmes in teacher training (5 years) or in vocational education (3 years) after the intermediate level. Those who excelled in their final examinations for these programmes could be admitted into colleges or universities to pursue higher degrees.

13 See Al-Rawi (1979: 229).

14 Ibid.

15 According to the *Report of the Second Conference on Illiteracy Eradication* (24–25 September 1979), before the campaign started, there were around 2,544,014 illiterate people in Iraq, of whom 1,798,851 were females. The 1995 *Human Development Report* maintains that in 1978 the illiterate Iraqi population among the 15 to 45 age group numbered 2,212,630, a rate of 48.4 percent of the total population. Of these, 676,693 were males and 1,535,937 were females (see UNDP and IEA, 1995: 45).

16 See CEDAW (1998).

17 See also UNESCWA (1994: 88).

18 See ABSP (1982a).

19 See ABSP (1982b: 167).

20 Ibid.

21 UNESCO Institute for Statistics, *Literacy Statistics*, 2003b.

     Online: HtmlResAnchor http://status.uis.unesco.or/TableViewer/tableView.aspx? ReportId=41 (Last accessed 16 September 2005); UNDP HDR (2002); *The World's Women 2000: Trends and Statistics*, UN Statistics Division. Online:HtmlResAnchor http://unstats.un.org/unsd/demographic/ww2000/table5d.htm.

     (Last accessed 23 August 2003). See also, Roudi-Fahimi and Moghadam (2003); Haub (2003).

22 Illiteracy rates among Iraqi males are also the highest among MENA countries. In 2000, the rate of illiteracy among males aged over 15 years was 45 percent, or 3,057,000, and the rate of illiteracy among males between 15 and 24 was 41 percent, or 962,000 males.

23 For example, compared with Egypt where per capita income in 2000 was US$3,670, the
    rate of illiteracy among women over 15 years of age was 56 percent; Indonesia's per capita
    income in 2000 was US$2,830, but only 18 percent of women aged over 15 were illiterate
    (see UNESCO Institute for Statistics. See *Literacy Statistics*, online UNESCO Institute for
    Statistics (2003b).

24 See Republic of Iraq, Ministry of Planning (1984: 212).

25 See UNESCO (2003: 29).

26 Ibid.

27 See UNICEF (2002b). In 2000, the total number of girls aged 5–14 was 2,972,917 girls
    out of Iraq's total population of 22,675,617 inhabitants. The number of girls enrolled in
    primary school was thus around half of the total number of girls eligible for school. See
    Republic of Iraq, *Annual Abstract of Statistics, 1998–99*: 47; and United States Census
    Bureau, population data/international data base: HtmlResAnchor http://www.census.gov/
    cgi-bin/ipc/idbagg; also: HtmlResAnchor http://www.census.gov/ipc/www/idbpyr.html
    (accessed 30 May 2005).

28 See UNESCO (2003a).

29 See Republic of Iraq, Central Statistical Organisation (1999: 376).

30 Gender inequality as a variable depends on a number of independent variables, including the
    economic (such as GNP and per capita income), the socio-economic (such as formal education
    and health), the social (such as legislation in favour of women's employment, female education,
    and family law), and the cultural (such as religious and ethnic specificities).

31 In the academic year 1970/71 there were only 47 female students in technology and
    engineering (i.e., only 7 percent of the total enrolment in the subject). In 1979/80, the
    number of females enrolled in technology and engineering increased to 399 students
    (22 percent). By 1982/83, the number of females enrolled had reached 1,724 (a rate of
    24 percent). As far as enrolment in Departments of Economics and Management Sciences
    was concerned, the rate of female students in 1970/71 was only 17 percent. This figure
    had increased to 38 percent of total enrolment in this field by 1979/80. In Agricultural
    Sciences, the rate of female students in 1970/71 was 5 percent. By 1979/80, the rate of
    female enrolment had increased to 20 percent. In Natural Sciences, female enrolment in
    1970/71 was at the rate of 30 percent, and had increased by 1979/80 to 39 percent (see
    Ministry of Planning, 1982: 225; and Ministry of Education, 1980: 1–6).

32 Following the increased demand for university enrolment, the state allowed the
    establishment of private universities and colleges in 1989. However, such permission was
    strictly limited to the BA degree in limited types of discipline only. Private colleges grant
    bachelor degrees in Business Administration, Accounting and Statistics, Computer
    Sciences, Law, Arabic, English, History, and Geography, as well as polytechnic level
    diplomas (see UNDP & IEA, 1995: 48–49).

33 See Musadeq (1987: 268); and Ministry of Planning (1987a: 248).

34 See Ministry of Planning (1987a). The duration of study at the Teacher Training Institutes
    is five years after intermediate school level, and at the Central Teacher Training Institutes
    is two years after secondary school level.

35 See UNESCO (2003: 30).

36 See UNDP & AFESD (2002: 54).

37 See UNICEF (1998: 80).

38 See UNICEF (1997: 89).

39 Ibid.

40 See UNESCO (2003: 15).

41 For example, in 1994 at the university level only, there were 4,778 new students at various academic levels who expected to be admitted (see UNDP, 2001: 51–62).

42 See UNESCO (2002).

43 Ibid.

44 See UNDP & IEA (1995: 52).

45 See Asquith (2003). Denis Halliday when reviewed the draft copy of this study stated that: 'Some 30,000 teachers left their jobs for lack of schools, books, and the poor salaries'. He added, 'I used to speculate that about 2 million Iraqi professional women and men went overseas and now we hear another 2 million have departed since the invasion. In short, Iraq now faces a brain drain problem of real size and loss'.

46 See UNESCO (2003).

47 See UNDP (2002: 53–54).

48 Ibid.

49 See Al-Ali and Husein (2003: 33–56).

50 Private college/university tuition costs range from ID 180,000–ID 300,000 per academic year (US$90–US$150 at exchange rate 1US$: ID 2000).

51 See UNDP & IEA (1995: 49).

52 See Republic of Iraq, Central Statistical Organization (1999: 411).

53 See UNDP & IEA (1995: 42–44); and UNDP & AFESD (2002: 51–55).

54 See UNESCO (2000).

55 See UNDP & IEA (1995: 42–44).

56 Total enrolment in vocational schools in 2000/01 was 65,750, including 61,861 in the Centre/South and 3,889 in the North. Nationally this was a decline of 55.6 percent in enrolment from 147,942 students in 1989/90. The situation deteriorated further when 10,976 students failed their examinations (see UNESCO, 2003: 63–64).

57 The Government of Iraq reported that this was the case in its most recent periodic report to CEDAW (the Committee for the Elimination of all forms of Discrimination Against Women) (see CEDAW, 1998: 12).

58 See UNDP & IEA (1995: 55).

59 See Dwyer and Bruce, eds. (1988); and Roudi and Moghadam (2003).

60 See Karshenas and Moghadam (2001); and El-Naggar, ed. (1993).

61 See Roudi-Fahimi and Moghadam (2003); and Dwyer and Bruce, eds. (1988).

62 A survey of the demographics and health of Egypt concluded that, among married Egyptian women aged, for example, 25 to 29 years, those with no education had married, on average, at age 18 and had produced a child by the age of 20, while those with secondary or higher education married at an average age of 23 years and had their first child by age 25 (see El-Zanaty and Way, 2001: tables 4.9, 8.4). Another survey on Turkey showed that in 1998, a significant percentage of 22 girls aged 15 to 19 who had no education or had not completed primary school were already mothers or pregnant (see Hacettepe University, Institute of Population Studies, 1999: esp. Table 3.9).

63 The findings of the survey by El-Zanaty and Way about Egypt reveals that women with more education also tend to have healthier families. For example, children born to mothers with no primary education were more than twice as likely to die as those born to mother who had completed secondary school. It shows, too, that women with less education were less likely to receive antenatal care (see El-Zanaty and Way, 2001: tables 9.9 and 11.5). Moreover, women with more education tended to know about a wider range of available methods and where to go to obtain contraception, and were more likely to discuss family planning issues with their husbands (Ibid: table 5.5).

64 See Garfield (1997: 1474–5) and (1999a) and (2000: 16–19).

65 See WHO (1996) and (1998b).

66 The Amended RCC Decision No. 1085 of 3 October 1983, stipulates that: 'The Ministry of Planning is responsible for the job distribution of all graduates, including vocational school graduates, teacher-training institutes graduates, university and college graduates, according to their specialties and the needs for their qualifications'.

67 See Caldwell (1982: 322).

68 An assumption that education affects western women differently from women in the developing countries suggests that female education in the West was not the only determinant force in improving women's status. This is not the case in the developing countries. In the West, classic patriarchy eventually evolved into a state welfare system or neo-patriarchy, and gendered class structures emerged when a capitalist market and liberal bourgeoisie ideology worked together to break private/public and male/female dichotomies (Mann, 1986: 52–53). However, while this by no means undermines the role of education in the lives of western women, it had 'provided western women with one of their furthest points of entry into the public sphere and into economic stratification' (Ibid).

69 See Mernissi (1987: xxv).

70 See Ismael (2004: 223).

71 These included a monthly sum for all students from limited income families, free accommodation for those from other provinces, and free books and notebooks for all students. The RCC Decision No. 1217 of 9 September 1981 stipulates that: 'According to the Law of Welfare (No. 126 of 1980), persons who are unable to work and students at university and colleges are entitled to a minimum monthly salary (ID 30 Equal to US$100), if the person has no other independent income'. The RCC Decision No. 277 of 8 March 1981 stipulates that: 'Students who receive a state monthly salary and accommodation allowance are not obliged to refund this money to the state'.

72 A number of analysts concur that economic, social, and political restrictions, including restrictions on Iraqi women's mobility, have placed extreme strain upon women (see UNOCHR, 2003; Zubaida, 2003; Ismael, 2004: 225; UNICEF, 1998).

Chapter 5

1 See Blumer (1990: 54).

2 See Kamrava (1993).

3 For further reading on the Arab family see Barakat (985: 27), Singerman (1995: 170–178), Joseph (ed.) (1999: 113–140), and Joseph (1996b).

4 See Al-Atiah (1994; and Al-Hassan (1994).

5 The classical Middle Eastern patriarchy has been pinpointed in societies where kinship is conterminous with society and where the dominance of male elders over kin groups is translated into a key force that dominates society in terms of organizing politics, economics, religion, and other social processes (see Joseph, 1999: 121; 1996a: 2–10); and Mann, (1986: 40–56).

6 See Mann (1986).

7 Suad Joseph's useful term "connectivity" is based on her experience of Lebanese society; she uses it to explain the psychodynamic process that characterises people as part of each other. She defines the connective relationship as: 'One's sense of self is intimately linked with the self of another so that the security, identity, integrity, dignity, and self-worth of

one is tied to the actions of the other' (see Joseph (ed.), 1999: 121). She suggests the construct of the Arab family is in a relational context and disagrees about views based on an individualist or corporatist context, arguing that the individualistic-based view is inadequate because it suggests that the socio-economic relations of the Arab family are mainly between individuals whereas group relations and formations in Arab society are rather weak. Joseph doubts the corporatist view, especially its functional definition of the Arab family. Corporatist-based analysis suggests that collective interests in the Arab society often override those of the individual. Joseph disagrees with this notion, which suggests that the deep integration of selves in the family is problematic for the society and the person because it would lead to a neglect of the interests of both (Joseph, 1999: 10–11).

8   As an example, women's mobility outside the country's borders was also restricted. Iraqi women under 45 years of age were officially barred from leaving the country without a male guardian (mehrim).

9   As an example, RCC Decision No. 632 of 13 May 1981 entitled men who aged 22 or over to a loan of ID 750 (equal to US$2,400) on favourable terms and a state grant of ID 500 (equal to US$1,600). If the man was a student, he was entitled to the same rights, in addition to free state housing and free public transport including air fares. See also RCC Decision No. 576 of 4 May 1981. A person who became handicapped and unable to work was eligible for a state grant for the purpose of marrying of ID 2000 (equal to US$6,400) for civilian and ID 3000 (equal to US$9,600) for military claimants.

10   Interview on 29 November 2001 with Dr Mohammed Ahmed Hamza, Department of Social Science, University of Baghdad.

11   The first part of the dowry is seen merely as a symbolic gift, given either to the bridegroom or the bride's guardian (usually male), or used by the new couple for furniture and/or by the bride for other needs. The second part of the dowry is symbolically intended to protect women, particularly against divorce. The issue of dowry has attracted much debate among scholars. Some argue that it is a practice intended to protect a woman's economic rights in the event of divorce or other kinds of abuse from the husband. Others see it as a bride price, affirming male dominance (cf. 'Izat, 1990).

12   Of 4200 women, 75 percent (3150) were unmarried. The study showed that 62 percent of these (1953 women) had never received a proposal of marriage, while among the remaining (1197) unmarried women, 57 percent (682 women) were engaged but had delayed entering marriage life because of lack of financial resources, while 34 percent (515 women) had dissolved their engagement to marry for other reasons. Of this latter group, 95 percent (489 women) had either been prevented from joining their partners outside the country or had given up on marriage after a long engagement period because of problems with housing and material resources (see Al-Banaa, 1996).

13   That is, marriage within the same lineage, sect, community, group, village, city, and/or neighbourhood. For more details see Al-Banaa (1996); and Al-Hassan (1986a).

14   See Al-Jenabi (1983: 16).

15   Ibid: 36.

16   During the Iraq-Iran war, women had to deal with the regime's attempts to raise the birth rate. Since the war had created many widows, the state tried initially to compensate these women by giving certain grants. Later on however, the state began to give grants to men as an incentive to marry the Iraqi widows.

17   Law No. 4, the Personal Status Law of 1978.

18   Al-Qur'an, Surat Al-Nessa'a, Verses 2 & 29 (Qur'an, Women Sura).

19 See UNICEF (1998: 9).

20 Among other see the following state-Decisions:

   1: RCC Decision No. 1611 of 31/12/1982 stipulates: 'the state forbids the sale of the house/flat if it is occupied by a widow as long she is alive'. Widows have the right to keep the dwelling, regardless of the reasons given for the sale. This decision can be disregarded only if the widow gives official consent to the sale.

   2: RCC Decision No. 2959 of 19/9/1983 and RCC Decision No. 970 of 5/9/1983, stipulate: 'wives of captives or lost husbands to be allowed special facilities for house-building loans by the Iraq Bank of Establishment'.

   3: RCC Decision No. 2828 of 4/5/1981 and RCC Decision No. 478 of 2/4/1981 stipulate: 'Families of martyrs are entitled a pension according to Pension Law and Social Welfare Law No. 39 of 1971 disregarding whether or not the father/brother was a civil servant within the government sector'.

   4: RCC Decision No. 2830 of 18/5/1981 and RCC Decision No. 558 of 3/5/1981 stipulate: 'Wives of martyrs (even if a man had more than one wife) are entitled to the equal rights and privileges'.

21 Referring to the principles of 'honour and shame' used by Al-Khayat, Iraqi women are supposed to be the guardians of their families' honour and must therefore protect it and safeguard it from outsiders (see Al-Khayat, 1990).

22 In general, the right of divorce is in the hands of men, but there are several conditions where a woman can initiate divorce without losing her legal rights. These are the following: 1) Personal Status Law No. 21 Paragraph 40 of 1978, amended by RCC Decision No. 23 of 5 January 1986, stipulates that a wife who is subjected to domestic violence confirmed by an official medical report has the right for divorce with full legal rights. 2) Law No. 125 of 1981, the seventh amendment of the Personal Status Law of 1978, stipulates that a wife has the right to initiate divorce in cases where the infidelity was committed by her husband. 3) Law No. 58 of 1981 Paragraphs 41 & 43, the seventh amendment of the Personal Status Law of 1978, stipulates that the wife has the right to divorce if the marriage was consummated when one or both partners was under the age of 18 without the consent of a state-authorized judge, or if it was a forced marriage, or in cases where the husband's marriage to another wife was without the consent of his first wife or/and the consent of a state-authorized judge. 4) Personal Status Law of 1978, Paragraph 43 & Law No. 45 of the Executive Law of 1980 stipulates that a wife has the right to divorce (a) if the husband is sentenced to imprisonment for a period of three years and more; (b) if the husband has abandoned his wife for a period of two years and more in which case, if the wife is not given alimony by the husband, she has the right to receive social security from the state; (c) if the marriage was not consummated for a period of two years after the execution of the marriage contact; (d) if the wife found the husband seriously ill (i.e., infertile); and (e) if the husband does not fulfil his responsibilities. 5) Law No. 77 of 1983 (concerning the Rights and Obligations of Divorced Women) stipulates that the divorced wife has the right to stay in the house/flat (owned by the husband) as long it is needed. If the house/flat was rented, the wife has the right to re-register it in her name. This right is not applicable if the reason for the divorce was infidelity by the wife, or was based on her demand without justification. 6) RCC Decision No. 1718 of 17 December 1981 stipulates that a wife has the right to divorce if her husband was officially deemed to have served the enemy or has escaped from military services for a period of more than six months. The law grants her full rights for housing and alimony, and if not paid by the husband, the state will be responsible for these

charges. 7) Law No. 51 of 1985 Para. 93(3) stipulates that a divorced woman has the right to compensation if she was injured by the man (divorced).

23   See Al-Khayat (1990: 187).

Chapter 6

1   It is important to note that this chapter looks at the issue of health under sanctions from a general concern, rather than providing a detailed analysis on this specific topic. The importance of health and the wide-scale and complex implications of sanctions for this viable sector have been a topic of concern by many professionals in the field.

2   Adopted by the General Assembly of the United Nations, resolution 48/104 of 20 December 1993.

3   See Schuler et al. (1996: 1729–42).

4   See ECLAC (1992).

5   See UNICEF (1989).

6   See UNCHR (2002).

7   For more reading on the issue see Ilkkaracan (2000); Keddie et al (eds.), (1991); Mayer (1995); Bouhdiba (1998); Sev'er & Yurdakul (2001: 964–998); and Mernissi (2000: 203–214).

8   See Sen (1999: 65–86).

9   The Code of Personal Status (CPS) of 1978, Law No. 21 Paragraph 40, amended by RCC Decision No. 23 of 5 January 1986, stipulates that a wife who is subjected to domestic violence confirmed by an official medical report has the right to divorce with full legal rights.

10   It is argued that in Middle Eastern societies, when a male's traditional role as provider is undermined, the potential abuse of women increases (see Mernissi, 1987). UNICEF reports speaking of many instances where the man insults and beats up his wife, blaming her, for example, for giving birth to a sick or malnourished child (see UNICEF 1997: 93).

11   See Kandiyoti (1988: 274–290).

12   For more details on the concept of 'honour and shame' see Shaaban (1988: 60); and Al-Khayyat (1990).

13   According to honour and shame ideology, the honour of any kinship group resides in the sexual conduct of its womenfolk. If a woman behaves immodestly or her modesty is violated she brings shame to all her kin. The act of an immodest woman is 'customarily' punishable by varying degrees of severity, starting with gossip, which immediately affects her reputation and consequently destroys her chance of marriage, and proceeding to her complete abandonment. In many cases, the punishment ends when the woman is killed by a male member of her paternal family (see Alwardi, 1996).

14   The 'ceremony' has to be held in this way, not because of fear of the killing itself, but for eventual protection of the honour of the male members of the particular family (see Omar, 1994).

15   The practice was first outlawed by the Code of Personal Status (CPS) of 1959, and continued to be outlawed by the CPS of 1978.

16   RCC Decree No. 111 of 17 February 1990, signed by Saddam Hussain, exempted from punishment or legal questioning men who murdered their mothers, daughters, sisters, paternal aunts, brothers' daughters or father's brothers' daughters if they were deemed guilty of "honour crimes", even if these women were raped.

17   See UNCHR (January 2002).

18 RCC Decree No. 39 of 11 January 1988, Law for the Elimination of Prostitution, No. 8 para.3 of 1988, stated that a person who was a broker or a manager of a brothel was to be punished for a period not exceeding seven years (*Al-Waqa'a al-iraqiyya*, No. 3186, 11 January 1988).

19 RCC Decree No. 155 of 21 October 1993, amendment of Law for the Elimination of Prostitution, No 8 Issue 42, section A, of 1988, stipulated, according to the Iraqi Constitution and the law, that 'the manager of a prostitution house, prostitution brokerage, and prostitution care is to be punished by sentence of death by execution' (*Al-Waqa'a al-iraqiyya*, No. 3482, 1 November 1993).

20 *Country Reports on Human Rights Practices-2003*, released by the Bureau of Democracy, Human Rights, and Labour (25 February 2004).

21 A few days after this action, Saddam Hussain appeared on Iraqi TV, expressing his regrets and speaking to a religious Shaikh (Sunni sect). The talk was symbolic and indirect. The killing was not specifically mentioned but it was obvious that they were referring to it. Saddam appealed to the Shaikh, saying that he thought he had done something awful, but that it had needed to be done. The Shaikh reassured Saddam that God would not punish him for that because God knew about his good intentions.

22 See Hoskins (1997), and (1992).

23 See UNICEF (1997: 72).

24 See United Nations UN (March 1999: para. 14).

25 See UNICEF (2002b: 12).

26 See Niblock (2001b: 59–67).

27 See UNICEF (1997: 32).

28 The government sometimes distributed subsidised foods such poultry and milk powder; however, the subsidy on such foods was only symbolic. For example, in 2000, the price of a kilo of poultry on the open market was ID 1,500 while the subsidised price was ID 1,350.

29 Notes given by Denis Halliday when reviewed the draft copy of this study.

30 See Drèze and Sen (1989: 20).

31 Respondents' basic needs were ranked accordance their importance: (1) food insecurity; (2) financial security and employment; (3) affordable housing; (4) good healthcare services; and (5) family security, including safety needs, belongingness and love needs.

32 See Garfield (1999b).

33 See WHO (1996: 10); Field (1993: 185–194); UNICEF (1997); and Garfield (1999a: 12).

34 See UNICEF (1997: 41).

35 See Garfield (1999a: 35).

36 See WHO (1998a) and (1998b); and CESR (1996).

37 See Garfield (2000: 16–19).

38 Ibid: 16.

39 See Garfield et al. (1997: 1474–5).

40 Ibid.

41 See UNICEF/Ministry of Health (1999a).

42 See Garfield et al. (1997).

43 See Garfield (1999a: 32–34), esp. Table 4.3.

44 Ibid: 35.

45 See WHO (1996).

46 See WHO (1998b: 11),

47 See WHO (1996: 17).

48 See UNICEF (1999a: 21).

49 Ibid.

50 See UNFPA (2003a).

51 Ibid.

52 According to the UNFPA Survey the number rose from 117 cases of maternal death per 100,000 live births in 1989 to 310 in 2002. See United Nations Population Fund (UNFPA) (2003b), *Reproductive Health Survey: Iraq – a Reproductive Health Assessment UNFPA, August 2003*, available online: HtmlResAnchor http://www.unfpa.org/rh/docs/iraq-rept04-08-03.doc (last accessed 16 September 2005).

Chapter 7

1 See UN International Law Commission (1980: 319).

2 See De Hoogh (1996: 44).

3 Article 30 of the Draft Article on the State Responsibilities, UN International Law Commission (ILC), 1980.

4 Sanctions that are authorized by the SC are mandatory. However there are other types of sanctions: the non-mandatory unilateral sanctions that are imposed by a country against specific target states. Unilateral sanctions have been a main tool of US foreign policy. For further reading on the use of unilateral sanctions see Hufbauer et al. (1990b, an update of Hufbauer and Schott, 1983); Baldwin (1985); also Galdi and Shuey (1997); and Martin (1992 and 1993). Sanctions in general include embargoes (exports-imports), commercial, and financial transactions, arms embargoes, diplomatic sanctions, sports sanctions, and cultural sanctions. For further reading see Hufbauer (1990a); Doxey (1996); and Shepherd (1991).

5 See Malanczuk (1987: 271).

6 The UN International Law Commission emphasized that the use of sanctions did not mean exclusively the taking of 'actions which infringe what in other circumstances would constitute a genuine right' (see UN ILC, 1979: 40).

7 Since its establishment in 1945 the SC has imposed either partial or comprehensive sanctions in 16 cases. Two cases (Rhodesia and South Africa) were in the period 1945–90; since 1990, the SC has evoked Chapter VII of the UN Charter in 14 cases of sanctions (the States of Former Yugoslavia; Haiti; Rwanda; Somalia; Libya; Liberia; Sudan; Angola; Côte d'Ivoire; the Democratic Republic of Congo; Ethiopia and Eritrea; Sierra Leone; Afghanistan; and Cambodia). In an unprecedented move, the SC also imposed sanctions on two non-state actors: the Khmer Rouge in Cambodia (formerly Kampuchea) and the National Union for the Total Independence of Angola (UNITA). The only comprehensive sanctions were those imposed on Haiti (for three years only) and Iraq (where they lasted over 13 years).

8 See Weiss et al. (1997: 15).

9 See Doxey (1996).

10 For more detailed analyses about this mainstream see: Davis (1991); Landgren (1989); Klinghoffer (1989); Gelb (1991); and Van Heerden (1991).

11 See Hufbauer el. al. (1990b: 2); and Doxey (1996: 92).

12 Among the 16 cases when the SC ordered sanction under Chapter VII of the UN Charter, three were cases of comprehensive sanctions (Rhodesia, Haiti, and Iraq). Rhodesia was the first (1965–79). The SC imposed comprehensive sanctions on Rhodesia on human rights grounds. However, although Rhodesia had continued to deny equal rights of the black majority with the white minority since 1960, the SC enforcement measures were

impaired, particularly by the UK veto (see Tomasevski, 1997: 99–100). Sanctions on Haiti (1991) were comprehensive in scope, but were lifted, when the legitimate government was restored to power in 1994. Sanctions on Iraq (1990–2003) were exceptional because they also paved the way for substantial military actions.

13 See Doxey (1996: 23–6).

14 For a detailed analysis see Hufbauer et al. (1990b); Mizea (1991: 97–108); Klotz (1995); and the United Nations (1994).

15 See Doxey (1996: 97).

16 See Baldwin (1985: 34–6).

17 See Doxey (1996: 93).

18 See EIU (1996: 13).

19 Ibid.

20 Sanctions on Iraq had some negative consequences for other states, especially poor workers from some Arab states (Egypt and Palestine) and South East Asia, but had no particular consequences for western states.

21 Scholars have also argued that behind the Gulf conflict (war and sanctions), countless reasons and looming uncertainties about the Arab world lay at the heart of the discourse (see Bennis, Moushabeck and Said, eds., 1998). The contributors to this book, including among others, Edward Said, Noam Chomsky, Ibrahim Abu-Lughod, Yvonne Haddad, Clovis Maksoud, and Hanan Ashrawi, contend that there is a policy of linkage between the Iraqi conflict and the Arab-Israeli conflict. They argue that false analogies were made in the press throughout the years in order to victimise Arabs.

22 Broadcast on Al-Jazeera TV [Arabic news], May 2003.

23 See publications of the US Commission on the Intelligence Capability of the United States regarding Weapons of Mass Destruction (WMD), Report to the President, March 31, 2005. Online: HtmlResAnchor http://www.wmd.gov/report/ (last accessed 23 May 2005).

24 See United Kingdom, (2002) 'Iraq's Weapons of Mass Destruction: The Assessment of the British Government 24 September 2002' [the British Dossier on Iraq]. An html version of the file is available online: HtmlResAnchor http://image.guardian.co.uk/sys-files/Politics/documents/2002/09/24/dossier.pdf. (Last accessed 16 September 2005).

25 United States Government (2005), *Commission on the Intelligence Capability of the United States Regarding Weapons of Mass Destruction (WMD), Report to the President, 31 March 2005* (Chapter One). Online: HtmlResAnchor http://www.wmd.gov/report/ (accessed 16 May 2005). The Commission was charged with reviewing the intelligence capabilities of the United States Intelligence Community – comprised of over a dozen intelligence agencies including the Central Intelligence Agency, the National Security Agency, and the Defence Intelligence Agency – with respect to threats such as those posed to the United States by Weapons of Mass Destruction (WMD). The Commission no longer exists.

26 See for example, Chandler (2003: 428–454); and Halliday (2005).

27 See Halliday (2005: 69).

28 Ibid.

29 Among others, see Reports of the UN Specialized Agencies, FAO, UNICEF, WFP, WHO, UNDP, WDP, and UN Special Missions on the Humanitarian impacts of the sanctions on Iraq, and reports by specialized groups and NGOs on the impact of sanctions on Iraq.

30 Before the Iraq case came into focus and international attention was drawn to the destructive effect of sanctions on the civilian population, a large body of literature existed about the domestic, political and economic impact of sanctions on South Africa and

Rhodesia (see e.g., Rowe, 1993: 59–110). However, the terminology and original critique were developed by Galtung (1967: 378–416).

31 See UN Inter-State Agency Standing Committee (1996a: Section 2).

32 See Boutros Ghali (1995: paras. 66–76).

33 UNICEF reported in April 2002 that over 1 in 5 Iraqis remained malnourished. See UNICEF (2002a), and (2002b).

34 When first introduced, the ration provided only 53 percent of daily caloric needs at nominal cost. In 1994, because of inadequate domestic production and a lack of foreign currency for imports, the ration was reduced to 34 percent of daily caloric needs (see UN FAO Report, 1995: 9).

35 See Boone, Gazdar and Hussain (1997: 32).

36 See Bossuyt (2000).

37 Stated in the Independent Inquiry Committee (Volcker) Report published online on 7 September 2005 at: HtmlResAnchor http://www.iic-offp.org/Mgmt_Report.htm.

38 For more detailed analysis of the term 'gender regime' see Connell (1990: 507 545), and Connell (1994: 29–40).

39 For example, middle-class urban Iraqi women tend to have better education and better employment opportunities than rural/peasant women. The latter are in a situation where the kinship system is much more persistent than it would be in an urban setting. In return, women's roles in production and work generally shape their class location, and reproductive practices. For more details see Moghadam and Khoury (1995: 11).

40 For example, RCC Decree No. 115, issued 1 November 1993, confirmed punishment by execution of those who owned prostitution houses and solicited for women. RCC Decree No. 175, issued 24 November 1993 facilitated the separation and divorce of women whose husbands 'switched' to serve the enemy (i.e., the political oppositions).

41 For example, RCC Decree No. 1110, issued 17 February 1990, where, in accordance with the Bedouin tradition that allows a woman's male blood relatives (but not her husband) to acquire legal rights over her. The decree: 'exempts from punishment or legal questioning men who murdered their mothers, daughters, sisters, paternal aunts, brothers' daughters and fathers' brother's daughters, if they were deemed guilty of 'honour crime' (illicit sexual contact)'. RCC Decree No. 1529, issued on 20 January 1986, facilitates the separation and divorce of Iraqi women from husbands who escaped or deserted from military services for a period of more than six months. The divorce was revocable in case the husband returned to military service, and irrevocable if he escaped again. RCC Decree No. 1610, issued on 23 December 1982, forbids Iraqi women to marry non-Iraqi citizens. If an Iraqi woman was already married to a non-Iraqi citizen, the decree prohibited her from transferring money or property to her non-Iraqi husband. The non-Iraqi husband was not eligible to inherit from his Iraqi wife, and in case of divorce, he was not eligible for any financial settlement or for custody of children.

42 See Rai (1996: 11).

43 The terms 'strong' and 'soft' state largely concern western definitions of the state. The term 'strong' state refers to a state's capacity to implement its political decisions 'logically', namely through the high degree of 'rationalized bureaucracy' of relations between the state and the 'pinnacle' of the interests of privileged groups (see the Weberian model of the state in Weber, 1978). A 'soft' state does not have these features. It is termed 'soft' because of a general inclination amongst the population to resist public control and political decisions (see for a detailed analysis, Mann, 1984). However, the term 'strong' state as used here refers to the 'infrastructural power' of the state. If the infrastructural

power is weak, 'the implementation of directives can become hostage to random factors outside the control of the state institutions' (see Rai, 1996: 15).

44   During the 1990s, in complete contrast to its policy during the 1970s, the Ba'th regime began to admire the centrality of the tribe in Iraq's social structure, and the virtues of tribal values and customs. The regime shifted from contemptuousness towards the tribalism and clan affiliations of the pre-crisis period to promoting tribalism as the official face of Iraq. In 1976, Saddam had made it an offence for public figures to use names showing regional or tribal affiliations, describing tribes and clans as 'The essence of backwardness and social reaction' (*Al-Thawra*, Baghdad, 18 November 1976).

45   For more detail see Dawisha (1999: 553–567); and Baram (1997: 1–17).

46   See HRW (July 2003).

47   While the wound of Abu-Ghraib prison was still not healed, the public learned of other shocking atrocities by American soldiers against Iraqi civilians, particularly children and women. These crimes include a summary execution of 24 unarmed civilians from one family in the town of Haditha (northwest of Baghdad), and a crime against the 14-year-old 'Abeer Al-Janabi', who was raped and killed and burned together with the rest of her family, including her 5-year-old sister, in Al-Mahmoudiya city (south of Baghdad). There is also an on-going investigation of British forces' involvement in crimes of killing and torturing Iraqi civilians and juveniles in the southern city, Basra.

48   Casualty count of the conflict in Iraq since 2003 up to 27 August 2006 shows: US soldiers killed – 2,653; U.K. solders killed – 117; other coalition forces killed –115. Foreign civilians killed: 258 private security personnel; more than 150 UN personnel; more than 30 journalists (see 'Iraq Coalition Casualties', *Iraq Casualty Count*. HtmlResAnchor http://icasualties.org/oif/ (Last accessed 4 September 2006). As for Iraqi civilian casualties up to 8 August 2006, a very rough estimate shows that a minimum of 39,702 and a maximum of 44,191 persons were reported killed (see Website: http://www.iraqbodycount.net/). The website released a report detailing that the US and its allies were responsible for 37 percent (24,865) of deaths while the remaining 63 percent of deaths were attributed to insurgent action, crimes and unknown reasons. The Iraqi military casualties varied considerably: during the 6 weeks of 'Major Combat' in March–April 2003; a very rough estimates show that 30,000 Iraqi soldiers were killed. As of 4 September 2006, 3,642 Iraqi policemen were reported killed. A study in *The Lancet*, September 2004, estimated that 200,000 persons were killed in the battle of Fallujah.

49   For more details see 'Study puts Iraqi toll at 100,000', *CNN*, 29 October 2004. On line: HtmlResAnchor http://www.cnn.com/2004/WORLD/meast/10/29/iraq.deaths/; 'Iraq Living Conditions Survey 2004', *United Nations Development Programme*. On Line: HtmlResAnchor http://www.iq.undp.org/ILCS/overview.htm , (last accessed 12 September 2006).

50   See Rehn and Sirleaf (2002).

51   Ibid.

52   For further reading see Dawisha (1999: 553–567).

53   According to the findings of a study by the Iraqi Health Ministry in cooperation with the Norwegian Institute for Applied International Studies and the UN Development Programme, published in November 2004, acute malnutrition among children in Iraq has nearly doubled since the US-led invasion. Acute malnutrition among the under-5s jumped from 4 percent in 2002 to 7.7 percent in 2004. This figure translates into around 400,000 children suffering from 'wasting; a condition characterised by chronic diarrhoea

and dangerous protein deficiencies. See the summary by Vick, 2004; also UNFAO and WFP, September 2003).

54 See Rehn and Sirleaf (2002).

55 For more details see Sardar-Ali and Mullally (1992: 113–123). In the context of the struggle for women's human rights within Islam, Sardar-Ali and Mullally stress that Islam permeates all aspect of Muslim life. Islam is not only a religion, but is thus an all-pervasive code of economic, social and political life (Sardar-Ali & Mullally, 1992: 119).

56 For further reading see Arkoun (1994); Sardar-Ali and Mullally (1992); Sardar-Ali (2000); and Sardar-Ali (2002).

57 See Arkoun (1994: 111 n.21).

58 See Sardar-Ali and Mullally (1992: 121).

59 See Sardar-Ali (2000: 41).

60 See Sardar-Ali (2002: 61–78).

APPENDIX

Chapter 1

Table 1.1
Iraq's oil revenue, oil output, gross domestic product,
and population (1950–90)

Year	Oil revenue ID/Bn	GDP ID/Bn	Oil revenue to GDP %	Oil output (MBD)	Population Million
1950	.005	.196	3	0.14	5.2
1955	.074	.413	18	0.70	6.1
1960	.095	.601	16	0.97	6.9
1964	.126	.805	16	1.3	7.8
1968	.203	1.1	18	1.5	8.9
1970	.214	1.3	16	1.5	9.4
1972	.219	1.5	15	1.5	10.0
1974	1.7	3.4	50	2.0	10.8
1976	3.1	5.4	57	2.4	11.5
1978	3.7	7.2	51	2.6	12.4
1980	8.9	15.8	56	2.6	13.2
1982	3.4	13.1	26	1.0	14.1
1984	3.0	14.8	20	1.2	15.4
1986	2.2	14.9	15	1.9	16.5
1988	3.5	17.4	20	2.7	17.6
1989	4.6	20.0	23	2.8	18.1
1990	2.9	23.9	12	2.1	18.9

Source:
1. Annual Abstracts of Statistics (Iraq, 1991).
2. Annual Statistical Bulletin; Central Bank of Iraq (1991).
Note: The official value of exchange rates in the period 1950–68 ID1:US$2,80. in 1969 ID1:US$2.,79; in 1970 ID1:US$2,78; in years 1971 & 1972 ID1:US$2,96; in the period 1973–81 ID1:US $3,38; and in the period 1982–90 ID1:US$3,21 (Iraq National Bank).

Table 1.2
Iraq's oil production and exports (thousand barrels/day)

Year	Production	Exports
1976–80	2,690	2,504
1981–86	1,263	961
1995	550	250
1996	580	275
1997	840	840
1998	2,110	1,635
1999	2,523	2,024
2000	2,568	2,243
2001	2,355	2,030
2002	2,014	1,689

Source: Economic Intelligence Unit (EIU), (Country Profile, 2003).

Table 1.3
Iraq oil production in year 2003

Year	Jan.	Feb.	Mar.	Apr.	May	Jun.	Jul.	Aug.	Sep.	Oct.	Nov.
2003	2,490	2,490	1,460	160	280	440	660	1,050	1,450	1,600	1,750

Source:
1. Organization for Oil-Producing Countries (OPEC, 2003).
2. International Energy Agency, *Oil monthly Report* (December 2003).

Table 1.4
Data on 'Holds' on contracts, Phases VI–XII, OFF Programme

Phase	Data	Total value of holds (million $US)	Number of applications on hold
VI	31/10/99	808	621
VII	31/03/00	1,957	1,203
VIII	31/10/00	2,600	1,293
IX	14/05/01	4,152	2,244
X	31/10/01	4,034	1.544
XI	17/05/02	5,170	N/A
XII	31/10/02	5,511	1,566

Source: Von Sponeck, H.C., "A Different Kind of War: The UN Sanctions Regime in Iraq" (2006: 284).

Table 1.5
Value of goods arrived under the OFF Programme

Phase	Data	Cumulative value of goods arrived (million $US)	Value of goods arrived in phase (million $US)
III	15/05/98	2,016	N/A
IV	10/31/98	3,532	1,516
V	31/03/99	4,744	1,213
VI	31/10/99	6,628	1,884
VII	01/06/00	8,071	1,443
VIII	31/10/00	8,834	763
IX	18/05/01	11,100	2,266
X	19/11/01	15,980	4,790
XI	17/05/02	22,000	6,110
XII	12/11/02	25,000	3,000
XIII	12/05/03	28,120	3,120

Source: Von Sponeck, H.C., "A Different Kind of War: The UN Sanctions Regime in Iraq" (2006: 285).

Table 1.6
Iraq's growth of national income and per-capita income (1970–80)

Year	National income ID/Million	Index	Per-capita Income ID	Index
1970	905,4	107	95.3	107
1971	1,021,2	120	1041	117
1972	1,111,1	131	1096	123
1973	1.339,4	158	1279	144
1974	2.847,1	335	2629	295
1975	3,491,9	411	3122	351
1976	4,826,1	568	4172	469
1977	5,386,1	637	4425	497
1978	6,709,9	789	5382	605
1979	10,588,5	1246	8259	928
1980	15,323,0	1803	11574	1300

Source:
1. Annual Abstracts of Statistics (Iraq, 1977: 128).
2. Annual Abstracts of Statistics (Iraq, 1987: 122).
Note: The official value of exchange rates in 1970 ID1:US$2,78; $2.96; in years 1971 & 1972 ID1:US$2,96; in the period 1973–81 ID1:US $3,38; and in the period 1982–90 ID1:US$3,21 (Iraq National Bank).

Table 1.7
Selective years of Iraq's GDP distribution by economic sectors

GDP by origin %	1975	1980	1981	1982	1984	1986	1988
Agriculture	8	5	9	10	13	15	16
Industry- total	57	66	37	32	34	27	33
(*Manufacturing*)	*7*	*4*	*7*	*7*	*8*	*11*	*12*
Construction	9	7	16	17	10	9	6
Trade	5	5	10	12	13	13	11
Transport and communication	5	4	7	7	5	7	7
Other activities	17	13	24	24	28	32	29

Source:

1. National Accounts Statistics: Main Aggregates and Detailed Tables, Part I (United Nations, 1989).
2. National Accounts Statistics: Analysis of Main Aggregates, 1988–89 (United Nations, 1991).

CHAPTER 2

Table 2.1
Division of economically active female in economic activities in 1977

Economic Sectors	Number female labour	Number Total labour force	% Female labour to total labour force	% Female labour to labour force in sector	% Female labour to total labour force
Agriculture, forestry & fishing	352824	943890	66.08	37.37	11.37
Mining & quarrying	2119	36835	0.40	5.75	0.06
Manufacturing industry	48618	284395	9.11	17.09	1.58
Water & electricity	949	23190	0.18	4.09	0.03
Construction & building	5136	321696	0.96	1.59	0.16
Commodity sectors	16155	224104	3.02	7.20	0.52
Transport, comm. & storage	4985	177799	0.93	2.80	0.16
Banking, ownership of dwelling & insurance	5066	31089	0.95	16.29	0.16
Service sector	86100	957979	16.13	8.98	2.81
Unknown+unemployed	11979	58237	2.21	20.56	0.39
Total	533931	3059214	100%		17.5

Source: Annual Abstract of Statistics (Iraq, 1977: 87–88).

Table 2.2
Female employments in public sector 1972–80

Sex	1968	1972	1973	1974	Year 1975	1976	1977	1978	1980
Male	240868	344422	354298	381549	413375	448779	491046	557818	641578
Female	35737	48532	50156	57448	68756	77799	89186	105038	144080
Total	276605	392954	404454	438997	482131	526578	580132	662856	785658
%	14.83%	14.09%	14.15%	15.05%	16.63%	17.33%	18.16%	18.83%	22.45%

Sources:
1. General Federation of Iraqi Women (GFIW), "Development of Female Participation in Economic Activities: Public Sector in Iraq During 1968–78" (GFIW Press, 1980: 45).
2. Ministry of Planning, "Employees in Public Sector in 1980", Survey by Social Statistics, Department for Labour Force in Public Sector (Iraq, 1980: 32).

Table 2.3
Division of female labour in economic activities according to
type of occupation in 1977

Profession	Female labour to total female labour force %	Female labour to total labour in profession %
Professional, technicians & related	11.9	32.4
Legislators, administrator chives & directors	0.1	3.0
Executive officials, clerks & related	5.2	7.3
Sales employees	1.7	6.9
Service employees	3.2	10.5
Employees in agriculture & forestry	65.7	37.8
Employees in production & related	9.7	5.5
Entrepreneurs	0.00	0.5
Unknown	2.6	4.5
Total	100.0	17.5

Source: General Abstracts of Statistics (Iraq, 1977: 126).

Table 2.4
Female labour force participation in economic sectors 1984

Economic Activities	Total (000)	Female (000)	Percent %
Agriculture	984	474	48.2
Services	1403	268	19.1
Industry	1084	114	10.5
Total	3471	856	24.7

Source:
1. Ministry of Planning, "The Situation of Population, Labour Force, and Wages for the period 1980–84", Department of Labour Force Planning, Ministry of Planning (Iraq, 1984:14).
2. General Federation of Iraqi Women (GFIW), "Iraqi Women's Participation in the Economic Development" (GFIW Press, 1983:10).

Table 2.5
Female labour force participation in economic activities of 1977–84

Economic activities	% Female labour to total labour in sector 1977	% Female labour to total labour in sector 1987	% Growth rates	Rank
Agriculture, forestry & fishing	37.4	48.2	10.8	(1)
Mining & quarrying	5.7	9.7	3.9	(6)
Manufacturing industry	17.1	20.5	2.8	(4)
Water & electricity	4.1	9.0	4.9	(7)
Construction & building	1.6	2.8	1.2	(9)
Commodity sectors	7.2	11.7	4.5	(5)
Transport, comm. & storage	2.8	5.6	2.8	(8)
Banking, ownership of dwelling & insurance	16.3	37.9	37.9	(2)
Service sector	9.0	26.1	26.1	(3)

Source: Derived from:
1. General Abstracts of Statistics (Iraq, 1977: 87–88).
2. Ministry of Planning, "The Situation of Population, Labour Force, and Wages 1980–1983", Department of Labour Force (Iraq, 1984).

Table 2.6
Distribution of female labour force in the economic activities in 1987

Economic sectors	Number female labour force	Number total labour force	% Female labour to total female labour force	% Female labour to total labour force in sector	% Female labour to total labour force
Agriculture, forestry & fishing	70741	493006	15.37	14.34	1.78
Mining & quarrying	4698	45137	1.06	10.40	0.11
Manufacturing industry	38719	266961	8.41	14.50	0.97
Water & electricity	4450	36236	0.96	12.28	0.11
Construction & building	8541	431186	1.85	1.98	0.21
Commodity sectors	24489	215605	5.32	11.35	0.61
Transport, comm. & storage	12155	224271	2.64	5.41	0.30
Banking, ownership of dwelling & insurance	10800	27015	2.34	39.97	0.27
Service sector	233068	1954816	50.64	11.92	5.89
Unknown	18232	167848	3.96	3.96	0.46
Unemployed	34326	184264	7.45	18.62	0.86
Total	460230	3956345	100%		11.68

Sources:
1. Annual Abstracts of Statistics (Iraq, 1987).
2. Kudhair, Nabil , "Employment in Relation to Recent Change in Iraq's Labour Market (1987–1991)", General Federation of Iraqi Women (GFIW Press, 1992: 30).

Table 2.7

Rates of female labour force in economic activities in years 1977–87

Economic sector	% Female in sector 1977 (1)	% Female in sector 1987 (2)	% Annual growth rate (2/1)
Agriculture, forestry & fishing	37.4	14.4	6.7-
Mining & quarrying	5.8	10.4	10.2
Manufacturing industry	17.1	14.5	7.7-
Water & electricity	4.1	12.3	30.7
Construction & building	1.6	2.0	5.5
Commodity sectors	7.2	11.4	4.3
Transport, comm. & storage	2.8	5.4	12.0
Banking, ownership of dwelling & insurance	16.3	40.0	9.4
Service sector	9.0	12.0	14.2
Unknown + unemployed	20.6	22.6	15.5
Total	17.5	11.6	8.7

Sources:

1. Mundher al-Badry, "Iraq's Labour Force During 1957 and 1977" (GFIW Press, 1980: 75).

2. Derived from selective data from the Annual Abstracts of Statistics (Iraq, 1989).

3. Ministry of Education, Survey of Labour Force in Government Institutions, Public and Mixed Sectors in 30/6/1990 (Iraq, 1993: 45).

Table 2.8
Female labour force division in occupation in years 1977–87

Profession	% Female labour to total female labour force		% Female labour to total labour in profession		Annual growth rate
	1977	1987	1977 (1)	1987 (2)	% (2/1)
Professional, technicians & related	11.9	39.2	32.4	43.9	13.6
Legislators, administrator chives & Directors	0.1	0.5	3.0	12.7	35.8
Executive officials, clerks & related	5.2	22.2	7.3	6.4	19.8
Sales employees	1.7	2.6	6.9	9.2	1.7
Service employees	3.2	6.5	10.5	15.8	5.4
Employees in agriculture & forestry	65.7	15.6	37.8	14.0	6.7-
Employees in production & related	9.7	10.2	5.5	4.1	1.3-
Entrepreneurs	0.00	0.00	0.5	0.00	0.00
Unknown	2.6	3.2	4.5	17.3	0.11-
Total	100.00	100.00			7.6

Sources:
1. Annual Abstract of Statistics, Ministry of Planning (Iraq, 1977: 126).
2. Ministry of Planning, Survey of Labour Force in the Socialist Sector (Iraqi Labour Force only) – 1981, Department of Social statistics (Iraq, 1981: 14).
3. Ministry of Planning, Renewed Survey of Labour Force in the Socialist and Mixed Sectors – 1987, Department of Labour force Statistics (Iraq, 1988: 10).
4. Ministry of Planning, labour Force in the State Institutions, Socialist and Mixed Sectors Until 30/6/1990, Department of Labour Force Statistics (Iraq, 1993: 16–17).

Table 2.9

Female labour force distribution in economic activities until 30/6/1990

Economic sectors	Number female labour force	Number total labour force	% Female labour to total female labour force	% Female labour to total labour in sector	% Female labour to total labour force
Agriculture, forestry & fishing	274715	895698	43.42	30.67	8.92
Mining & quarrying	3162	30738	0.49	10.28	0.10
Manufacturing industry	35132	216748	5.55	16.20	1.14
Water & electricity	4374	30807	0.69	14.19	0.14
Construction & building	8090	288424	1.27	1.98	2.80
Commodity sectors	30957	381395	4.89	8.11	1.0
Transport, comm. & storage	11328	319034	1.79	3.55	0.36
Banking, ownership of dwelling & insurance	18531	45334	2.92	40.87	0.60
Service sector	217304	611498	34.35	35.53	7.06
Unknown	407	5883	0.06	6.91	0.01
Unemployed	28597	251208	3.57	11.38	0.92
Total	632597	3076776	100%		23.97

Source:

1. Ministry of Planning, Survey of Labour Force in Government Institutions, Public and Mixed Sectors for 1990 (Iraq, 1993).
2. Ministry of Planning, "The Perspectives of Unemployment in Iraq", Department of Labour Force Planning Vol. 952 (Iraq, 1992).

Table 2.10
Composition of female labour in economic activities during
1987 – until 30/6/1990

Economic sector	Female labour to total female labour force % 1987	Female labour to total female labour force % 1990
Agriculture, forestry & fishing	15.4	43.4
Mining & quarrying	1.0	0.5
Manufacturing industry	8.4	5.5
Water & electricity	0.1	1.0
Construction & building	1.9	1.3
Commodity Sectors	5.3	4.9
Transport, comm. & storage	2.6	1.8
Banking, ownership of dwelling & insurance	2.3	2.9
Service sector	50.6	34.3
Unknown + unemployed	22.6	18.3
Total	11.6	23.97

Source:
1. Annual Abstract of Statistics (Iraq, 1989).
2. Ministry of Planning, Survey of Labour Force in Government Institutions, Public and Mixed Sectors in 30/6/1990 (Iraq, 1993).

CHAPTER 3

Table 3.1
Numbers of male and female employees in the public sector
by year of appointment as at 31/12/1998

Year of appointment	Male (000)	Female (000)	Total (000)
50 & less	219	35	254
1951–55	1023	186	1209
1956–60	6095	1486	7581
1961–65	13765	4690	18455
1966–70	23657	5431	29088
1971–75	70816	23774	94590
1976–80	150598	63683	214281
1981–85	58115	88386	146501
1986–90	69710	67483	1137193
1991–95	95524	66293	1618817
1996–98	22525	19813	42338
Total	512047	341260	853307

Source: Planning Commission, Annual Abstract of Statistics, Board of Ministry (Iraq, 1998/1999: 122).

Table 3.2
Number of employees in public sector in Baghdad city from
31/12/1997 to 31/12/1998

Year	Male	Female	Total
31/12/1997	134940	128692	263632
31/12/1998	130640	127547	258187

Source: Planning Commission, Annual Abstract of Statistics, Board of Ministry (Iraq, 1998/1999: 123–24).

CHAPTER 4

Table 4.1

Selected socio-economic indicators in the Middle East and North Africa in year 2000

Middle East & North Africa	Population, 2000 (Million)	Percent of population over age 15 who are illiterate, 2000		Number of people over age 15 who are illiterate (000), 2000		Percent of population ages 15–24 who are illiterate, 2000		Number of people ages 15–24 who are illiterate (000), 2000	
		Female	Male	Female	Male	Female	Male	Female	Male
All Countries	343	42	22	50,057	26,671	23	11	8,585	4,573
Algeria	31,2	43	24	4,211	2,360	16	7	530	227
Bahrain	0,64	17	9	32	25	1	2	1	1
Egypt	70,5	56	33	12,253	7,374	37	24	2,500	1,678
Iran	65,7	31	17	6,696	3,819	9	4	655	296
Iraq	22,7	77	45	5,070	3,057	71	41	1,593	962
Jordan	5	16	5	220	78	1	1	3	5
Kuwait	2	20	16	103	130	7	8	15	19
Lebanon	3,6	20	8	246	91	7	3	23	9
Libya	5,1	32	9	533	168	7	0.5	43	1
Morocco	30,1	64	38	6,286	3,702	42	24	1,265	750
Oman	2,5	38	20	246	155	4	0.5	9	1
Plaestine*	3,1	16	6	136	48	–	–	–	–
Qatar	0,74	17	20	21	57	3	7	1	3
Saudi Arabia	23,1	33	17	1,723	1,092	10	5	187	101
Syria	16,3	40	12	1,879	566	21	5	376	85
Tunisia	9,6	39	9	1,307	621	11	3	106	27
Turkey	65,6	24	7	5,453	1,539	6	1	392	81
United Arab Emirates	2,4	21	25	117	345	6	13	10	29
Yemen	17,5	75	33	3,525	1,444	54	17	874	292

Sources:

1. UNESCO institute for Statistics, "Literacy Statistics, 2003" (HtmlResAnchor www.uis.unesco.org)
2. United Nations Development Programme, Human Development Report (2002).
3. UN Statistics Division, The World's Women 2000: Trends and Statistics (August 2003) (HtmlResAnchor http://unstats.un.org/unsd/demographic/ww2000/table5d.htm.)
4. Roudi-Fahimi, "Women's Reproductive Health in the MENA" (2003).
5. C. Haub, World Population Data Sheet (2003).

Table 4.2

Selective data of female enrolment in primary schools in the period 1968–2000

Year	No. Female (000)	(%)
1968–69	0,298,589	29.9
1978–79	1,058,695	43.0
1987–88	1,352,580	45.1
1988–89	1,341,253	44.5
1990–91	1,479,897	44.5
1991–92	1,267,584	44.9
1992–93	1,277,056	44.7
1993–94	1,295,906	44.7
1994–95	1,298,973	44.6
1995–96	1,301,852	44.8
1996–97	1,322,622	44.8
1997–98	1,351,421	44.6
1998–99	1,392,892	44.5
1999–00	1,433,495	44.5
2000–01	1,776,212	44.0

Sources:

1. Annual Abstracts of Statistics (Iraq, 1984: 212).
2. Annual Abstract of Statistics, 1987 (Iraq, 1989: 206–208).
3. Baghdad Chamber of Commerce, Department of Research and Statistics, "The Position of Iraqi Women in Paid Labour Force" (Iraq, 1991: 7).
4. Board of Ministries, Planning Commission, Central Statistical Organisation, Annual Abstract of Statistics (Iraq, 1999: 369).

Table 4.3

Selected data: primary school enrolment ratios in MENA countries in the 1990s

Middle East & North African Countries	Primary											
	Gross enrolment ratio (%)						Net enrolment ratio (%)					
	Total 1990/96		Male 1990/96		Female 1990/96		Total 1990/96		Male 1990/96		Female 1990/96	
Algeria	100	107	108	113	92	102	93	93	99	97	87	91
Bahrain	110	106	110	105	110	106	99	99	99	97	99	99
Egypt	94	101	101	108	86	94	–	–	–	98	–	88
Iraq	111	85	120	92	102	78	–	–	–	81	–	71
Jordan	–	–	–	–	–	–	–	–	–	–	–	–
Kuwait	60	77	62	78	59	77	45	45	45	62	44	61
Lebanon	118	111	120	113	116	108	–	–	–	–	–	–
Libya	105	–	108	–	102	–	–	–	–	–	–	–
Morocco	67	86	79	97	54	74	58	58	68	83	48	65
Oman	86	76	90	78	82	74	70	70	73	70	68	68
Plaestine*	–	–	–	–	–	–	–	–	–	–	–	–
Qatar	97	86	101	87	94	86	87	87	87	–	86	59
Saudi Arabia	73	76	78	77	68	75	59	59	65	63	53	60
Syria	108	101	114	106	102	96	98	98	100	95	93	87
Tunisia	113	118	120	122	107	114	94	94	97	99	90	96
United Arab Emirates	104	89	106	91	103	87	94	94	95	79	93	78
Yemen	–	70	–	100	–	40	–	–	–	–	–	–

Sources: UNESCO (2000), Secondary Education: Duration, Population, and Enrolment Ratio (Online).

Note: Gross Enrolment Ratio is the number of students, regardless of age, enrolled in school, divided
by the total number of people in the appropriate age range for the level of schooling.

* Not available.

Table 4.4
Secondary school enrolment ratios in MENA countries in the 1990s

Middle East & North African Countries	Secondary											
	Gross enrolment ratio (%)						Net enrolment ratio (%)					
	Total 1990/96		Male 1990/96		Female 1990/96		Total 1990/96		Male 1990/96		Female 1990/96	
Algeria	62	63	67	65	54	62	54	56	60	58	48	54
Bahrain	62	63	67	65	54	62	54	56	60	58	48	54
Egypt	76	75	84	80	68	70	–	67	–	71	–	87
Iraq	47	42	57	51	36	32	–	–	–	–	–	–
Jordan	–	–	–	–	–	–	–	–	–	–	–	–
Kuwait	51	65	51	65	51	65	45	61	46	62	45	61
Lebanon	74	81	71	78	76	84	–	–	–	–	–	–
Libya	86	–	–	–	–	–	–	–	–	–	–	–
Morocco	35	39	41	44	30	34	–	–	–	–	–	–
Oman	46	67	51	68	40	66	–	–	–	–	–	–
Plaestine*	–	–	–	–	–	–	–	–	–	–	–	–
Qatar	81	80	77	80	85	79	67	–	64	–	70	–
Saudi Arabia	44	58	49	62	39	54	31	48	34	54	28	41
Syria	52	42	60	45	44	40	46	38	52	40	39	36
Tunisia	45	65	50	66	40	63	43	–	46	–	39	–
United Arab Emirates	67	80	63	77	72	82	59	71	56	68	63	74
Yemen....	–	34	–	53	–	14	–	–	–	–	–	–

Source: UNESCO (2000), Secondary Education: Duration, Population, and Enrolment Ratio (Online).
* Not available.

Table 4.5

Selected socio-economic indicators in the Middle East and North Africa in year 2003

Middle East & North African Countries	Popul	Gross Enrolment Ratio (%)[a]				Women as a Share of University Enrolment (%)	Public Education as a Share of Total Convergent Expenditure (%)	Percent of People Ages 15 and Older in Labour Force †		Women as Percent of Labour Force †	Total Fertility Rate
		Primary		Secondary							
		Female	Male	Female	Male			Female	Male		
All MENA Countries 2000		91	100	62	71	–	–	20	73	20	3.3
Algeria	31,2	107	116	73	68	–	16	–	–	–	2.8
Bahrain	0,63	103	103	105	98	60	12	19	65	17	2.6
Egypt	70,5	96	103	83	88	–	15	20	74	21	3.5
Iran	65,7	85	88	75	81	47	18	11	75	12	2
Iraq	22,7	91	111	29	47	34	–	17	75	18	5.4
Jordan	5	101	101	89	86	51	20	22	76	21	3.7
Kuwait	2	95	93	57	55	68	14	43	83	25	4
Lebanon	3,6	97	101	79	72	52	8	27	76	28	2.4
Libya	5,1	117	115	–	–	48	–	23	78	21	3.7
Morocco	30,1	88	101	35	44	44	25	30	79	28	2.7

Oman	2,5	71	74	67	69	58	16	16	79	14	4.1
Plaestine*	3,1	109	107	86	80	47	–	10	67	13	5.7
Qatar	0,74	104	105	92	86	73	–	35	92	13	3.5
Saudi Arabia	23,1	–	–	–	–	56	23	15	80	11	5.7
Syria	16,3	105	113	41	46	–	14	21	83	20	3.8
Tunisia	9,6	115	120	80	76	48	20	24	73	24	2.1
Turkey	65,6	96	105	48	67	41	15	26	72	27	2.5
United Arab Emirates	2,4	99	99	80	71	–	20	31	92	12	3
Yemen	17,5	61	96	25	96	21	22	19	82	27	7

Sources:

1. UNESCO institute for Statistics, "Literacy Statistics" (March 2003) (HtmlResAnchor www.uis.unesco.org).
2. United Nations Development Programme, Human Development Report (2002).
3. UN Statistics Division, The World's Women 2000: Trends and Statistics (HtmlResAnchor http://unstats.un.org/unsd/demographic/ww2000/table5d.htm)
4. Roudi-Fahimi, "Women's Reproductive Health in the MENA" (2003).
5. C. Haub, World Population Data Sheet (2003).

a Gross enrolment ratio is the number of students, regardless of age, enrolled in school, divided by the total number of people in the appropriate age range for that level of schooling.

† Data on Labour force participation may include foreign workers.

* Not available

Table 4.6

Development of female enrolment in vocational schools from 1978–2000

Type of schools	Number schools	Number female students	(%) Total
Technical			
1978–1979	38	3300	3.1
1987–1988	122	6211	6.3
1999–2000	163	2923	5.6
Agricultural			
1978–1979	25	629	8.3
1987–1988	24	824	11.3
1999–2000	10	000	0.00
Commercial			
1978–1979	39	8640	69.5
1987–1988	102	33278	74.4
1999–2000	61	5917	70.5

Sources:

1. Annual Abstract of Statistics (Iraq, 1984: 212–224).
2. Annual Abstract of Statistics (Iraq, 1987: 221).
3. Board of Ministries, Planning Commission, Annual Abstract of Statistics (Iraq, 1999: 390–91).

Table 4.7
Development of female enrolment in high education 1968–2000

Year	Number of female students	(%)	Total number
1968–69	9877	24	41159
1969–70	8045	22	37290
1972–73	11743	23.9	49194
1978–79	26576	31.8	83593
1980–81	30217	31.4	96301
1985–86	43864	32.1	136688
1986–87	47783	34.7	137627
1987–88	53353	35.8	148987
1988–89	61531	35.0	175766
1989–90	61204	34.0	180277
1990–91	62267	35.5	175422
1991–92	68708	35.6	193005
1992–93	67175	34.9	192215
1993–94	63164	35.0	180531
1994–95	68457	35.1	194921
1995–96	77388	34.3	225644
1996–97	85889	34.3	250132
1997–98	90220	34.8	259130
1998–99	87068		
Private Colleges	6096		
Total	93164	34.4	270471
1999–00	85836		
Private Colleges	6355		
Total	92191	34.7	265595

Sources:
1. Annual Abstracts of Statistics (Iraq, 1987: 228 & 256).
2. Annual Abstract of Statistics (Iraq, 1984: 230–238).
3. Musadaq Jamil Habib, "Education and Economic Development", (Baghdad: 1981: 267).
4. Baghdad Chamber of Commerce, "Position of Iraqi women in Paid Labour Force" (Iraq, 1991:9).
5. Annual Abstract of Statistics, Central Statistical Organisation (Iraq, 1999: 303–410).

Table 4.8

Development of female enrolment in postgraduate
studies for the periods from 1970/71 – 1999/2000

Academic year	Male	Female
1970–71	97	42
1986–87	2370	700
1997–98	6558	3296
1998–99	8136	4268
1999–00	8799	4883
Total	23493	12447

Source: Annual Abstract of Statistics, Planning Commission (Iraq, 1999: 421–424).

Table: 4.9

Development of female employment in education (teachers) 1948–88

Year	Primary school teachers	%	Secondary school teachers	%	Vocational school teachers	%	High-education teachers	%
1968–1969	16448	34.9	3059	32.6	344	34.3	210	11.2
1973–1974	20697	35.4	5214	35.4	301	24	325	13
1976–1977	28923	40.8	8062	41.2	298	15.6	580	13.5
1978–1979	37748	43.3	8127	41.5	412	17.6	706	17
1984–1985	63078	59.8	17562	52.4	2163	40.7	1348	19.4
1985–1986	68838	66.5	19189	54.7	2640	41.2	1483	20.4
1986–1987	80394	65.7	20803	53.2	3314	43.3	1692	21.3
1987–1988	39907	67	22140	54.8	3755	45.1	1885	22

Sources:
1. Annual Abstracts of Statistics, Various Issues (Iraq: 1984, 1985, 1986, & 1987).
2. Ministry of Education, "Education Under Auspices of the Revolution" (Iraq, 1987: 215).

Table 4.10

Number of students and teaching staff in the teacher training institutes and central teacher training institutes for the academic years 1992/93 – 1998/99

Year	Number of institutes	Number of students admitted (000)			Number of students in all classes (000)			Number of teaching staff (000)		
		Males	Females	Total	Females	Males	Total	Males	Females	Total
1992/93	41	3946	5306	9306	12711	18984	31695	1047	785	1832
1993/94	38	2802	4002	6804	11647	1682	28468	817	842	1659
1994/95	36	1597	2752	4349	10502	15567	26069	663	836	1499
1995/96	35	1540	3121	4661	9414	14393	23807	616	793	1409
1996/97	35	1898	3448	5346	9636	14078	23714	594	806	1400
1997/98	54	2735	5158	7893	11071	19496	30567	569	877	1446
1998/99	81	3383	6773	10156	13841	26259	40100	579	991	1570

Source: Annual Abstract of Statistics, Board of Ministries, (Iraq, 1999: 396).

Table 4.11

Number of teachers in the teaching training institutes and in state-sponsored universities and private colleges for the academic years 1998/99 – 1999/2000

Type of Education	Academic year	Number of teaching staff		
		Males	Females	Total
Teachers Training Institutes	1998/1999	574	979	1553
	1999/2000	552	1038	1590
Universities & Technical Institutes	1998/1999	8259	3366	11619
	1999/2000	7932	3545	11577
Private universities & Colleges	1998/1999	318	119	437
	1999/2000	244	80	324

Source: Annual Abstract of Statistics, Board of Ministries, (Iraq, 1999: 397–398 & 414–417 & 394–402).

Table 4.12
Selective data of students failures and dropouts in the 1990s

Type of education Number of failures (000) Male Male	Academic year Number of dropouts (000)	Number of students (000) Female Female
Vocational Schools	1997–1998	14917
12367		766
1397		387
	1999–2000	15185
13012		838
954		381
Central Institutes for Teachers Training	1997–1998	3046
1703		872
116		355
	1999–2000	5241
2499		1837
304		601

Source: Annual Abstract of Statistics, Board of Ministries, (Iraq, 1999: 394–402).

BIBLIOGRAPHY

'Abdallah, Jasim A. (1987), "Harakat al-tashgil al-niswi fi al-irak" [The movement toward women's employment in Iraq], in *Al-Mar'a al-'Arabiyya* [Arab Women], Vol. 5: 59–78.

Abdel-Fadil, Mahmoud (1989), "Labour in the Unorganized Sector", *Al-Ahram al-Iqtisadi*, issue no. 6, November 1989: 18–21.

Abdel-Khalek, Gouda (2001), *Stabilization and Adjustment in Egypt: Reform or De-Industrialization?* Cheltenham, U.K.: Edward Elgar.

Abu Khalil, Assad (1993), "Toward the Study of Women and Politics in the Arab World: The Debate and the Reality", *Feminist Issues*, Vol. 13, no.1. : 3–22.

Abu-Nasr, J. Ulinda, Khoury & Azzam, T. H., (1985), *Women, Employment, and Development in the Arab World*, Berlin: Mouton.

Afshar, Haleh (1985), "Women, State and Ideology in Iran", *Third World Quarterly*, Vol. 7, no. 2.

——, and Carolyne Dennis (eds.) (1992), *Women and Adjustment Policies in the Third World*, London: Macmillan.

Ahtissaari, Martti (1991), *Report to the Sectary-General on Humanitarian Needs in Kuwait and Iraq in the Immediate Post-Crisis Environment*, New York, UN Report no. S122366, March 1991.

Al-Ali, Nadje (2000), *Secularism, Gender, and the State in the Middle East: the Egyptian Women's Movement*, Cambridge: Cambridge University Press.

——, (2005), "Gendering Reconstruction: Iraqi Women between Dictatorship, Wars, Sanctions and Occupation", *Third World Quarterly*, Vol. 26, no. 4–5: 739–758.

——, and Yasmin Hussein (2003), "Iraq", in Ali Akbar Mahdi, ed., *Teen Life in the Middle East: Teen Life Around the World*, Westport, Connecticut & London: Greenwood Press. : 33–57

Allen, Judith (1990), "Does Feminism Need a Theory of the State?" in Sophie Watson ed., *Playing the State*, New York: Verso. : 21–37

Alnasrawi, Abbas (1994), *The Economy of Iraq: Oil, Wars, Destruction of Development and Prospects, 1950–2010*, London: Greenwood Press.

Alvesson, Mats, and Kaj Sköldberg (2000), *Reflexive Methodology: New Vistas for Qualitative Research*, London and Thousand Oaks CA, Sage Publications.

Alwardi, Ali (1996), *Derassha fi tabi'at al-mujtama'a al-iraqy* [A study of the society of Iraq], new ed., Iraq, University of Baghdad.

Al-Alusi, Manal, (1985), *Values Related to Women in President Saddam Hussain's Addresses to Women*, Baghdad, GFIW. [Original in Arabic]

Al-Ameen, Abdul Wahab (1981), "Investment Allocations and Plan Implementation: Iraq's Absorptive Capacity, 1951–1980", *Journal of Energy and Development*, Vol. 6, no. 2: 263–275.

Anan, Kofi (1998a), *Report of the Secretary-General Pursuant to Paragraph 10 of the SCR 1153*, New York: United Nations *S/1998/1100*, 19 November; Online at: HtmlResAnchor www.un.org/Depts/oip/reports/180days4.html (Last Accessed 18 April 2003).

——, (1998b), *Report of the Secretary-General to the Security Council Pursuant to Paragraph 7 of Resolution 1143* ("To prevent further deterioration in the humanitarian conditions, health, and nutritional status of the Iraqi population"), New York: United Nations, S/RES/90 para. 66, February 1998.

——, (2001), *Report of the Secretary-General*, United Nation Doc.S/2000/1132:2, New York: United Nations, 2 March 2001.

Anker, Richard (1998), *Gender and Jobs: Sex Segregation of Occupation in the World*, Geneva: International Labour Organization (ILO).

Arab Ba'th Socialist Party Doctrine (ABSP), (1974a), *The Ba'th Law No. 142*, Political Report of the Ba'th Eight Regional Congress, Baghdad, Arab Ba'th Socialist Party.

——, (1974b), *Revolutionary Iraq: 1968–1973. Al-taqrir al-qutri al-thamin le-hizb al-ba'th al-'arabi al-ishtirakiy, quter al-iraq* [The Political Report adopted by the Eight Regional Congress of the Arab Ba'ath Socialist Party], Baghdad: Al-Thawrah Publications.

——, (1976), *The Ba'th Socialist Party Constitution (14 April 1949)*, in Nidal al-Ba'th: al-Mu'tamarat al-Qawmiyya al-Sab'a al-Ula 1947–64, Beirut.

——, (1982a), *Central Report of the Ninth Regional Conference of the Arab Ba'th Socialist Party* (ABSP), Baghdad, Dar Al-Huriyya Publications. [Original in Arabic]

——, (1982b), *The Political Report of the Ninth Regional Congress*, Arab Ba'th Socialist Party (ABSP), Baghdad: Al-Thawrah Publications. [Original in Arabic]

Arab Monetary Fund (AMF) et al. (1992), *Joint Arab Economic Report 1992*, Arab Fund for Social and Economic Development, Joint Annual Arab, and OAPEC: Abu Dhabi.

——, Arab Republic of Egypt (2001), *Ministry of Health and Population Health Survey 2000*, Ministry of Health & National Population Council: Egypt, Cairo.

Arkoun, Muhammed (1994), "Human Rights" in M. Arkoun, ed., *Rethinking Islam Common Questions, Uncommon Answers,* Boulder, CO: Westview Press.

Asquith, Christina (2003), "Iraq's Students Say 'Welcome back Professor'", *World Education News and Reviews*, November-December 2003.

Assaad, Ragui (2000), *The Transformation of Egyptian Labour Market: 1988–1998, Final Report for the Egypt Labour Market Project*, Economic Research Forum for the Arab Countries, Iran and Turkey, Cairo.

Al-Atia, Fawzia (1990), *Ta'thirat tahwil ba'dh ajzza'a al-tijara al-dakhliya wal al-kharijiya illa al-kata'a al-khas 'ala al-mar'a wal al-'a'ila al-irakiyya* [The Impacts of the Shift of some Internal and External Trades to the Private Sector on Iraqi Women and the Household], Report for Department of Studies and Research, Baghdad, Ministry of Education.

——, (1994), "Al-'a'iliah al-iraqiyya wa tahadyat al qern al wahed wal 'eshreen [The Iraqi family and the challenges of the twenty-first century], paper at seminar organised by the General Federation of Iraqi Women (GFIW) on *The Arab Family in the Twenty-first Century*. Baghdad, May 1994.

Ayubi, Nazih (1997), "Etatisme Versus Privatization: The Changing Economic Role of the State in Nine Arab Countries", in Heba Handoussa, ed., *Economic Transition in the Middle East: Global Challenges and Adjustment Strategies,* Cairo, The American University of Cairo Press.

——, (1995), *Overstating the Arab State: Politics and Society in the Middle East*, London, I.B.Tauris.

Badran, Margot (1991), "Competing Agendas: Feminism, Islam and the State in Nineteenth and Twentieth-Century Egypt", in Deniz Kandiyoti, ed., *Women, Islam, and the State*, London: Macmillan. : 201–236

——, (1993), "Independent Women: More than a Century of Feminism in Egypt", in Judith Tucker, ed., *Arab Women: Old Boundaries – New Frontiers*, Bloomington, Indiana University Press. : 129–148

Baldwin, David A. (1985), *Economic Statecraft*, Princeton: Princeton University Press.

Al-Banaa, Thekraa (1996), *Al-Zawaj wal talaaq tahta t'atheer al-hessar al-iqtisadi* [The Impact of the economic sanctions on marriage & divorce in Iraq], unpublished PhD thesis, Baghdad University, Iraq.

Barakat, Halim (1985), "The Arab Family and the Challenge of Social Transformation", in Elizabeth Warnock Fernea, ed., *Women and the Family in the Middle East: New Voices of Change*, Austin: University of Texas Press. : 27–48

Baram, Amatzia (1997), "Neo-Tribalism in Iraq: Saddam Hussein's Tribal Policies, 1991–1996", International *Journal of Middle East Studies*, Vol. 29: 1–17

Barber, James (1979), "Economic Sanctions as a Policy Instrument", *International Affairs*, Vol. 55: 367–384.

Baron, Beth (1994), *Women's Awakening in Egypt: Culture, Society and the Press*, New Haven and London: Yale University Press.

Barrett, Michèle, and Mary McIntosh (1985), "Ethnocentrism and Socialist Feminism", *Feminist Review*, Vol. 20: 22–42.

Barsoum, Ghada (1998), "Female Graduates in Egypt: The Jobs Dilemma", in Mohamed Farag, ed., *Proceedings of the Sixth American University in Cairo Research Conference on Human Development for the Twenty-first Century*, Cairo: The AUC Press.

Batatu, Hanna (1978), *The Old Social Classes and the Revolutionary Movements of Iraq: A Study of Iraq's Old Landed and Commercial Classes and of its Communists, Bathists, and Free Officers*, Princeton, NJ, Princeton University Press.

Bennis, Phyllis, Michel Moushabeck and Edward W. Said, eds (1998), *Beyond the Storm: A Gulf Crisis Reader*, Northampton: Interlink Publishing Group.

Bhatty, Zarina (1987), "Economic Contribution of Women to the Household Budget: A Case Study of the Beedi Industry", in A. M. Singh and A, K. Viitanen, eds., *Invisible Hands: Women in Home-based Production*, India: Sage Publications. : 35–50

Bibars, Iman (2001), *Victims and Heroines: Women, Welfare and the Egyptian State*, London and New York: Zed Books, 2001.

Blumberg, Rae Lesser (1991), "Introduction: The Triple Overlap of Gender Stratification, Economy, and the Family", in Rae Lesser Blumberg, ed., *Gender, Family, and the Economy: The Triple Overlap*, Newburg Park, CA: Sage. 1–33

Blumer, Herbert (1990), *Industrialisation as an Agent of Social Change: A Critical Analysis*, Hawthorne, NY: Aldyne de Gruyter.

Boone, Peter, Haris Gazdar and Athar Hussain (1997), *Sanctions against Iraq: Cost of Failure; The Impact of UN Imposed Sanctions on the Economic well-being of the Civilian Population of Iraq*, report for the Center for Economic and Social Rights (CESR), New York, November 1997.

Boserup, Esther (1987), *Women and Economic Development*, 2nd ed., New York: St. Martin's Press.

Bossuyt, Marc (2000), *The Adverse Consequences of Economic Sanctions on the Enjoyment of Human Rights*, Economic and Social Council, Commission on Human Rights, United Nations Document E/CN.4/Sub.2/2000/33, Geneva: United Nations, June 2000.

Bouhdiba, Abdelwahab (1998), *Sexuality in Islam*, London: Saqi Books.

Boutros Ghali, Boutros (1995), *Supplement to Agenda for Peace*, with the new Supplement and UN Documents, New York: United Nations.

——, (1996), An Agenda for Peace, New York, United Nations.

Brand, Laurie A. (1998), *Women, the State, and Political Liberalization: Middle Eastern and North African Experiences*, New York: Columbia University Press.

Bulloch, John, and Harvey Morris (1991), *Saddam's War: The Origins of the Kuwait Crisis and the International Response*, London: Faber and Faber.

Bureau of Democracy, Human rights, and Labour (2004), *Country Reports on Human Rights Practices – 2003*, Released by the Bureau of Democracy, Human Rights, and Labour, February 2004.

Burstyn, Varda (1983), Masculine Dominance and the State, in R. Milibend and J. Saville, ed., *Socialist Register.*

Butler, Judith (1992), "Contingent Foundations: Feminism and the Question of Postmodernism" in Judith Butler and Joan W. Scott, eds., *Feminists Theorize the Political*, New York: Routledge. : 3–21

Cainkar, Louise (1993), "The Gulf War, Sanctions, and the Lives of Iraqi Women", *Arab Studies Quarterly*, Vol. 15: 15–49.

——, (1998), "Desert Sin: A Post-War Journey Through Iraq", in Phyllis Bennis and Michel Moushabeck, eds., *Beyond the Storm*, Northampton: Interlink Publishing Group. :335–355

Caldwell, John C. (1982), *Theory of Fertility Decline*, London: Academic Press.

Center for Economic and Social Rights (CESR) (1996), *Unsanctioned Suffering: A Human Rights Assessment of United Nations Sanctions on Iraq*, New York, May 1996.

Chan, Steven, and Cooper A. Dury (2001), *Sanctions As Economic Statecraft: Theory & Practice*, International Political Economy Series, Basingstoke and New York: Palgrave Macmillan.

Chandler, David (2003), "Rhetoric Without Responsibility: The Attraction of 'Ethical' Foreign Policy", *The British Journal of Politics & International Relations*, Vol. 5, no. 3: 428–454.

Charlton, Ellen Sue (1989), *Women, the State, and Development*, Albany: State University of New York Press.

Charrad, Mounira (1993), *States and Women's Rights: A Comparison of Tunisia, Algeria and Morocco*, Berkeley CA: University of California Press.

Chase-Dunn, Christopher (1989), *Global Formation: Structures of the World-Economy*, Cambridge: Basil Blackwell.

Chaudhry, Kiren A. (1991), "On the Way to Market: Economic Liberalization and the Iraq Invasion of Kuwait", *Middle East Report*, Vol. 21, no. 3, May/June 1991.

——, (1997), "Economic Liberalization and Lineage of the Rentier State: Iraq and Saudi Arabia Compared", in Nicholas S Hopkins and Saad Eddin Ibrahim, eds., *Arab Society: Class, Gender, Power, and Development*, 3rd ed., Cairo, The American University in Cairo Press. :357–384

Chomsky, Noam (1998), "After the Cold War: U.S. Middle East Policy", in Phyllis Bennis and Michel Moushabeck, eds., *Beyond the Storm: A Gulf Crisis Reader*, Northampton: Interlink Publishing Group.

Cinar, Mine, ed. (2001), *The Economics of Women and Work in the Middle East and North Africa*, Chicago: Loyola Chicago.

Clark, Roger, et al. (1991), "Culture, Gender, and Labour Force Participation: A Cross-National Study", *Gender and Society*, Vol. 5, no. 1: 47–66.

Clegg, Steven (1988), *Frameworks of Power*. London: Sage Publications.

Cobbett, Deborah (1989), Women in Iraq" in *Saddam's Iraq: Revolution or Reaction*. London: Zed Books for CARDRI.

Cockburn, Cynthia (1999), "Gender, Armed Conflict and Political Violence", keynote paper at *Conference on Gender, Armed Conflict and Political Violence*, convened by the World Bank, Washington DC, June 1999.

Collier, Paul (1993), "The Impact of Adjustment on Women", in L. Demery, M. Ferroni, C. Grootaert with J. Worg-Valle (ed.). *Understanding the Social Effects of Policy Reform.* Washington DC: World Bank. : 183–197

Committee for the Elimination of all Forms of Discrimination Against Women (CEDAW) (1998), *The Second and Third Periodic Reports of State Parties: Republic of Iraq*, CEDAW/C/IRQ/2–3, Iraq, 19 October 1998.

Connell, Robert W. (1987), *Gender and Power*, Stanford CA:, Stanford University Press.

——, (1990), "The State, Gender and Sexual Politics: Theory and Appraisal", *Theory and Society*, Vol. 9, no. 5: 507–545.

——, (1994), "Gender Regimes and the Gender Order", *Gender Studies*, Polity Reader, Cambridge: Polity Press. : 29–40

Cortright, David & George A. Lopez, eds.(1995), *Economic Sanctions: Panacea or Peacebuilding in Post-Cold War World?* Boulder & Oxford: Westview Press.

Cox, Robert W., and Timothy J. Sinclair (1996), "Social Forces, States, and World Orders: Beyond International Relations", in Robert W. Cox and Timothy J. Sinclair, eds., *Approaches to World Order*, Cambridge: Cambridge University Press. : 87–107

Curtiss, Richard H. (1996), "Women's Rights: An Affair of State for Tunisia", in Suha Sabbagh, ed., *Arab Women: Between Defiance and Restraint*, New York, Olive Branch Press. : 33–41

Daoudi, M. S., and M. S. Dajani (1983), *Economic Sanctions: Ideals and Experience*, London, Routledge and Kegan Paul.

Davis, Eric, and Nicola Gavrielides, eds. (1991), *Statecraft, Historical Memory, and Popular Culture in Iraq and Kuwait*, Miami FL, Florida International University Press.

Davis, Eric (1991). "Theorizing Statecraft and Social Change in Arab Oil-Producing Countries", in Eric Davis and Nicola Gavrielides, eds., *Statecraft in the Middle East; Oil, Historical Memory, and Popular Culture*, Miami FL, Florida International University Press. : 1–35

Davis, Stephen P. (1991), "Economic Pressure on South Africa: Does It Work", in *Effective Sanctions on South Africa: The Cutting Edge of Economic Intervention*, New York, Westport.

Dawisha, Adeed (1999), "Identity and Political Survival in Saddam's Iraq", *Middle East Journal* (Middle East Institute), Vol. 53, no. 4: 533–567.

——, (2003), *Arab Nationalism in the 20th Century: from Triumph to Despair*, Princeton NJ: Princeton University Press.

De Hoogh, André (1996), *Obligations Egra Omnes and International Crimes: A Theoretical Inquiry into the Implementation and Enforcement of International Responsibility of State*, The Netherlands: Kluwer Law International.

Delmar, Rosalind (1986), "What is Feminism?", in Juliet Mitchell and Ann Oakly, eds., *What is Feminism?* New York: Pantheon Books. : 8–33

Dex, Shirley (1985), *The Sexual Division of Work: Conceptual Revolutions in Social Sciences*, Brighton: Harvest Press.

Doallar, David, and Aart Kraay (2001), *Trade, Growth, and Poverty*, New York: World Bank, (mimeo).

Doling, John, and Roziah Omar (2000), "The Welfare State System in Malaysia", *Journal of Societal and Society Policy*, Vol. 1, no. 1: 33–47.

Doxey, Margaret P. (1990), "International Sanctions", in David G. Haglund and Michael K. Hawes, eds., *World Politics: Power, Interdependence and Dependence*, Toronto, Harcourt Brace Jovanovich. :243–261

———, (1996), *International Sanctions in Contemporary Perspective*, 2nd ed., London, Macmillan.

Drèze, Jean, and Amartya K. Sen (1989), *Hunger and Public Action*, Oxford: Clarendon Press.

———, and Haris Gazdar (1991a), *Income and Economic Survey: Health and Welfare in Iraq after the Gulf War Crisis, An In Depth Assessment*, New York, International Study Team (IST), October.

———, (1991b), *Hunger and Poverty in Iraq*, Development Economics Research Programme, no. 32, London: London School of Economics.

Dunning, John H. (1995), *Globalisation, Economic Restructuring and Development*, UNCTAD/ EDM/ERCP/7/1994, Reviewed by Terutomo Ozawa in Transnational *Corporations*, vol. 4, no.3: 167–170.

Dwyer, Daisy, and Judith Bruce, eds. (1988), *A Home Divided: Women and Income in the Third World*, Stanford, CA: Stanford University Press.

Economic Commission for Latin America and the Caribbean (ECLAC) (1992), *Domestic Violence against Women in Latin America and the Caribbean: Proposals for Discussion*, ECLAC, Social Development Division. Santiago, Chile.

Economic Intelligence Unit (EIU) (1981), Economic Review of Iraq, London: EIU.

———, (1984), *Economic Review of Iraq* (4), London: EIU.

———, (January 1996), *Country Profile Iraq, 1995–6*, London EIU.

———, (March 1997), *Country Report Iraq*, London: EIU.

———, (2000), *Country Profile Iraq*, London: EIU.

———, (January 2000), *Country Report Iraq, 1999–2000*, London: EIU.

———, (January 2001), *Country Profile Iraq*, London: EIU.

———, (September 2003), *Country Report Iraq*, London: EIU.

———, (December 2003), *Country Report Iraq*, London: EIU.

Economic Research Forum for the Arab Countries, Iran and Turkey (ERF) (2002), *Economic Trends in MENA Region, 2002*. Cairo: The American University in Cairo Press. : Chapter Five

Efrati, Noga (1999), "Productive or Reproductive? The Roles of Iraqi Women during the Iraq-Iran War", *Middle Eastern Studies*, London: Frank Cass, Vol. 35. no. 2: 27–44.

Eisenstein, Zillah R. (1979), "A Theory of Capitalist Patriarchy and Socialist Feminism", in Zillah R. Eisenstein, ed., *Capitalist Patriarchy and the Case of Socialist Feminism, New* York: Monthly Review Press.

Al-Emari, Zakia (1994), "Al 'a'ila al-iraqiah: adawrahaa wa ta'theer al-hissar 'alayha" [The impact of sanctions on the Iraqi family functions], paper at GFIW seminar on *Arab Family in the Twenty-first Century*, Baghdad: General Federation of Arab Women Press.

Elson, Diane (1991), "Male Bias in the Development Process: The Case of Structural Adjustment", in Diane Elson, ed., *Male Bias in the Development Process*. London: Macmillan. : 69–99

Enloe, Cynthia (1988), *Does Khaki Become You? The Militarism of Women's Lives*, 2nd ed., London, Pandora.

———, (1990a), *Bananas, Beaches, and Bases in Making Feminist Sense of International Politics*, Berkley CA: University of California Press.

———, (1990b), "Womenandchildren: Making Feminist Sense of the Persian Gulf Crisis", *The Village Voice, 25* September 1990.

——, (1993), *The Morning After: Sexual Politics at the End of the Cold War*, Berkeley CA: University of California Press.

——, (2000), *Manoeuvres: The International Politics of Militarising Women's Lives*. Berkeley CA: University of California Press.

——, (2004), "'Gender' is not enough: the need for a feminist Consciousness" Abstract/ Comment on Gillian Young's article 'Feminist International Relations: A Contradiction in Term? Or: Why Women and Gender are Essential to Understanding the World 'we' Live In', *International Affairs*, Vol. 80, no.1: 95–98.

Evan, Peter B. (1985), "Bringing the State Back In: Strategies of Analysis", in Peter B. Evan, Dietrich Rueschemeyer and Theda Skocpol, eds., *Bringing the State Back In*, Cambridge: Cambridge University Press. : 58–101

Fahimi, Roudi-Farzaneh (2003), *Women's Reproductive Health in the Middle East and North Africa* (MENA). Washington, DC: Population Reference Bureau.

Farahni, Nader (1986), *The Impact of Oil Market Change on Employment in the Arabic Oil-Producing Countries*, Morocco. Arab Organisation for Employment.
[Original in Arabic].

Farouk-Sluglett, Marion, and Peter Sluglett (1990), "Iraq Since 1986: Strengthening of Saddam", *Middle East Report*, no. 167: 19–25, November/December 1990.

Farouk-Sluglett, Marion (1993), "Liberation or Repression? Pan-Arab Nationalism and the Women's Movement in Iraq", in Derek Hopwood, Habib Ishow and Thomas Koszinowski, eds., *Iraq: Power and Society*, Reading: Ithaca Press. 51–73

Farsoun, K. Samih, ed. (1985), *Arab Society: Continuity and Change*, London: Croom Helm.

——, (1997), "Class Structure and Social Change in the Arab World", in Nicholas S. ed., *Arab Society: Class, Gender, Power and Development*, Cairo: The American University Press. : 11–27

Fernea, Elizabeth Warnock, ed. (1985), *Women and the Family in the Middle East: New Voices of Change*, Austin: University of Texas Press.

Field, John (1993), "From Food Security to Food Insecurity: The Case of Iraq", *Geo-Journal*, (Kluwer Academic Publishers), Vol. 30, no. 2: 185–194, June 1993.

Flax, Jan (1990), "Postmodernism and Gender Relations in Feminist Theory", in Linda J. Nicholson, ed., *Feminism/Postmodernism*, New York: Routledge. : 39–62

Foucault, Michel (1978), *The History of Sexuality*, Vol. 1: Introduction, trans. Robert Hurley, New York: Pantheon.

Franzway, Suzanne, D. Court and Robert W. Connell (1989), *Staking a Claim: Feminism, Bureaucracy and the State*, London: Paladin.

Friedland, William H. (1969), "A Sociological Approach to Modernization", in Chandler Morse et al., eds., *Modernization By Design: Social Change in the Twentieth Century*, London: Cornell University Press.

Galdi, Theodore and Robert Shuey (1997), *U.S. Economic Sanctions Imposed against Specific Countries: 1979 to the Present*, Washington, DC: Congressional Research Service.

Galtung, John (1967), "On the Effects of International Economic Sanctions, with Examples from the Case of Rhodesia", *World Politics*, Vol. 19, no. 3: 378–416.

Garfield, Richard, S. Zaidi and J. Lennock (1997), "Medical Care in Iraq after Six Years of Sanctions", *British Medical Journal*, no. 315: 1474–5.

Garfield, Richard (1999a), *Morbidity and Mortality among Iraqi Children from 1990 through 1998: Assessing the Impact of the Gulf War and Economic Sanctions*, Columbia University Press.

——, (1999b), *The Impact of Sanctions on Health and Well-being*, Overseas Development Institute (ODI), London, November 1999.

——, (2000), "The Public Health Impact of Sanctions: Contrasting Responses of Iraq and Cuba", *Middle East Report*, no. 215: 16–19.

Gazdar, Haris (1997), "The Economy under Sanctions", paper presented to the conference on *Frustrated Development: The Iraqi Economy in War and in Peace* organised by the Centre for Arab Gulf Studies, University of Exeter, in collaboration with the Iraqi Economic Forum, Exeter, 9–11 July 1997.

Gelb, Stephen (1991), "South Africa's Economic Crisis: An Overview", in Stephen Gelb, ed., *South Africa's Economic Crisis*, Cape Town: David Philip. : 1–32

Gellman Barton (1991), "Allied Air War Struck Broadly in Iraq; Officials Acknowledge Strategy Went Beyond Military Targets", *Washington Post* (23), June 1991.

Gellner, Ernest (1983), *Nations and Nationalism*, Oxford: Basil Blackwell.

General Federation Of Iraqi Women (GFIW) (1980), *Development of Female Participation in Economic Activities: Public Sector during 1968–1978*, Baghdad: The General Federation of Iraqi Women (GFIW). [Original in Arabic]

——, (1983a), *The National Campaign to Increase Women's Participation in the Economic Development Process,* Baghdad: The General Federation of Iraqi Women (GFIW), December 1983. [Original in Arabic]

——, (1983b), *Women's Participation in the Economic Development*, Baghdad: The General Federation of Iraqi Women (GFIW). [Original in Arabic]

——, (1985), *Report of the GFIW Secretariat and Public Relations*, Meeting of the World in Baghdad, Baghdad: The General Federation of Iraqi Women (GFIW), March 1985. [Original in Arabic]

——, (1987), *Situation of Unemployment in Iraq and Perspectives for Solution, Study No. 952*, A Study by General Federation of Iraqi Women to the Department of Labour Force Planning. Baghdad: Ministry of Planning Publications. [Original in Arabic]

——, (1989), "Mukhtarat min ahadith al-qa'ed saddam hussain [Collection of the Leader's Speeches], Baghdad: General Federation of Iraqi Women (GFIW).

——, (1990), *The Impacts of the Privatisation on Iraqi Women and the Household,* Department of Studies and Research. Baghdad: The General Federation of Iraqi Women (GFIW). [Original in Arabic]

——, (1994a), *Demographic, Economic, Educational, and Social Development of Iraqi Women during 1977–1988*, Studies and Research Centre. Baghdad: The General Federation of Iraqi Women (GFIW). [Original in Arabic]

——, (1994b), *National Report on the Development of the Iraqi Women 1985–1995*, Preparatory Committee for the Fourth International Women Conference. Baghdad: The General Federation of Iraqi Women (GFIW).

Goldstein, Joshua S. (2001), *War and Gender: How Gender Shapes the War System and Vice Versa*, Cambridge: Cambridge University Press.

Graham-Brown, Sarah (1999), *Sanctioning Saddam: The Politics of Intervention in Iraq*, London and New York: I.B.Tauris.

——, (2002), "Humanitarian Needs and International Assistance in Iraq", in Kamil A. Mahdi, ed., *Iraq's Economic Predicament*, Reading: Ithaca Press. : 267–288

Grant, Rebecca, and Kathleen Newland, eds. (1991), *Gender and International Relations*, Milton Keynes, Open University Press.

Grant, Rebecca (1992), "The Quagmire of Gender and International Security", in V. Peterson, ed., *Gendered States: Feminist (Re)Visions of International Relations Theory*, Boulder CO: Lynne Rienner Publishers. : 83–97

Grosz, Elizabeth A. (1990), "A Note on Essentialism and Difference", in Sneja Manna Gurew, ed., *Feminist Knowledge as Critique and Construct*. London: Routledge. : 332–344

Hacettepe University, Institute of Population Studies (1999), Turkey Demographic and Health Survey 1998, Final Report, Turkey, Calverton, MD, USA & ORC Macro.

Hajjar, Sami G. ed. (1985), "Introduction: The Middle East from Transition to Development", in *Sociology and Social Anthropology, International Studies*, The Netherlands: Lieden E.J. Brill. :1–17.

Halliday, Fred, and Hamza Alavi (1988), "Introduction", in Fred Halliday and Hamza Alavi, eds., *State and Ideology in the Middle East and Pakistan*, London: Macmillan Education. : 1–9

Halliday, Fred (1991), "Hidden from International Relations: Women and the International Arena", in Rebecca Grant and Kathleen Newland, eds., *Gender and International Relations*. Bloomington: Indiana University Press. : 158–169

——, ed. (1994), "State and Society in International Relations", in *Rethinking International Relations*. London: Macmillan Press.

——, (2000), *Nation and Religion in the Middle East*, London: Saqi Books.

——, (2005), *One Hundred Myths about the Middle East*, London: Saqi Books.

Hamadeh, Najla S. (1999), "Wives or Daughters: Structural Differences Between Urban and Bedouin Lebanese Co-Wives", in Suad Joseph, ed., *Intimate Selving in Arab Families: Gender, Self, and Identity*, Syracuse: Syracuse University Press. : 141–173

Hanson, Gordon H., and Ann E. Harrison (1999), "Who Gains from Trade Reforms? Some Remaining Puzzles", *Journal of Development Economics*, Vol. 5: 315–324

Harding, Sandra, ed. (1987), *Feminism and Methodology: Social Science Issues*, Bloomington: Indiana University Press.

Hart, Keith (1973), "Informal Income Opportunities and Urban Employment in Ghana", *Journal of Modern African Studies*, Vol. 11: 61–89.

Harvard Study Team (1991a), *Public Health in Iraq after the Gulf War*, New York, May 1991.

——, (1991b) (International Study Team), Health and Welfare in Iraq after the *Gulf War: An In-Depth Assessment*, New York, August (an update of May 1991 report).

Al-Hassan, Mohammed Ihsan (1981), *Al-tasni'a wa ta'atheeraho a'la al-mujtama'a* [The Social impact of industry], Beirut: Dar al-Tali'a.

——, (1986a), *Al-'a'iliah wal qarabah wal al-zawaj* [The family Kinship ties and marriage], 2nd Edition, Beirut: Dar al-Tali'a.

——, (1986b), *Al-tasne'a wa tagheer al mujtama'a* [Industry and social change], 2nd.ed. Baghdad: Ministry of Information Press.

——, (1985), *Thaar al-tasni'a fi bina'a wa wadha'ef al-'a'iliah al-irakiyya* [Impact of industry on the functions of the Iraqi family], Vol. 11, Baghdad: Al-Mustansiriyya University Press.

——, (1994), "Waq'e al 'elaqaat al- usaraiah fi al-irak" [Family relations in Iraq], Paper at seminar on *The Arab Family in the Twenty-first Century* organised by the General Federation of Iraqi Women (GFIW), Baghdad, May 1994.

Hassan, Nagah (2000), *Female Labour Market Entrants in Egypt*, Cairo, Population Council (mimeo).

Hatem, Mervat (1987), "Class and Patriarchy as Competing Paradigms for the Study of Middle Eastern Women", *Comparative Studies in Society and History*, Vol. 29, no. 4: 811–818.

——, (1992), "Economic and Political Liberalization in Egypt and the Demise of State Feminism", *International Journal of Middle East Studies,* Vol. 24: 231–251.

——, (1993), "Toward the Development of Post-Islamist and Post-Nationalist Feminist Discourses in the Middle East", in Judith Tucker, ed., *Arab Women: Old Boundaries, New Frontiers*, Bloomington: Indiana University Press. : 195–207

——, (1994), "Privatisation and the Demise of State Feminism in Egypt", in Pamela Starr, ed., *Mortgaging Women's Lives: Feminist Critique of Structural Adjustment*, London: Zed Books. : 40–56

——, (1995), "Political Liberalization, Gender, and the State", in Rex Brynen, Bahgat Korany and Poul Noble eds., *Political Liberalization and Democratization in the Arab World: Theoretical Perspectives*, Vol. I: 187–208, London: Lynne Rienner Publishers.

——, (1998), "Secularist and Islamist Discourses on Modernity in Egypt and the Evolution of the Postcolonial Nation-State", in Y. Haddad and J. Esposito, eds., *Islam, Gender, and Social Change*, Oxford: Oxford University Press. : 85–99

Haub, Carl (2003), Press Release of *the World Population Data Sheet*, 2003, Population Reference Bureau. Online at: HtmlResAnchor http://www.prb.org/Content/NavigationMenu/PRB/Journalists/PressReleases/PressConference_Release_of_the_2003_World_Population_Data_Sheet.htm (Last accessed 22 February 2005).

Al-Haza'a', Sannah (1999), *Al-hajjat al-a'sasiya alti tatatala'a ilihaa al-mara'a al-iraqiya li marhala ma ba'da al-hissar* [Iraq women; perceptions of needs after lifting the sanctions], unpublished Masters Thesis in Psychology, University of Baghdad, Iraq.

Hernes, Helga M. (1984), "Women and the Welfare State: The Transition from Private to Public Dependence", in Harriet Holter, ed., *Patriarchy in Welfare Society*, Oslo: Norwegian University Press. : 26–45

——, (1987), *Welfare State and Women Power: Essays in State Feminism*, Oslo: Norwegian University Press.

Heydermann, Steven, ed. (2000), *War, Institutions and Social Change in the Middle East*. Berkley CA: University of California Press.

Hijab, Nadia (1988), *Womenpower: The Arab Debate on Women at Work*, Cambridge: Cambridge University Press.

——, (1996), "Women and Work in the Arab World", in Suha Sabbagh, ed., *Arab Women: Between Defiance and Restraint*, New York: Olive Branch Press. : 41–53

Hiro, Dilip (1991), *The Longest War: The Iran-Iraq Military Conflict*, New York: Routledge.

——, (1992), *From Desert Shield to Desert Storm,* New York: Routledge.

Holton, Robert J. (1998), *Globalisation and the Nation-State*, New York: St. Martin's Press.

Hopkins, Nicholas S. ed. (1991), *The Informal Sector in Egypt*, Cairo Papers in Social Science, Vol. 14, no.4.

Hoskins, Eric (1992), "The Truth Behind Economic Sanctions: A Report on the Embargo of Food and Medicines to Iraq", in Ramsey Clark et al., *War Crimes: A Report on United States War Crimes Against Iraq*, Washington, D.C.: Maisonneuve Press.

——, (1997), "The Humanitarian Impact of the Economic Sanctions and War on Iraq", in Tomas G Weiss, David Cortright, George A. Lopez, and Larry Minear, eds., *Political Gain and Civilian Pain: Humanitarian Impact of Economic Sanctions,* Boulder: Rowman & Littlefield Publisher, Inc. : 57–90.

House of Commons (2000), "International Development/Second Special, Session 1999–2000, *International Development Committee Publications.* Online at: HtmlResAnchor http://

www.parlament.the-stationery-office.co.uk/pa/cm199900/cmselect/cmintdev/473/
47302.htm
(Last Accessed on March 2004).

Hufbauer, Gary (1985), *History and Current Policy*, Washington DC, Institute for International Economices.

——, (1990a), *Economic Sanctions Reconsidered: History and Current Policy*, 3rd Ed. Washington D.C.: Institute for International Economics.

Hufbauer, Gary C., Jeffrey J. Schott, and Kimberly Ann Elliott, eds. (1990b), *Economic Sanctions Reconsidered: Supplemental Case Histories* (an update of Hufbauer and Schott, 1983), Washington, D.C.: Institute for International Economics.

Human Rights Watch (HRW) (2003/2005), *Climate of Fear: Sexual Violence and Abduction of Women and Girls in Baghdad*, (HRW), vol. No. 7(E) (July/2003 and February 2005). Online HtmlResAnchor http://www.hrw.org (Last accessed 19 May 2005)

Ilkkaracan, Pinar, ed. (2000), *Women and Sexuality in Muslim Societies*. Istanbul: Kadinin Insan haklari Piujesi.

International Labour Organization (ILO) (1972), *Employment, Income and Equality: A Strategy for Increasing Productive Employment in Kenya*, Geneva ILO.

——, (1991), *The Dilemma of the Informal Sector*, International Labour Conference, 78th Session, Report of the Director-General, Geneva, ILO.

——, (1995), *Economically Active Population, Statistical Sources and Methods*, Vol. 3. Geneva, ILO.

——, (1999), *Economically Active Population Statistical Sources and Method* (ILO), Vol. (3): 183–184.

Ismael, Shereen T. (2004), "Dismantling the Iraqi Social Fabric: From Dictatorship Through Sanctions to Occupation", *Journal of Comparative Family Studies*, Vol. 35, no.2: 220–339.

'Izat, Fatah (1990), *Al-zawaj w'al-talaaq fi al-irak* [Marriage and Divorce in Iraq], Baghdad Ministry of Justice.

Jabri, Vivienne, and Eleanor O'Gorman, eds. (1999), "Locating Difference in Feminist International Relations", in Vivienne Jabri and Eleanor O'Gorman, eds., *Women, Culture, and International Relations*, Boulder, CO: Lynne Rienner Publishers. : 1–15

Jameson, Fredric and Masao Miyoshi, eds. (1998), *The Culture of Globalisation*, London and Durham NC: Duke University Press.

Jayawardena, Kumari (1988), *Feminism and Nationalism in the Third World*, London: Zed Press.

Al-Jenabi, A'idaa (1983), *Al-mutghiraat al-ijtema'iyya wal thaqafiyya li dhaherat ta'adud al-zawjat fi al-irak* [Social and cultural variables of the phenomenon of polygamy], Baghdad, Dar Al-Huriyya.

Jiyad, Ahmed M. (1997), "Iraq's Indebtedness: From Liquidity to Unsustainability", paper at conference on *Frustrated Development: The Iraqi Economy in War and in Peace*, University of Exeter, Centre for Arab Gulf Studies, July 1997.

——, (1998), "Human Development Paradigm under Globalization Environment: The Arab Gulf", paper at *The Middle East in Globalizing World*, Fourth Nordic Conference on Middle Eastern Studies, Oslo, Norway, 13–16 August 1998.

——, (2002), "The Development of Iraq's Foreign Debt: From Liquidity to Un-sustainability", in Kamil A. Mahdi, ed., *Iraq's Economic Predicament*, Exeter Arab and Islamic Series, Reading, Ithaca Press. : 141–169

Johnson, Susan and Ben Rogaly (1997), *Microfinance and Poverty Reduction*, Oxfam Development Guidelines, Oxfam: Oxfam.

Jones, Adam (1996), "Does 'Gender' Make the World Go Round? Feminist Critique of International Relations", *Review of International Studies*, Vol. 22, no. 4: 405–429.

Joseph, Suad (1982), "The Mobilization of Iraqi Women into the Wage Labour Force", Studies in Third World Societies, Vol. 16: 69–90.

——, (1991), "Elite Strategies for State Building: Women, Family, Religion and State in Iraq and Lebanon", in Deniz Kandiyoti, ed., *Women, Islam, and the State*, London: Macmillan. : 176–200

——, (1993), "Gender and Civil Society", *Middle East Report*, no. 183: 14–26, July–August, 1993.

——, (1996a), "Gender and Citizenship in Middle Eastern States" *MERIP* Vol. 26, no.1. 1996: 2–10

——, (1996b), "Gender and Family in the Arab World", in Suha Sabbagh, ed., *Arab Women: Between Defiance and Restraint*, New York: Olive Branch Press. : 194–203

——, (1999), "Brother-Sister Relationships: Connectivity, Love, and Power in the reproduction of Patriarchy in Lebanon", in S. Joseph, ed., *Intimate Selving in Arab Families: Gender, Self, and Identity*, Syracuse: Syracuse University Press. : 113–141

Al-Jumai'i', Fu'ad, and Hanna Hadi Mohammed-'Ali (1989), "Assaliib ziadet musahamet a'enaath fi al-qaw al-a'milah al-iraqiyya [Methods for increasing female labour participation], *Journal of Gulf and Arab Peninsula Studies*, Vol. 25, no. 158: 195–222, Kuwait University Press.

Kamrava, Mehran (1993), *Politics and Society in the Third World*, London and New York: Routledge.

Kandiyoti, Deniz (1977), "Sex Roles and Social Change: A comparative Study of Turkey's Women", *Signs*, Vol. 3: 57–73.

——, (1988), "Bargaining with Patriarchy", *Gender & Society*, Vol. 2, no. 3: 274–290.

——, ed. (1991a), "Introduction", in *Women, Islam and the State*, London: Macmillan. : 1–18

——, ed. (1991b), "End of Empire: Islam, Nationalism and Women in Turkey", in *Women, Islam and the State*, London: Macmillan. : 22–44

——, (1991c), "Identity and Its Discontents: Women and the Nation", *Millennium*, Vol. 20 No. 3: 429–445.

——, (1991d), "Islam and Patriarchy: A Comparative Perspective", in N. R. Keddie and B. Baron, eds., *Shifting Boundaries: Women and Gender in Middle Eastern History*, New Haven: Yale University Press.

——, ed., (1996), "Contemporary Feminist Scholarship and Middle East Studies", in *Gendering the Middle East: Emerging Perspectives*, London: I.B.Tauris. : 1–19

Karam, Azza (1998), *Women, Islamism and the State: Contemporary Feminisms in Egypt*, London and New York, Macmillan/St Martin's Press.

Karshenas M., and Valentine V. Moghadam (2001), "Female Labour Force Participation and Economic Adjustment in MENA Region", in E. Mine Cinar, ed., *The Economics of Women and Work in the Middle East and North Africa*, Amsterdam: JAI-Elsevier Science. : 51–74

Karshenas, Massoud (1996), "Economic Liberalization, Competitiveness and Women's Employment in the Middle East and North Africa", paper presented at the Annual Conference of the Economic Research Forum for Arab Countries, Iran and Turkey, 28 August–1 September 1996, APSA, San Francisco, CA.

Keddie, Nikki R. (1988), "Ideology, Society and the State in Post-Colonial Muslim Societies", in F. Halliday and H. Alavi, eds., *State and Ideology in the Middle East and Pakistan*, London: Macmillan. : 9–30

Keddie, Nikki R. and Beth Baron, eds. (1991), *Women in Middle Eastern History: Shifting Boundaries in Sex and Gender*, New Haven CN: Yale University Press.

Al-Khalidi, Dhokaa M. (1989), "State Legislation during 1985–1990", *paper at Sixth Conference of the Institute of Economics and Management Status of Iraqi Women's Participation in Labour Force*, Baghdad: Al-Mustansiriyya University, 29–31 March 1989. [Original in Arabic]

——, (1991), *Role of Iraqi Working Women: Participation in Development and Future Perspectives*, Baghdad: GFIW Publications. [Original in Arabic]

Khan, Aga Sadruddin (1991), *Report to the Secretary-General on the Humanitarian Needs in Iraq*, UN Doc. S/22799, July 1991.

Khandker, Shahid (1998), *Fighting Poverty with Microcredit: Experience in Bangladesh*. Oxford: Oxford University Press.

Khatib, Hisham (1997), "A Human Capital for the Future", in *Economic Trends in the MENA Region*, Economic Research Forum, Cairo.

Al-Khayyat, Sana (1990), *Honour and Shame: Women in Modern Iraq*, London, Saqi Books.

Klinghoffer, J. Arthur (1989), *Oiling the Wheels of Apartheid*, Boulder Co.: Lynne Rienner Publishers.

Klotz, Audie (1995), *Norms in International Relations: The Struggle against Apartheid*, Ithaca, NY, Cornell University Press.

Knauss, Peter (1987), *The Persistence of Patriarchy: Class, Gender and Ideology in Twentieth Century Algeria*, New York: Praeger.

Krippendorf, Ekkehart (1987), "The Dominance of American Approaches in International Relations", *Millennium*, Vol. 16, no. 2: 207–214.

Kudhair, Nabil (1992), "Employment in Relation to Recent Change in Iraq's Labour Market, 1987–1991", paper at seminar organised by the General Federation of Iraqi Women (GFIW), Baghdad.

Laclau, Ernesto, and Chantal Mouffe (1985), *Hegemony and Socialist Strategy*, London: Verso.

Landgren, Signe (1989), *Embargo Disimplemented: South Africa's Military Industry*, New York: Oxford University Press.

Lentin, Ronit, ed. (1997), *Gender & Catastrophe*, New York: Zed Books.

Lenway, Stefanie Ann (1988), "Between War and Commerce: Economic Sanctions as a Tool of Statecraft", *International Organization*, Vol. 42, no. 2: 397–420.

Leyton-Brown, David, ed. (1987), *The Utility of International Economic Sanctions*, London: Macmillan.

Lobban, Richard A. Jr., ed. (1998), "Introduction", in *Middle Eastern Women and the Invisible Economy*, Gainesville FL: University of Florida Press. : 1–42

Lopez, George A., and David Cortright (1995), "The Sanctions Era: An alternative to Military Intervention", *Fletcher Forum for World Affairs*, Vol. 19, no. 2, Summer/Fall.

Lorber, Judith (1994), *Paradoxes of Gender*, New Haven and London: Yale University Press.

MacEwen Alison Scott (1994), *Gender Segregation and Social Change*, Oxford: Oxford University Press.

Machiavelli, Niccolo (1995), *The Prince*, ed. and trans. Stephen Milner, London: Everyman.

Maguire Robert, et al. (1996), *Haiti Held Hostage: International Responses to the Quest for Nationhood, 1986–1996*, Occasional Paper 23, Providence RI: Watson Institute.

Mahdi, Kamil A. (1998), "Rehabilitation Prospects for the Iraqi Economy", *The International Spectator* (Journal of Istituto Affari Internazionali, Rome), Vol. 33, June 1998. (See also online: HtmlResAnchor http://www.casi.org.uk/info/mahdi98.html. (Internet version posted November 1999)

Maher, Vanessa (1978), "Women and Social Change in Morocco", in Lois Beck and Nikki Keddie, eds., *Women in the Muslim World*, Cambridge, MA: Harvard University Press.

Malanczuk, Peter (1987), Countermeasures and Self-defence", in *United Nations Codification of State Responsibility*, New York: United Nations.

Manal Yunis (1985), *Values Related to Women in President Saddam Hussain's Addresses to Women*, Baghdad: GFIW Publications.

Mann, Michael (1984), "The Autonomous Power of the State", *Archives of European Sociology*, Vol. 15, no. 2.

——, (1986), "A Crisis in Stratification Theory?" in Rosemary Crompton and Michael Mann, eds., *Gender and Stratification*, Cambridge: Polity Press.

Martin, Lisa (1992), *Coercive Cooperation: Explaining Multilateral Economic Sanctions*, Princeton NJ: Princeton University Press.

——, (1993), *Political Symbol or Policy Tool? Making Sanctions Work*, Muscatine, Iowa: Stanley Foundation

Mayer, Ann Elizabeth (1995), "Cultural Particularism as a bar to Women's Rights: Reflections on the Middle Eastern Experience", in Julie Peters and Andrea Wolper, eds., *Women's Rights Human Rights: International Feminist Perspectives*, New York: Routledge.

Mazumdar, Dipak, (1976), The Urban Informal Sector, *World Development*, Vol. 4: 655–679.

Middle East Economic Digest (MEED), October 1982.

Middle East Economic Digest (MEED), Vol. 21, no. 49, 9 December 1977.

Middle East Economic Digest (MEED), Vol. 24, no. 35, 29 August 1980

Middle East Economic Digest (MEED), *Quarterly Report,* June 1990

Middle East Economic Digest (MEED), *Quarterly Report,* July 1991

Middle East Economic Survey (MEES), 18 September 1989

Middle East Economic Survey (MEES), 23 January1989

Meghdessian, Rafidi Samira (1980), *The Status of the Arab Women*, Westport: Greenwood Press.

Mehdi, Amin Sharawardi and Oliver Robenson (1983), "Economic Development and the Labour Market in Iraq", *International Journal of Manpower*, Vol. 4, no. 2: 18–26.

Mehdid, Malika (1992), "Feminist Debate on Women and the State in the Middle East", *Middle East Report*, Vol. 22, no.1.

Mernissi, Fatima (1978), "The Degrading Effects of Capitalism on Female Labour", *Mediterranean People*, Vol. 6: 16–25, January–March, 1978.

——, (1987), *Beyond the Veil: Male-Female Dynamics in Modern Muslim Society*, rev. ed., Bloomington: Indiana University Press.

——, (1988), *Doing Daily Battle: Interviews with Moroccan Women*, trans. Mary Jo Lakeland, London: The Women's Press.

——, (2000), "Virginity and Patriarchy", in Pinar Ilkkaracan, ed., *Women and Sexuality in Muslim Societies,* Istanbul: Women for Women's Rights. : 203–214

Mies, Maria (1986), *Patriarchy and Accumulation on a World Scale*, London, Oxford University Press.

Minear, Larry , et al. (1993), *United Nations Coordination of the International Humanitarian Response to the Gulf Crisis, 1990–1992*, Occasional Paper 13, Providence RI: Watson Institute.

Mizea, Timothy (1991). "Chronology of Arms Embargoes against South Africa", in George W. Shepard Jr., ed., *Effective Sanctions on South Africa: The Cutting Edge of Economic Intervention*, New York: Praeger. : 97–108

Moghadam, Valentine M., and Nabil F. Khoury (1995), "Introduction and Overview", in V. Moghdadm and P. Khoury, eds., *Gender and Development in the Arab World, Women's Economic Participation: Patterns and Politics*. London: Zed Books. : 1–6

Moghadam, Valentine M. (1988), "Women, Work and Ideology in the Islamic Republic", *International Journal of Middle East Studies*, Vol. 20, no.: 221–243.

——, (1993), *Modernizing Women: Gender & Social Change in the Middle East*, Boulder and London: Lynne Rienner Publishers.

——, ed. (1994), *Gender and National Identity: Women and Politics in Muslim Societies*, London, Zed Books. Esp.1–17

Moghadam, Valentine M. (1995a), *Economic Liberalization and women's Employment in the Middle East and North Africa*. Helsinki: United Nations University (UNU)/WIDER World Development Study Series, Vol. 1: 22–45.

——, (1995b), "The Political Economy of Female Employment in the Arab Region", in V. Moghadm and P. Khoury (eds.), *Gender and Development in the Arab World, Women's Economic Participation: Patterns and Politics*. London: Zed Books. : 6–34

——, (1995c), *Gender and Development: Rethinking Modernization and Dependency Theory*, Boulder and London: Lynne Rienner Publishers.

——, (1998), *Women, Work, and Economic Reform in the Middle East and North Africa*, Boulder and London: Lynne Rienner Publishers.

Mohammad, Rajaa Q. (1984), *Working Women in Iraq: Social, Demographic Study of the Role of Iraqi Working Women*, Unpublished Master's Thesis, Baghdad, University of Baghdad. [Original in Arabic]

Moore, Henrietta (1988), *Feminism and Anthropology*, Cambridge, Polity Press.

——, (1994), *The Cultural Constitution of Gender*, (Polity Reader in Gender Studies series), Cambridge: Polity Press. : 14–21

Morganthau, Hans (1948), *Politics Among Nations: The Struggle for Power and Peace*, New York: Knopf, reprinted 1960.

Morsy, Soheir A. (1990), "Rural Women, Work and Gender Ideology: A Study in Egyptian Political Economic Transformation", in Seteney Shami, et al., *Women in Arab Society: Work Patterns and Gender Relations in Egypt, Jordan, and Sudan*, Providence RI, Berg, for UNESCO. : 87–159

Moskoff, William (1982), "Women and Work in Israel and the Islamic Middle East", *Quarterly Review of Economics and Business*, Vol. 22. no. 4: 89–104.

Musadeq, Jamil Habib (1987), *A Study of Educational and Economic Development in Iraq*, Baghdad: al-Rasheed Publishing House. [Original in Arabic]

Mustafa-Yasin, Adnan (1990), *Women and Development in an Urban Context: A Study of Women Migrants in Mosul City (Iraq)*, Unpublished PhD thesis, University of Hull.

El-Naggar, Said, ed. (1993), *Economic Development of the Arab Countries*, Washington DC.: International Monetary Fund (IMF) Publications.

Nagy, Thomas J. (2001), "The Secret Behind the Sanctions: how the U.S. intentionally destroyed Iraq's water supply", *The Progressive*, September 2001.

Naylor, Larry L. (1996), *Culture and Change: An Introduction*, Westport CT and London: Bergin and Carvey.

Nellis, John, and Sunita Kikeri (1989), "The Privatisation of Public Enterprises", in Said El-Naggar, ed., *Privatisation and Structural Adjustment in Arab Countries*, Washington, DC: International Monetary Fund (IMF).

Niblock, Tim (1991), "International and Domestic Factors in the Economic Liberalization Process in Arab Countries", paper presented at symposium on *Economic Liberalization: its Social and Economic Effects*, University of Exeter, September 1991.

——, (2001a), *Pariah States and Sanctions in the Middle East: Iraq, Libya, Sudan*, Boulder CO and London: Lynne Rienner Publishers.

——, (2001b), "The Regional and Domestic Political Consequences of Sanctions Imposed on Iraq, Libya, and Sudan", *Arab Studies Quarterly* (ASQ), Vol. 23, no. 4: 59–67.

Niblock, Tim, and Rodney Wilson, eds. (1999), *The Political Economy of the Middle East*, Vol. IV: *Economic and Political Liberalization*, London: Edward Elgar.

Nicholson, Linda (1994), "Interpreting Gender", *Signs* (*A Journal of Women and Culture in Society*), Vol. 20, no.1: 79–105.

Nincic, Miroslav and Peter Wallensteen (eds) (1983), *Dilemmas of Economic Coercion*, New York: Praeger Publishers.

Nossal, Richard Kim (1989), "International Sanctions as International Punishment", International Organization, Vol. 43, no. 3: 301–322.

——, Lori Buck and Nicole Gallant (1998), "Sanctions as Gendered Instrument of Statecraft: The Case of Iraq", The British International Studies Association (BISA), Review of International Studies, issue 24: 69–84, January 1998.

Olson, Richard Stuart (1979), "Economic Coercion in World Politics: with a Focus on North South Relations", *World Politics*, Vol. 31: 471–494.

Omar, Suha (1994), "Women: Honour, Shame and Dictatorship", in Fran Hazelton, ed., *Iraq Since the Gulf War: Prospects for Democracy*, London: Zed Publications. : 60–71

Ottoman, M. Saad (1980), *The Theoretical Principle of the Implementation of Socialism in Iraq*, Baghdad: Dar-Al-Hurriyya. [Original in Arabic]

Paidar, Parvin (1995), *Women and the Political Process in Twentieth-century Iran*, Cambridge: Cambridge University Press.

Papps, Ivy (1993), "Attitudes to Female Employment in Four Middle Eastern Countries", in Haleh Afshar, ed., *Women in the Middle East: Perceptions, Realities and Struggles for Liberation*, London: Macmillan.

Patman, Carole (1988), *The Sexual Contract*, Stanford CA: Stanford University Press.

Payson, Parker (1991), "Figure it Out", in *The Washington Report on Middle East Affairs*, May/June 1991. Online at:
HtmlResAnchor http://www.washington-report.org/backissues/0491/910455.htm. (Last accessed on 13 September 2005).

Pegg, Scott (2003), *Poverty Reduction or Poverty Exacerbation?* World Bank Support Group for Extractive Industries in Africa, Indianapolis, Indiana and Purdue Universities (IUPUI), April 2003.

Peterson, Spike V. (1992a), "Introduction", in Spike V. Peterson, ed., *Gendered States: Feminist (Re) Vision of International Relations Theory*, Boulder CO: Lynne Rienner Publishers. : 1–29

——, (1992b), *Gendered States: (Re)visions of International Theory Challenge.* Boulder CO: Lynne Rienner Publishers.

——, (1992c), "Security and Sovereign States: What Is at Stake in Taking Feminism Seriously", in Spike V. Peterson, ed., *Gendered States; Feminist (Re)Visions of International Relations Theory*, Boulder CO, Lynne Rienner Publishers. : 31–64

——, and Anne Sisson Runyan (1993), *Global Gender Issues: dilemmas in World Politics*, Boulder CO.: Lynne Rienner Publishers.

Pettman, Jindy J. (1996), *Worlding Women: A Feminist International Politics*, London and New York: Routledge.

Poggi, Gabriella (1978), *The Development of the Modern State*, Stanford CA: Stanford University Press.

Poulantzas, Nicos (1973), *Political Power and Social Classes*, London: New Left Books.

Power, Grant (1997), "Globalization and its Discontents", *Development*, Vol. 40, no. 2: 75–80.

Pringle, Rosemary, and Sophie Watson (1992), "Women's Interest's and the Post-structuralist State", in M. Barrett and M. Philips, eds., *Destabilizing Theory*, Cambridge: Polity Press. : 53–73

Puggie, Mary (1984), *The State and Working Women*, Princeton NJ: Princeton University Press.

Al-Qusairy, En'aam (1988), *Al-tadhamun al-ijtema'I fi al-usrra al-irakyya khalal fatrat al-harb al-irakiyya al-iraniyya* (Social solidarity in the Iraqi family in the time of Iraq-Iran War), unpublished Masters thesis, Baghdad University, Iraq.

Radtke, Lorraine H., and Hendrikus J. Stam (1994), "Introduction", in H. L. Radtke and H. J. Stam, eds., *Power/Gender: Social Relations in Theory and Practice*, London: Sage Publications. : 1–14

Rai, Shirin M. (1996), "Women and the State in the Third World: Some Issues for Debate", in Shirin M. Rai and Geraldine Lievesley, eds., *Women and the State: International Perspectives*, London; Bristol, PA: Taylor & Francis. : 1–22

——, (2001), "Gender and Globalisation and Women's Activism: Critical Engagements", *Law, Social Justice and Global Development* (LGD), Vol. 1. Online at: HtmlResAnchor http:// elj.warwick.ac.uk/global/issue/2001–1/rai.html (Last Accessed on 21 June 2001)

Rassam, Amal (1992), "Political Ideology and Women in Iraq: Legislation and Cultural Constraints", in Nancy W. Jabbra and Joseph G. Jabbra, eds., *Women and Development in the Middle East and North Africa*, Leiden: E. J. Brill. : 82–95

——, (1982), "Revolution Within the Revolution? Women and the State in Iraq", in Tim Niblock, ed., *Iraq: The Contemporary State*, London: St. Marin's Press. : 88–99

Al-Rawi, Mansoor (1979), *Reading in Illiteracy Eradication and Education of Adults*, Baghdad: Ministry of Education Press. [Original in Arabic]

Rehn, Elisabeth, and Ellen Johnson Sirleaf (2002), "Women, War, Peace: The Independent Experts' Assessment on the Impact of Armed Conflict on Women and Women's Role in Peace-Building", *United Nations Development Fund for Women (UNIFEM)*, *October 2002*. Online at: HtmlResAnchor http://www.unifem.undp.org/resources/assessment/ index.html.
(Last accessed on 28 August 2003)

Reinharz, Shulamit (1992), *Feminist Methods in Social Research*, Oxford: Oxford University Press.

Renwick, Robin (1981), *Economic Sanctions*, Harvard Center for International Affairs, Cambridge MA, Harvard University Press.

Republic of Iraq (1971), Collection of Laws and Regulations Relating to the Formation of Planning System in Iraq and Laws of Development Programmes and Economic Plans 1950–70, Iraq. [Original in Arabic]

Republic of Iraq, Ministry of Education (1980a), *The Development of Iraqi Women in Higher Education in the period 1970–1971/ 1979–1980*", Baghdad, May 1980. [Original in Arabic]

Republic of Iraq, Ministry of Education (1980b), *Report of the Second Conference on Illiteracy Eradication*, High Committee for the Compulsory Illiteracy Eradication Campaign 24– 25 September 1979. [Original in Arabic]

Republic of Iraq, Ministry of Oil (1973), *Iraq National Oil Company and Direct Exploitation of Oil in Iraq*, Baghdad.

Republic of Iraq, Ministry of Planning (1970), *Law of National Development Plan for the Fiscal Years 1970–1974*, Iraq.

——, (1971a), "Situation and Development of Iraq's Labour Force: A Detailed Study", *Department of Labour Force*, Iraq.

——, (1971b), *Guide to the National Development Plan*, 1970–1974, Iraq.

——, (1977a), *National Development Plan Law No. 89 of 1977*, Article 1 &3, Iraq.

——, (1977b), "Planning Labour Force: Second Part (1976–1980)", *Department of Labour Force*, Iraq.

——, (1978a), *Annual Abstract of Statistics*, Iraq.

——, (1978b), *National Development Plan Law*, Iraq.

——, (1978c), *Man, the Objective of Revolution*, Iraq.

——, (1979), *Annual Abstract of Statistics 1978–1980*, Iraq.

——, (1980), *Employment in the Public Sector in 1980*, Baghdad, *Department for labour Force in the Public Sector*, Ministry of Planning, Iraq.

——, (1983a), *Annual abstract of Statistics (1978–1982)*, Iraq.

——, (EPC) (1983b), *The Economic Planning Commission*. Iraq.

——, (1984), *The Situation of Population, Labour Force, and Wages for the period 1980–1984*, Iraq, Department of Labour Force, Ministry of Planning, Iraq.

——, (1987a), *Annual Abstract of Statistics*, Iraq

——, (1987b), Situation of Unemployment in Iraq and Perspectives for Solution, Study No. 952, *Department of Labour Force*, Iraq.

——, (1991), *Annual Abstract of Statistics*, Iraq.

Republic of Iraq, Central Statistical Organisation (1999), *Annual Abstract of Statistics (1998–1999)*, Baghdad: Board of Ministries, Planning Commission.

Reuters, News Agency (2000), *"Top UN Official Leaves Iraq, says programme failed"* [reporting on resignations of Hans Von Sponek from OFF], 29 March 2000.

Reynolds, Lioyd G. (1985), *Economic Growth in the Third World, 1950–1980*, New Haven and London: Yale University Press.

Richards, Alan, and John Waterbury (1990), *A Political Economy of the Middle East: State, Class and Economic Development*, Boulder CO: Westview Press.

Ridd, Rosemary, and Helen Callaway, eds. (1981), *Caught up in Conflict: Women's Responses to Political Strife*, London: Macmillan.

Roudi-Fahaimi, F, & Moghadam, V.M. Empowering Women, Developing Society: Female Education in Middle East and North Africa. *Women's Education in the Middle East and North Africa*. Population Reference Bureau (PRB), 2003. Online at: HtmlResAnchor http://www.eldis.org/static/DOC14160.htm. (Last accessed 15 September 2005)

Rowe, Mathew David (1993), *Surviving Economic Coercion: Rhodesia's Responses to International Economic Sanctions*, unpublished PhD dissertation, Duke University, North Carolina USA.

Rugh, Andrea (1984), *Family in Contemporary Egypt*, Syracuse, NY: Syracuse University Press.

Rush, Michael (1992), *Politics and Society: An Introduction to Political Sociology*, Hertfordshire: Harvester Wheatsheaf.

El-Saadawi, Nawal (2002), "Globalisation and the Middle East", *Socialist Review*, no. 264.

S'aid, Mohammed Kareeb (1993), "Malameh al-usra fi al-khalij al-Arabi wal mushkilat alti twajehaa" [Features of the family in the Arab Gulf states, and the problems it faces], *Dirassat al-Khalij al-'Arabi* [Arab Gulf Studies], Vol.24, no 1.

Sabbagh, Suha, ed., (1996), *Arab Women Between Defiance and Restraint*, New York: Olive Branch Press.

Sardar-Ali, Shaheen, and Siobhan Mullally (1992), "Women's Rights and Human Rights in Muslim Countries; a Case Study", in Hilary Hinds, Ann Phoenix and Jackie Stacey, eds., *Working Out: New Directions for Women's Studies*, London: Falmer. : 113–123

Sardar-Ali, Shaheen (2000), *Gender and Human Rights in Islam and International Law: Equal Before Allah, Unequal Before Man?* The Hague; London; Boston: Kluwer Law International.

——, (2002), "Women's Rights, CEDAW, and International Human Rights Debates: Towards Empowerment?", in S. Rai, J. Parpart and K. Staudt, eds., *Rethinking Empowerment: Gender and Development in a Global/Local World*, London: Routledge. : 61–78

Schuler, Sidney R., Syed Hashemi, Ann P. Riley and Shireen Akhter (1996), "Credit Programs, Patriarchy and Men's Violence against Women in Rural Bangladesh", *Social Science Medicine*, Vol. 43, no. 12: 1729–42.

Scott, Catherine V. (1995), *Gender and Development: Rethinking Modernisation and Dependency Theory*, London, Lynne Rienner Publishers.

Scott, Joan Wallach (1996), "Gender: A Useful Category of Historical Analysis", in Joan Wallach Scott, ed., *Feminism and History*, New York: Oxford University Press. : 152–180

Sen, Puma (1999), "Enhancing Women's Choices in Responding to Domestic Violence in Calcutta: A Comparison of Employment and Education", *The European Journal of Development Research*, Vol. 11, no. 2: 65–86.

Sev'er, Aysan, and Cökçeçiçek Yurdakul (2001), "Culture of Honour, Culture of Change: A feminist Analysis of Honour Killings in Rural Turkey", *Violence against Women*, Vol. 7, no. 9: 964–998.

Shaaban, Bouthaina (1988), *Both Right and Left Handed: Arab Women Talk About Their Lives*, Indianapolis: Indiana University Press.

Shaban, Radwan, Ragui Assaad, and Sulayman S. Al-Qudsi (1995), "The Challenge of Unemployment in the Arab Region", *International Labour Review*, vol. 135, no. 1. Online Library at: HtmlResAnchor http://www.questia.com/SM.qst (Last 12 July 2001).

Sharabi, Hisham, and Mukhtar Ali (1977), "The Impact of Class and Culture on Social Behaviour: The Feudal-Bourgeois Family in Arab Society", in L. Carl Brown and Norman Itzkowitz, eds., *Psychological Dimensions of Near Easter Studies*, Princeton NJ, Darwin Press. : 240–256

Sharabi, Hisham (1975), *Muqaddamat li dirasat al-mujtama' al-'arabi* (Introduction to the Study of Arab Society), Jerusalem: Dar Salah Eddin.

——, (1985), "The Dialectics of Patriarchy in Arab Society", in Samih K. Farsoun, ed., *Arab Society: Continuity and Change*, London, Croom Helm. : 83–104

——, (1988), *Neopatrirachy: A Theory of Distorted Change in Arab Society*, Oxford: Oxford University Press.

Sharma, Ursula (1986), *Women's Work, Class, and the Urban Household: A study of Shimla Community, North India*, London: Tavistock Publications.

Al-Sharqi, Amal (1982), "The Emancipation of Iraqi Women", in Tim Niblock, ed., *Iraq: The Contemporary State*, London, Croom Helm. : 74–87

Shaw, R. Paul (1983), *Mobilizing Human Resources in the Arab World*, London: Kegan Paul International.

Shendel, Abdul Khadem (1975), *Athar Al-Sena'ah fi 'a'lakat al-mara'a al-'a'milah fi al-usrra Al-Irakiayya; m'a' al-tarkeez 'ala al-ness'a' al-mutazawijaat* [The impact of industry on the relation between women and the family; with specific emphasis on married women], unpublished Masters thesis, Baghdad: Baghdad University.

Shepherd, George W. (1991), *Effective Sanctions on South Africa: The Cutting Edge of Economic Intervention*. New York: Praeger Publishers.

Simons, Geoff (1998), *The Scourging of Iraq: Sanctions, Law, and National Justice*, London: Macmillan Press.

———, (1999), *Imposing Economic Sanctions: Remedy or Genocidal Tool?* London: Pluto Press.

———, (2002), *Targeting Iraq: Sanctions and Bombing in US Policy*, London: Saqi Books.

Singerman, Diane (1995), *Avenues of Participation: Family, Politics, and Networks in Urban Quarters of Cairo*, Cairo: American University of Cairo Press.

Skocpol, Teda (1979), *States and Social Revolutions*, Cambridge: Cambridge University Press.

Sluglett, Peter, and Marion Farouk Sluglett (1992), "Iraq", in Joel Krieger, ed., *Oxford Companion to Politics of the World*, Oxford: Oxford University Press.

Smart, Carol (1989), *Feminism and the Power of Law*, London: Routledge.

So, Alvin Y. (1990), *Social Change and Development: Modernization, Dependency, and World-System Theories*, London: Sage Publications.

Solomon, Semere (1999), *The Iraqi Educational System- A Review*, Baghdad: UNESCO, March 1999.

Sparr, Pam, ed. (1994), *Mortgaging Women's Lives: Feminist Critiques of Structural Adjustment*, London: Zed Books.

Springborg, Robert (1999), "Infitah, Agrarian Transformation, and Elite Consolidation in Contemporary Iraq", in Tim Niblock and Rodney Wilson, eds., *The Political Economy of the Middle East: Economic and Political Liberalisation*, London: Edward Elgar. : 33–52

Spybey, Tony (1992), *Social Change: Development & Dependency*, Cambridge: Cambridge Polity Press.

Stauth, George (1991), *Gamaliyya. Informal Economy and Social Life in a Popular Quarter of Cairo*, Cairo Papers in Social Science, Vol.14, Cairo: American University in Cairo (AUC) Press. : 78–103

Stean, Jill (1998), *Gender and International Relations: An Introduction*, Cambridge: Polity Press.

Stichter, Sharon (1990), "Women, Employment and the Family: Current Debates", in Sharon Stichter and Jane Parpart, eds., *Women, Employment and the Family in the International Division of Labour*, Lonodon: Macmillan. : 11–71

Stiehm, Judith (1983), *Women's and Men's Wars*, Oxford: Oxford University Press.

———, (1989), *Arms and the Enlisted Women,* Philadelphia PA, Temple University Press.

Stienstra, Deborah (1994), *Women's Movements and International Organizations*, London: Macmillan. : 1–22

Strasser, Hermann, and Susan Randall (1981), *An Introduction to Theories of Social Change*, London: Routledge and Kegan Paul.

Theordorson, George A., and Achilles G. Theordorson (1969), *A Modern Dictionary of Sociology*, New York: Thomas Y. Crowell.

Thies, Cameron G. (2004), "Are Two Theories Better Than One? A Conservative Model of the Neorealist-Neoliberal Debate", *International Political Science Review*, Vol. 25, no. 2: 159–183.

Tickner, Jan J. (1992), *Gender in International Relations: Feminist Perspectives on Global Security*, New York: Columbia University Press.

———, (2001), *Gendering World Politics: Issues and Approaches in the Post-Cold War Era*, New York: Columbia University Press.

Tilly, Charles, ed. (1975), *The Formation of National States in Western Europe*, Princeton, NJ: Princeton University Press.

Tjaden, Patricia, and Nancy Thoennes (2000), *Full Report of the Prevalence, Incidence, and Consequences of Violence against Women: Findings from the National Violence against Women Survey (U.S): Research Report.* Washington, D.C.: National Institute of Justice and the Centers for Disease Control and Prevention.

Tomasevski, Katarina (1997), *Between Sanctions and Elections; Aid Donors and their Human Rights Performance*, London & Washington: Printer.

Townsend, John (1984), "Economic and Political Implications of the War: The Economic Consequences for the Participants", in M. S. El Azhary, ed., *The Iran-Iraq War: A Historical Analysis*, New York: St. Marin's Press.

Tripp, Charles (2000), *History of Iraq*, 2nd ed., Cambridge: Cambridge University Press.

Tsebelis, George (1990), "Are Sanctions Effective? A Game-Theoretic Analysis", *Journal of Conflict Resolution*, Vol. 34, no. 1: 28.

Ullman, H. Richard, ed. (1996), *The World and Yugoslavia's Wars*, New York: Council on Foreign Relations.

United Kingdom (2002), "Social Indicators", Research Paper 02/01, 9 January 2002. Online at: HtmlResAnchor http://www.parliament.uk/commons/lib/research/rp2002/rp02–001.pdf

(Last Accessed on 12 December 2004).

United Kingdom, (2002), "Iraq's Weapons of Mass Destruction: The Assessment of the British Government, 24 September 2002" [the British Dossier on Iraq]. The file is available online: HtmlResAnchor http://image.guardian.co.uk/sys-files/Politics/documents/2002/09/24/dossier.pdf.

(Last accessed 16 September 2005).

United Nations (UN) (1991), *National Accounts Statistics: Analysis of Main Aggregates 1988–1989*. New York, United Nations. : 126–197

——, (1994), *The United Nations and Apartheid: 1948–1994*. New York: United Nations,

——, (1996a), *Respect for Humanitarian Mandates in Conflict Situation*, New York: United Nations, Inter-Agency Standing Committee.

——, (1996b), *Memorandum of Understanding between the Secretariat of the United Nations and the Government of Iraq on the implementation of Security Council Resolution 986, S/1996/356"*. New York: United Nations, March 1996.

——, (1996c) *The United Nations and Iraq-Kuwait Conflict, 1990–96, Letter of the Iraqi Foreign Minister to the UN Secretary-General*, New York: United Nations.

——, (1999), *Special Topics on Social Conditions in Iraq, An Overview Submitted by the UN system to the Security Council Panel on Humanitarian Affairs*. New York: United Nations, 24 March 1999.

——, *Reports of the Secretary General Pursuant to OFF Resolutions*, online: HtmlResAnchor http://www/casi.org.uk/info/scriraq.html#1990 (Last accessed 12 September 2005).

——, Office of Iraq (UNOIP), *OFF Programme, Press Releases*, Office of Iraq (UNOIP), *OFF Programme*, online:

HtmlResAnchor http://www.un.org/Depts/oip/sector-displaced.html (Last accessed 12 September 2005)

——, OIP, See also "Weekly Update": HtmlResAnchor www.un.org/Depts/oip/latest/wu02521

(Last accessed 13 July 2002). See also: HtmlResAnchor http://www.un.org/news & HtmlResAnchor http://www.un.org/depts/oip/ (Last accessed 12 September 2005).

United Nations, Commission on Human Rights (UNCHR) (2002), *UN Special Rapporteur for Violence against Women*, United Nations Commission on Human Rights Situation in Iraq (UNCHR). E/CN.4/2002/83, January 2002.

United Nations, Department of Humanitarian Affairs (UNDHA) (1995), *United Nations Humanitarian Cooperation Programme for Iraq, Mid-Term Review*, UNDHA.

United Nations Development Programme (UNDP) (1994), *Human Development Report*, Oxford: Oxford University Press, for UNDP.

———, (1997), *The State in Changing World:* HtmlResAnchor World Development Report 1997 Washington DC: World Bank, for UNDP, September 1997.

———, (2001), *Human Development Report 2001*. New York & Oxford: Oxford University Press, for UNDP.

———, (2002), *Human Development Report*, Oxford: Oxford University Press for the UNDP.

———, and the Iraqi Economists' Association (IEA) (1995), "The Cumulated Economic Cost to Iraq as a Result of the Sanctions", *Arab Human Development Report,* Baghdad: UNDP and the IEA.

———, and Arab Fund for Economic and Social Development (UNDP & AFESD) (2002), *Arab Human Development Report 2002: Creating Opportunities for Future Generations*, New York: United Nation.

UNDP HDR (2002), *The World's Women 2000: Trends and Statistics*, UN Statistics Division, online HtmlResAnchor http://unstats.un.org/unsd/demographic/ (Last accessed 23 August 2003).

United Nations Economic and Social Commission for West Asia (UNESCWA) (1994), *Arab Women in ESCWA Member States*, E/ESCWA/STAT/1994/17- 1994, Beirut.

United Nations Educational, Scientific and Cultural Organization (UNESCO) (2000), *Situational Analysis of General Education in Iraq, Mission Report of UNEDBAS* (Regional Office for Education Based in the Arab States), (UNESCO). United Nations: Beirut, March 2000.

———, Educational Sectoral Working Group (EDSWG) (2002). *Hygiene and Sanitation in Primary Schools*, EDSWG: Printing Press Report.

———, *Situation Analysis of Education in Iraq (2003)*, UNESCO: Paris, April 2003a.
Also available online at: HtmlResAnchor http://unesdoc.unesco.org/images/0013/00/308/130838e.pdf
(Last accessed 11 September 2005).

———, UNESCO Institute for Statistics (2003b), *Literacy Statistics*. Online at: HtmlResAnchor http://status.uis.unesco.or/TableViewer/tableView.aspx? ReportId=41 (Last accessed 16 September 2005).

United Nations Food and Agriculture Organisation UN FAO (1995), Evaluation of Food and Nutrition Situation in Iraq, *Terminal Statement Prepared for the Government of Iraq*, Rome: Technical Cooperation Programme, September 1995.

———, and World Food Program (FAO/WFP) (2003), *Crop, Food Supply and Nutrition Assessment Mission to Iraq*, Special Report by FAO/WFP, September 2003.

United Nations Population Fund (UNFPA) (2003a), *Reproductive Health Survey: Prepares to Aid Pregnant Iraqi Women*, New York: UNFPA HQ/2003/6, Press Release, 21 March 2003. Online at: HtmlResAnchor http://www.unfpa.org/news.cfm?ID=179&Language=1
(Last accessed 18 September 2005).

United Nations Population Fund (UNFPA) (2003b), *Reproductive Health Survey: Iraq – a Reproductive Health assessment UNFPA*, August 2003. Online at: HtmlResAnchor http://www.unfpa.org/rh/docs/iraq-rept04-08-03.doc
(Last accessed 16 September 2005).

United Nations Humanitarian Panel (UNHP) (1999a), *Report of the second panel established pursuant to the note by the president of the SC of January 30/1999 Concerning the Current Humanitarian Situation in Iraq*, United Nations Humanitarian Panel (UNHP), United

Nations Document S/1999/356, Annex II (S/1999/100 March 30/1999:§ 25), March 1999.

——, (1999b) *United Nations Report on the Current Humanitarian Situation in Iraq submitted to the Security Council*, United Nations Humanitarian Panel (UNHP), United Nations Document (S/1999/356), March 1999.

United Nations Children Fund (UNICEF) (1989), *Invisible Adjustment: Poor Women and Economic Crisis*, The Americas and Caribbean Regional Office, Santiago: UNICEF.

——, (1997), *Women and Children: A Situation Analysis of Children and Women in Iraq"*, New York: UNICEF.

——, (1998), A Situation Analysis of Children and Women in Iraq, UNICEF/Iraq, 30 April 1998. Online at: HtmlResAnchor http://www.childinfo.org/Other/Iraq_sa.pdf. (Last accessed on 16 September 2005).

——, and Iraqi Ministry of Health (1999a), *Child and Maternal Mortality Survey 1999*, Preliminary Report, July 1999.

——, (1999b), *Mortality among Women and Children in Iraq*, Al-Mustaqbal Al-'Arabi, issue (248), October 1999.

——, (2002a), *Profile of Women & Children in Iraq*, New York: UNICEF, April 2002.

——, (2002b), *Situation of Children in Iraq*, UNICEF, February 2002.

United Nations Independent Commission of Inquiry (2004), *Status Report issued by the independent international Commission of Enquiry into Oil For Food in Iraq* [Volcker Commission reports]. Online at: HtmlResAnchor http://www.iic-offp.org/documents.htm & HtmlResAnchor http://www.un.org/Depts/oip (Last accessed 10 September 2005).

——, (2005) *The Management of the United Nations Oil-For-Food Programme* (September 2005) [Volcker Commission]. Online at: HtmlResAnchor http://www.iic-offp.org/Mgmt_Report.htm. (Last accessed 20 September 2005).

United Nations International Law Commission (UNILC) (1979), "Draft Articles on State Responsibility, Report on the Commission to the General Assembly on the work of its twenty-fifth session", in *Yearbook of the International Law Commission* (UNILC), Vol. 11, Doc. A/9010/REV.1. New York: United Nations.

——, (1980), "Draft Articles on States Responsibility, Report of the Commission to the General Assembly on the work of its thirty-first session, International Law Commission (ILC)", in *Yearbook of the International Law Commission*, Vol. II, Part 2, Doc. A/34/10. New York, United Nations, 1980.

——, (2004), *Draft Article on Minimum Standards for Imposing Economic Sanctions*, New York: United Nations International Law Commission (UNILC), November 2004.

United Nations Office of the Humanitarian Coordinator for Iraq (UNOCHR) (2003), *Occasional Paper: Situation of Women in Iraq*, (UNOCHR). Iraq, May 2003.

United States Census Bureau, Population Data/International Database. Online at: HtmlResAnchor http://www.census.gov/cgi-bin/ipc/idbagg & HtmlResAnchor www.census.gov/ipc/www/idbpyr.html (Last accessed 30 May 2005)

United States Government (2005), *Commission on the Intelligence Capability of the United States regarding Weapons of Mass Destruction (WMD), Report to the President, March 31, 2005*. online at: HtmlResAnchor http://www.wmd.gov/report/ (Last accessed 23 May 2005).

Ursel, Jane (1986), "The State and the Maintenance of Patriarchy", in J. Dickinson and B. Russell, eds., *Family, Economy and the State*, Beckenham UK, Croom Helm. : 150–191

Van der Stoel, Max (1991), *Report on the Situation of Human Rights in Iraq to the General Assembly*, UN document A/46/467, New York: United Nations, Commission on Human Rights November 1991.

Van Eeghen, William (2000), *Education and Economic Growth in Middle East and North Africa*, New York: The World Bank. Online at: HtmlResAnchor http://www.worldbank.org/wbi/mdf/mdf1/edecmen.htm
(Last accessed 20 September 2005).

Van Heerden, Auret (1991), "Trade Union Gains from Sanctions", in *South Africa's Economic Crisis*, Cape Town: David Philip.

Vick, Karl (2004), "Children pay Cost of Iraq's Chaos", *Washington Post Foreign Service*, Sunday, 21 November 2004.

Von Sivers, Peter (1987), "Life Within the Informal Sectors", in G. Stauth and S. Zubaida, eds., *Mass Culture, Popular Culture, and Social Life in the Middle East*, Frankfurt am Main: Campus.

Von Sponeck, Hans (1999), *Report of a meeting with a delegation from Physicians for Social Responsibility on 5 April 1999*. Online at:
HtmlResAnchor www.scn.org/ccpi/UNandUSreports.html, (Last accessed 12 September 2005)

——, (2001), "Open Letter to Mr. Peter Hain", *The Guardian* (newspaper), 3 January 2001.

——, (2006), "A Different Kind of War: The UN Sanctions Regime in Iraq", New York. Oxford: Berghahn Books.

Walby, Sylvia (1989), "Theorizing Patriarchy", *British Journal of Sociology* Vol. 23, no. 2: 213–234.

——, (1988), "Introduction", in Sylvia Walby, ed., *Gender Segregation at Work*, Milton Keynes: Open University Press. : 1–13

——, (1992), "Post-Post-Modernism? Theorizing Social Complexity", in Michele Barrett and Anna Philips, eds., *Destabilizing Theory; Contemporary Feminist Debates*, Cambridge, U.K.: Polity Press. : 31–52

Weber, Max (1978), *Economy and Society*, vol. 2, Berkeley and Los Angeles, CA: University of California Press.

Weedon, Chris (1987), *Feminist Practice and Post-Structuralist Theory*, Oxford: Basil Blackwell.

Weiss, Thomas G., D. Cortright, G. A. Lopez and L. Minear, eds. (1997), *"Political Gain and Civilian Pain: Humanitarian Impacts of Economic Sanctions"*, Boulder: Rowman & Littlefield Publisher, Inc.

Whitworth, Sandra (1994), *Feminism and International Relation: Towards a Political Economy of Gender in Interstate and Non-Governmental Institutions*, New York, St. Martin's Press.

Wilson, Elizabeth (1977), *Women and the Welfare State*, London: Tavistock,

Winters, Alan (2000), *Trade and Poverty: Is There a Connection? Special Study for the World Trade Organization*, Geneva, WTO.

World Bank (1980), *Women in Development*, World Bank. New York, August 1980.

——, (1994), *World Development Report: Infrastructure for Development*, Oxford: Oxford University Press for the World Bank.

——, (1995), *Workers in an Integrating Economy*, Oxford: Oxford University Press for the World Bank.

——, (1998) *World Development Indicators*, Washington DC, World Bank.

——, (2000), *Attacking Poverty*, HtmlResAnchor World Development Report 2000, Washington DC: World Bank, September 2000.

——, (2003), *Gender and Development in Middle East and North Africa: women in the Public Sphere*, Washington DC: World Bank, September 2003

World Health Organisation (WHO) (1996), *The Health Conditions of the Population in Iraq since the Gulf Crisis*. Rome: WHO, Doc. WHO/EHA/96.1, March.

——, (1998a), *Current Emergencies in Iraq*. Rome: WHO, August 1998.

——, (1998b) *Health Conditions of the Population in Iraq Since the Gulf Crisis*. World Health Organization (WHO), Resource Centre, Rome.

——, and World Food Program (FAO/WFP) (2003), Crop, Food Supply and Nutrition Assessment Mission to Iraq, *Special Report (FAO/WFP)*, Rome, September 2003.

Youngs, Gillian (1999), *International Relations in a Global Age: A Conceptual Challenge*, Cambridge: Polity Press.

Yuval-Davis, Nira, and Floya Anthias, eds. (1989), "Introduction", in N. Yuval-Davis and F. Anthias, eds., *Women – Nation – State*, London: Macmillan. : 1–16

Yuval-Davis, Nira (1991), "The Citizenship Debate: Women, the State And Ethnic Processes", *Feminist Reviews*, No. 39: 58–68.

——, (1997), *Gender and Nation*, London, Thousand Oaks & New Delhi: Sage Publications.

Zalewski, Marysia (1995), "Well, What Is the Feminist Perspective on Bosnia?", *International Affairs*, Vol. 71, no. 2: 339–356.

El-Zanaty, Fatma, and Ann Way (2001), *Egypt Demographic and Health Survey (DHS) 2000*. Calverton, MD: Ministry of Health and Population (Egypt). National Population Council, and ORC Macro. Online at: HtmlResAnchor http://www.measuredhs.com/pubs/pdf/FR1171/00FrontMatter.pdf (Last accessed on 22 May 2002).

Zubaida, Sami (1993), *Islam, the People and the State: Political Ideas and Movements in the Middle East*, 2nd ed. London: I. B. Tauris.

——, (2002), "The Fragments Imagine the Nation: The Case of Iraq", *International Journal of Middle East Studies*, Vol. 34: 205–215.

——, (2003), *The Rise and Fall of Civil Society in Iraq* (February 2003). Online at: HtmlResAnchor http://www.opendemocracy.net/content/articles/PDF/953.pdf (Last accessed 3 June 2004).

Sources for the cited Iraqi Law and Legislation [In Arabic]:

Al-Waqa'e al-irakyya [The Iraqi Gazette]

Al-Adalah al-Iraqiyya [Iraq Gazette]

Al-Jumhuriyya (Iraq's official newspaper)

Al-Thawra (Iraq's official newspaper – Baghdad)

Laws of General Federation of Iraqi Women (GFIW) no. (139), 1972 [amended]

Law of Personal Status no. (188), 1959 [and its amendments]

Law of Personal Law no. (188), 1978 [amended]

Law of Compulsory Education no. (118), 1976

Law of Civil Pension no. (33), 1966

The Agrarian Reform Law no. (117), 1970 [amended, and its amendments]

Social Security Law no. (140), 1964

Pension and Social Security Law no. (39), 1971 [amended]
Social Security Law no. (126), 1980
Protection of Juvenals Law no. (78), 1980
Protection of Juvenals Law no. (76), 1983
Law of Divorced Women's Rights in Marital Property no. (77), 1983
Public Health Law no. (89), 1981
Labour Law no. (1), 1985 [and its amendments]
Labour Law no. (151), 1970 [and its amendments]
Labour Law no. (71), 1987
Equality of Men and Women in Financial Rights and Obligations no. (191), 1970
Republic of Iraq's Constitution(s) of 1964
Republic of Iraq's Constitution of 1985
Republic of Iraq's Constitution of 1968
Republic of Iraq's Constitution of 1970

INDEX OF SUBJECTS

INDEX OF NAMES

228   WOMEN IN IRAQ

ABOUT THE BOOK

In this important new book, Yasmin Husein Al-Jawaheri argues that the explosion of violence against Iraqi women since the removal of Saddam Hussain should not have taken people by surprise. The deterioration of gender relations was in fact, as she vividly demonstrates, a direct result of a decade of international economic sanctions.

Al-Jawaheri explores the gender-related impact of those sanctions in the areas of employment, education, family relations, and domestic responsibilities. Also focusing on how the 2003 invasion and subsequent upsurge in sectarianism have intensified the problem, she assesses the prospects for women's rights in Iraq.

Yasmin Husein Al-Jawaheri is an Iraqi-born scholar and writer. She holds a Ph.D. in Middle East Studies from the University of Exeter and a degree in international law from Lund University.